THE
ART OF WAR IN ANCIENT INDIA

THE
ART OF WAR IN ANCIENT INDIA

By

P.C. CHAKRAVARTI, M.A. (DAC.), PH.D. (LOND.)

Sir Asutosh Mukherji Gold Medalist (Cal.).

Lecturer in History, University of Dacca.

KALPAZ

ISBN: 978-93-5128-539-7

First Published in 1941
Indian Reprint in 2017

Published by

Kalpaz Publications
C-30, Satyawati Nagar,
Delhi – 110052
E-mail: kalpaz@hotmail.com
Website: kalpazpublications.com
Ph.: +91-9212142040

Cataloging in Publication Data—DK
Courtesy: D.K. Agencies (P) Ltd. <docinfo@dkagencies.com>

Chakravarti, P. C. (Prithwis Chandra), 1904-1969, **author.**
The art of war in ancient India / by P.C. Chakravarti (M.A. (DAC.), PH.D. (Lond.)).
pages cm
"First published in 1941"—Title page verso.
Includes bibliographical references and index.
ISBN 9789351285397

1. Military art and science—India—History—To 1500. 2. India—History, Military—To 1500. I. Title.

U29.C43 2017 DDC 355.00934 23

TO THE MEMORY OF MY FATHER

PREFACE

Early in 1927 when I was awarded a Research Studentship by the University of Dacca, I began my study of the materials bearing on the Art of War in Ancient India. A year later I submitted a thesis entitled "Archery in Ancient India," which won me the Sir Asutosh Mukherji Gold Medal of the Calcutta University. Then for several years I could not proceed with the work owing to private preoccupations. It was, however, resumed in 1936 when I went to England on study leave. By and large, the present volume embodies the results of investigations carried out at London during the academic sessions, 1936-7 and 1937-8.

Strictly speaking, this is not a pioneer work. Others have laboured in the same field, the most notable among them being E. W. Hopkins, H. C. Ray and G. T. Date. Hopkins' article in particular on the Social and Military Position of the Ruling Caste, published in the *Journal of the American Oriental Society,* 1888, will ever remain a monument of critical scholarship. I have sometimes drawn upon his work, in so far as the Epic materials are concerned; but I have also covered fresh ground and arrived at conclusions which are not always in conformity with his. Mr. Date's essay bears the same title as mine, but we differ as widely in method and approach as in the range of materials utilised.

With regard to the spelling of names and the use of diacritical marks, I am afraid I have not been consistent all through. Arabic and Persian names have been generally written without diacritical marks, but there are exceptions. For instance, Mahmud has been written as

Maḥmūd, and Beruni as Berūnī. In regard to Sanskritic names, however, the spelling has been more consistent.

Two chapters of this work were published beforehand as articles in the *Indian Historical Quarterly* and the *Dacca University Studies*. I am grateful to the editors of these journals for permission to incorporate them in this volume with some modifications.

Although a formal acknowledgement is at best inadequate, I would here express my indebtedness to Dr. R. C. Majumdar, M.A., Ph.D., Vice-Chancellor, Dacca University, who first suggested to me this subject for work and initiated me in the methods of historical research. I owe also grateful thanks to Dr. L. D. Barnett, M.A., Litt.D., C.B., under whose supervision this work was mostly carried out, and to Professor H. C. Ray Chaudhuri, M.A., Ph.D., for his interest and advice on a number of difficult points. To Mr. G. H. Langley, M.A., formerly Vice-Chancellor, Dacca University, and Sir John Marshall, K.C.I.E., Litt.D., I am indebted for the readiness with which they read through portions of this thesis. My thanks are also due to my friend and colleague, Mr. Parimal Roy, M.A., who kindly, yet critically, read the proofs, and to the staff of the British Museum and India Office libraries for their courteous help.

P. C. CHAKRAVARTI

UNIVERSITY OF DACCA,
February, 1941

TABLE OF CONTENTS

CHAPTER VII

CHAPTER VIII

CHAPTER IX

SOME ASPECTS OF MILITARY ADMINISTRATION

CHAPTER X

ARMY ON THE MARCH

CHAPTER XI

CHAPTER XII

ARMY IN THE FIELD

CHAPTER XIII

FORTIFICATION AND SIEGECRAFT

CHAPTER XIV

NOTES ON ARMS AND ARMOUR

CHAPTER XV

ABBREVIATIONS

Ag. P.	Agni Purāṇa.
A. S. R.	Annual Report of the Archeological Survey of India.
C. I. I. or Corp. Inscr. Ind.	Corpus Inscriptionum Indicarum.
Ep. Ind.	Epigraphia Indica.
Gaṇ.	Arthaśāstra of Kauṭilya, edited by Ganapati Sastri.
Ind. Ant.	Indian Antiquary.
Ind. Hist. Quart. ..	Indian Historical Quarterly.
J. A. O. S. ..	Journal of the American Oriental Society.
J. B. O. R. S. ..	Journal of the Behar and Orissa Research Society.
J. B. A. S. ..	Journal of the Bengal Asiatic Society.
J. B. B. R. A. S. ..	Journal of the Bombay Branch Royal Asiatic Society.
Mat. P.	Matsya Purāṇa.
S. I. I. or South. Ind. Inscr.	South Indian Inscriptions.
Nītiv.	Nītivākyāmṛta of Somadeva.
Nīti-p.	Nīti-prakāśikā of Vaiśampāyana.
Shām.	Arthaśāstra of Kauṭilya, edited by R. Shamasastry.
Śār.	Śārṅgadhara Paddhati.
Vaś.	Dhanur-veda Saṁhitā of Vaśiṣṭha. (Bengal ed.)
Z. D. M. G. ..	Zeitschrift der Deutschen Morgenlandischen Gesellschaft.

INTRODUCTION

The Hobbesian dictum that man is a fighting animal is fundamentally true. There are two instincts which lie deep down in man's nature. One is the instinct of self-preservation, the other that of self-expansion. Right through the ages, man has always fought in response to one or other of these two basic facts of his nature. At first he fought man against man. Then he fought clan against clan. Still later he fought state against state. And the process continues.

India was no exception to this general rule. From the days of King Divodāsa in the Ṛgveda till the closing years of the twelfth century, when the Turkish tempest swept down upon the plains of northern India, the country passed through an endless series of battles, wars and revolutions. Kingdoms rose and fell in never-ending succession. Mighty conquerors sped across the land from one end to another in search of wealth, territory, glory and adventure. *Dig-vijaya* (conquest of regions) was held up as a righteous ideal, and empires were built up through the same mechanism of bloody strife and diplomacy as the later-day empires of the Moghuls, the Marathas and the British. From the 5th century B.C. onwards there were periodical incursions of foreign military adventurers and migratory tribes, and countless wars and battles were fought to keep them at bay. Porus and Candragupta, Puṣyamitra and Skandagupta, Ānandapāla and Pṛthvīrāja—these are but a few of those valiant generals, who, like Aëtius and Charles Martel in Europe, stood athwart the path of alien invaders and fought in defence of their country and religion. Fortune did not always bless their efforts with success, but the goddess of battle found in them votaries of unbending courage and determination.

Yet such names as these, of whom any country in the world might legitimately feel proud, would have been completely lost in oblivion but for the records of foreign historians and the happy discovery of a few epigraphic records in India. It is a well-known fact that ancient India, in spite of its multifarious literary activities, produced no historical literature worth the name. Until almost the close of our period, the muse of history remained immutably mute. The result has been that though wars like the Peloponnesian war were fought on the soil of India in ancient times, there was no Thucydides to record them—at any rate with that scientific precision and attention to authentic details which constitute the core of history.

This lack of historical literature makes the task of writing a military history of ancient India a well-nigh impossible task. What has been attempted in the following pages is not, strictly speaking, a military history, but an account of the art of war as known to, and practised by, the ancient Hindus. It is a study of one aspect—and an important aspect—of the institutional life of ancient India. By 'ancient' is here meant the period of Indian history, commencing roughly from the sixth or fifth century B.C. and extending to the conquest of Islam in the 11th and 12th century A.D. Though the period prior to the 5th or 6th century B.C. has frequently been brought in as a sort of background, it is mainly upon the period subsequent to that date that the real emphasis has been laid. At the beginning of this period, the military institutions of India had reached a stage of evolution from which, generally speaking, there was no violent departure during the next millennium and a half. Modifications and changes there undoubtedly were from age to age; ethnic, geographic and climatic factors often conspired to produce and develop local and regional differences. It is not always possible to trace these, but they have been traced as far as the materials permit. On the whole, however, the basic structure remained fundamentally the same. The four-fold army of the Jātakas and the Epics remained four-fold till about the 8th century A.D.; elephants, which formed the chief strength of Porus, constituted also the chief strength of Pṛthvīrāja; the chief implements of war, which were used by Hindu armies fighting against the invading hordes of Islam, were already well-known in the 4th century B.C.; and the principles of fortification enunciated by Kauṭilya guided the builders and architects of the following ages.

Broadly speaking, the materials used for the present study fall under two heads: literary and archeological. Archeological evidence consists mainly in the remains of old towns and forts, ancient sculptures, paintings, coins and inscriptions. These are often of high illustrative value, throwing a flood of light on methods of fortification, equipment and arms. The literary sources, again, are of two kinds: viz., indigenous and foreign. The chief importance of foreign notices about India lies in the fact that they are generally dated, and we know with perfect certainty to which epoch they must be referred. As is well-known, these foreign notices come primarily from three sources: Greek and Graeco-Roman, Chinese and Muhammadan. Of these, the first apppears to be by far the most important for our purpose. Notwithstanding certain obvious defects, the classical accounts constitute a real treasure-house of information regarding the art of war as practised in India in the fourth and third century B.C. The accounts of the Chinese pilgrims, though they are of inestimable value as contemporary descriptions of religious, social and even political institutions, contribute comparatively little information which can be utilized for the purposes of the present study. The early Muhammadan chronicles are more helpful than the Chinese; they are valuable authorities on the gradual conquest of India by. the armies of Islam. But they lack the range and catholicity of the classical writers, and they usually present only one side of the picture.

Among indigenous literary works, the most important for the purpose of the present study—are the two Sanskrit epics, the Rāmāyaṇa and the Mahābhārata, treatises on arthaśāstra and nīti, and extant manuals on Dhanur-veda and other cognate topics. As regards the interpretation of these works the greatest difficulty arises from the uncertainty of their chronology. Yet chronology has been called the very "eye of history", and all historical discussion must be based on some sort of chronological framework.

Since the basic theme of both the epics is war, they naturally throw a flood of light on the military ideas, customs and usages of ancient India. But it is no easy task to delimit their chronological setting. A well-known critic remarks that, strictly speaking, there is no such thing as an epic age. For, the epics, especially the Mahābhārata, represent a veritable museum in which relics of different ages have been stored in a hopelessly ill-assorted and confused manner. Professor Winternitz has pointed out that there are "myths, legends and poems" in the Mahābhārata, which reach back to the time of the Veda. There are, again, many moral narratives and sayings which "belong to the ascetic poetry", drawn upon from the 6th century B.C. onwards also by Buddhists and Jains. But most scholars agree that other portions of the great epic could not have been composed until many centuries later. The Rāmāyaṇa, which is certainly a more homogeneous work than the Mahābhārata, nevertheless betrays the same process of extension and growth. Scholars have pointed out that certain parts of the Rāmāyaṇa, especially Books I and VII (Bāla-kāṇḍa and Uttara-kāṇḍa), are separated from the genuine Rāmāyaṇa of Books II to VI by a long interval of time. This fact of gradual extension and elaboration in the two epics has rendered the task of assigning a definite date to them an exceedingly difficult proposition. It is no wonder, therefore, that discussion on the subject has led to the growth of a bewildering mass of opinions and theories; and it is not unlikely that the last word by scholarship on the question has not yet been pronounced.[1]

But whatever be the age when the mass of the epic poems was composed—whether between the 5th century B.C. and the 2nd century A.D., or between the 4th century B.C. and the 4th century A.D.,[2]—they seem, on the whole, to embody traditions of an age anterior to that of Alexander and the Mauryas. These traditions, enshrined in ballads, lived on in the memory of the people; and these ballads formed the basis of both the Rāmāyaṇa and the Mahābhārata. We may here refer to two facts which illustrate our point of view. The Greek writers make it abundantly clear (even if we leave aside the evidence of Kauṭilya on the point) that in the 4th century B.C. the Indians placed their chief reliance in warfare on elephants tamed and trained for the purpose. In the epics, however, the chief strength of the army consisted in car-warriors. Bhīṣma and Arjuna, Karṇa and Droṇa and all the front-rank knights of the Mahābhārata were redoubtable car-warriors, and if one or two of them occasionally appear (as Duryodhana does) on the battle-field riding on war-elephants, these are exceptions rather than the rule. The other fact to which attention may be drawn is the manner in which the epic commanders are elected and consecrated. We have graphic descriptions of this in the Udyoga-parva, chs. 151 and 155, Droṇa-parva, ch. 5, and Karṇaparva, ch. 10. As soon as there is a vacancy in the office, the chiefs and knights assemble in conclave. The king opens the discussion and requests one of the attending knights to propose a name for the office. This knight then makes a short speech and suggests a name. Sometimes one or two other knights come forward to support the proposal, but more often the king, gauging the sense of the assembly, evades further discussion and straight

[1] For some opinions on the subject, see Macdonell, *History of Sanskrit Literature*, London, 1928, pp. 285-7 309 etc.; Winternitz, *History of Indian Literature*, 1927, Vol. I, pp. 454-475, 500-517; Hopkins, *Epic Mythology*. 1915, p. 1.; Hopkins, *The Great Epic of India*, 1901, pp. 386-402; Cambridge History of India, Vol. I, p. 258; Wilson's view on the date of the Rāmāyaṇa is to be found in Ind. Ant., 1884, p. 229; Jacobi's in ibid., 1894, pp. 54 ff.; Keith's in J. R. A. S., 1915, p. 327.

[2] Macdonell assigns them to the period from the 5th century B.C. to the 3rd century A.D. Hopkins in his Epic Mythology, (op. cit.), considered 300 to 100 B.C. to be the probable date of the Mahābhārata, but in Cambridge History, I, 258, he gives the limits 4th century B.C. to the 4th century A.D. So does Winternitz in his History of Indian Literature. Professor Krishnaswami Aiyangar (*Beginnings of South Indian History*, 1918, p. 64) says that both the works "may have to be referred to the 5th century B.C.", but he gives no reasons in support of his view.

away requests the proposed knight to assume the leadership of the army. There is scarcely any disagreement among the chiefs, and the ordinary troops take no part in the election except by sitting up, waiting for the decision and acclaiming the new commander when the choice is known. The election is immediately followed by an installation ceremony. The knight-in-command is made to sit on a wooden seat, bathed with sacred water and invested with the *saināpatya* "according to the rites enjoined in the scriptures."

There are obvious resemblances between the installation ceremony of an epic commander and the coronation ceremony of a Vedic king. But whether the description is applicable to kingship or generalship, it is for obvious reasons not applicable to the Mauryan or post-Mauryan epoch. These facts, then, largely justify our assumption that the military traditions of the epics should be placed somewhere before the 4th century B.C. We are conscious that so simple a generalization may not stand the test of a comprehensive scrutiny and that there are details even in the military picture which are obviously late. But it is not always easy to distinguish between older and newer elements; and the demands of synthetic treatment sometimes make strict adherence to chronology neither possible nor desirable. In view of these considerations, we have, as a rule, put the bulk of the epic evidence on our subject of enquiry prior to that of the classical authors and the Arthaśāstra, though it is not implied thereby that these always represent an earlier cultural stratum.

We now proceed to a consideration of the works on arthaśāstra and nīti, the value of which for a study of the ancient Indian military system can hardly be over-estimated. They supply us with the theoretical background of the system, and reveal the ideas and principles on which the structure stood. Though primarily concerned with statecraft, the writers of the arthaśāstra and nīti seldom kept war-craft out of their purview. For they seem to have believed, like the German military philosopher, Clausewitz, that "war was nothing but a continuation of policy by other means."

It is well-known that of all the works of this kind which have come down to us, the earliest and yet the most comprehensive is the Arthaśāstra of Kauṭilya. It contains the most complete statement of Hindu ideas on government, law and war. It was also the progenitor and in certain respects the model of numerous later works.[1] The problem of its age and authorship has in recent years aroused much animated discussion. There are some who believe

[1] It was, for instance, the model after which Vātsyāyana Mallanāga formed his Kāmasūtra.

in the theory, first propounded by Shamasastry and Fleet, that it is really a work composed by Cānakya, the minister of Candragupta Maurya. There are others who contend that this traditional ascription of the Arthaśāstra to the Mauryan minister is not justified by internal evidence and that the work as we have it could not have been composed earlier than the first or second century A.D. We do not agree with those who regard the Arthaśāstra as "The Imperial Gazetteer" of the early Mauryan empire; at the same time we do not subscribe to the view that it is "merely the work of a Pandit."[1] Though primarily a theoretical work, it is essentially the work of a practical administrator little interested in political theories. Though formally a *śāstra,* it is unquestionably based on the realities of civil and military administration.[2] In regard to the age of the Arthaśāstra we maintain that even though it was composed in the first or second century of the Christian era, and Johnston has shown that it could not have been later,[3] it largely portrays the theories and institutions of an earlier epoch. It is generally recognized that there are some remarkable points of resemblance between the administrative and economic system of the Mauryas and that of the Arthaśāstra. Moreover, the author begins his work with the statement that it is "a compendium of almost all the Arthaśāstras, which in view of acquisition and maintenance of earth, have been composed by ancient teachers." Within the book itself, he frequently quotes the opinions of several previous authors and schools It is, therefore, reasonable to assume that the ideas and customs embodied in the Arthaśāstra are applicable not merely to the age of its author, but also to a long period anterior to this. In other words, we may assign the military ideas and institutions of Kauṭilya's work roughly to the period from 300 B.C. to 100 A.D.

But whatever be its actual date, the Arthaśāstra compresses within itself a vast mass of useful information regarding the military ideas and practices of the ancient Hindus. It describes

[1] For the former view, compare B. K. Sarkar, *Positive Background of Hindu Sociology*, 1914, p. 7.; K. P. Jayaswal, *Hindu Polity*, 1924, Vol. I, p. 4. For the latter, see Winternitz, *Some Problems of Indian Literature*.

[2] This double character of the Arthaśāstra is asserted by the author himself:

Sarva-śāstrā-nukramya prayogam-upalabhya ca
Kauṭilyena narendrārthe śāsanasya vidhiḥ kṛtaḥ.

(Bk. II. ch. 10)

[3] On the basis of a comparison with some Buddhist works, E. H. Johnston concludes that the Arthaśāstra is not separated by a great interval from Aśvaghoṣa, and is distinctly earlier than the Jātakamālā of Āryasūra. (J. R. A. S., 1929, pp. 77 et. seq.).

the composition of the army, and the relative value of its different branches. It speaks of the duties of various military officers, and defines the functions of the different arms. It contains detailed rules for stabling and training horses and elephants, for marching and camping, for fortification and siegecraft. Moreover, Kauṭilya's maxims on tactics and strategy are at once wise and sound, and often remind us of the articles and sayings of the Chinese masters—Suntzu and Wutzu. He insists throughout on the necessity for constant precaution, on the avoidance of risks, on protection by means of energetic entrenching and vigilant sentries. He emphasises the need for accurate topographical information and recommends the utilization of natural features in battles and attention to climatic and metereological changes. He recognises the absolute necessity of a reserve in battle. Without a reserve, he categorically maintains, the king should never attempt to fight, "for it is by the reserved force that dispersed troops are collected together." (Bk. X. ch. 5).

It should be noted, however, that Kauṭilya was no war-monger by temperament. If the end could be achieved by non-military methods, even by methods of intrigue, duplicity and fraud, he would not advocate an armed conflict. In Bk. VII, ch. 11, he says: "When the advantages derivable from peace and war are of equal character, one should prefer peace; for disadvantages, such as the loss of power and wealth, sojourning and sin, are ever attending upon war." Again, in Bk. X, ch. 6, he writes: "The arrow shot by an archer may or may not kill a single person; but skilful intrigue, devised by wise men, may kill even those who are in the womb."[1]

This brings us to the consideration of another important characteristic of Kauṭilya's mental make-up, viz., his predilection for fraud and duplicity, in other words, his non-moral attitude. Almost every chapter of the Arthaśāstra bears the impress of this Machiavellian outlook. Like Machiavelli, Kauṭilya apparently believed in the theory of the end justifying the means. Like him, he did not feel the slightest scruple in the employment of wine, women, poison or spies for the achievement of the objective. Like him, too, he would not allow the intrusion of ethics into a discussion of politics and war. There is, however, one slight difference. In his *Discourses*, the Florentine Secretary protests that it is only from warfare that he would exclude ethics as irrelevant. In the Arthaśāstra, Kauṭilya makes no protestation; he tacitly warns morality from the threshhold.

[1] Elsewhere, however, in an altogether different context, Kauṭilya says: "Whoever is inferior to another shall make peace with him; whoever is superior in power shall wage war." (Bk. VII. ch. I.)

The successors of Kauṭilya in the field of political and military writing were but shadows of the great master. The Nītisāra of Kāmandaka, which is usually assigned to the 8th century A.D., is merely a metrical version of Kauṭilyan teachings with certain important omissions. The Nītivākyāmṛta of Somadeva Sūri (tenth century A.D.), though written with some freshness and originality of style, seldom treads upon new ground. Both these authors, moreover, are archaeological in their taste and outlook, and their teachings, therefore, do not seem to be always in conformity with the realities of daily life.[1] More important, from our point of view, are the two works known as Yukti-kalpataru and Mānasollāsa. The former is attributed to King Bhoja of Dhārā in Malwa, the great patron of Sanskrit learning in the eleventh century. It purports to give "an account of all requirements in a royal court," and is, in fact, a miscellany of information on polity, buildings, furniture, precious stones, ornaments, etc. But there are sections in the work which deal with certain aspects of the art of war, and especially with the implements, animals and vehicles needed for war-like purposes. The Mānasollāsa is said to have been composed by the Cāḷukyan emperor, Someśvara III ("Bhū-loka-malla"), who reigned between 1127 and 1138 A.D. It is a metrical treatise on the Arthaśāstra, written in an easy and florid style. Like the Yukti-kalpataru it deals with a variety of subjects. It has chapters, for instance, devoted to moral and religious duties of kings, functions of all kinds of officials and court menials, taxation and treasury, methods of diplomacy, fortresses, army and war.

Two other works of considerable importance from our point of view are the Nīti-prakāśikā of Vaiśampāyana and the Nītisāra of Śukra. Though bearing the title of *nīti,* the former is really a work on the art of war. Of its eight chapters or cantos, four (II-V) are devoted to the classification and description of the various kinds of arms and weapons, two (VI-VII) to the composition and constitution of the army, military arrays, rules regarding marching and camping, allowances and rewards for officers and privates, etc., and only one (VIII) to the general duties of the king in the government and administration of his kingdom. The Nītisāra of Śukra is a well-known manual of the Arthaśāstra type, and an inestimable source of information regarding Hindu ideas on politics, sociology and war. Once again, however, we are faced with the intricate problem of date. With indiscreet zeal, the late Dr. Oppert identi-

[1] Compare, for instance, their references to the "four-fold" army. They continue to describe the functions of chariots, although, as will be proved later, chariots had by this time ceased to be employed as instruments of war.

fied Vaiśampāyana and Śukra, the supposed authors of these two works, with the eponymous sages of the Mahābhārata; and on the basis of this precarious hypothesis he drew the conclusion that they belonged to about the same age. Much discussion has taken place since his time; and although nothing like unanimity has yet been achieved, it is generally agreed that neither of the two manuals in their present form could have been composed earlier than about the 16th century A.D.[1] On the other hand, it is very probable that the present versions of the Nīti-prakāśikā and Śukranīti are based on more ancient texts, and many of the passages in both can be easily traced in such standard works as the Mahābhārata, Manu, Kāmandākīya and Agni Purāṇa.[2] What, then, should be our attitude towards these works? Should we reject their evidence as of no value in relation to the period we have selected, or should we accept them, without discrimination, as illustrating the customs and usages of ancient India? We believe wholesale rejection would be as rash as wholesale acceptance. Both works have no independent value but when their evidence is of a corroborative nature, illustrating or clarifying facts known from recognized ancient sources, it must not be ignored.

We may now pass to an examination of the extant treatises on Dhanurveda and other cognate topics. There are references to

[1] The issue has been decided chiefly on the ground that they contain references to guns and gun-powder. Cf. Keith, *History of Sanskrit Literature*, p. 464. It may be pointed out, however, that unlike the Śukranīti, the Nīti-p. contains *no* formula for the preparation of gun-powder, and the passages in the text which have been taken by Oppert as meaning guns and rockets may bear altogether different interpretations. Cf. e.g. *yantrāgāra* in VI. 22, which Oppert translates as "arsenal for guns." But *yantra* need not mean a gun at all. It is mentioned in most ancient texts, and it usually meant a mechanical contrivance of any kind (see Ch. XIV). Again, *nalikā* mentioned in II. 17, has been translated as "musket." In IV. 40, it is described as a kind of missile, straight, thin and penetrating, but with a hole in the middle, and discharged from a *droṇi-cāpa*. This *droṇi-cāpa* appears to have been a mechanism of the nature of a cross-bow. Be it noted, further, that *nālīka*, as a kind of arrow, is mentioned in the epics. In the Droṇa-parva 188,11, it is included in a list of a dishonourable weapons. The commentator here explains by defining *nālīka* as an arrow that enters, breaking in the flesh, and cannot be withdrawn on account of its small size. Cf. also Anuśāsana-parva 104,34; Rām. VI. 20, 26, etc. The *dhūma-gulikā* mentioned in Nīti-p. V. 54, should perhaps be interpreted as a bullet, but it might be explained as a stinkball as well.

[2] Cf. e.g. Nīti-p. I, 51, 53, 54 and VI, 89 with Kām. V, 78-79; XIII, 61 and XIV, 7; VIII, 18, 24 and XIX, 18. Also Nīti-p. VII, 45 and Manu VII, 90; Nīti-p. V, 31-34 and Śalya-parva 57, 16 ff.

Dhanurveda in ancient literature and inscriptions.[1] In the Viṣṇu Purāṇa,[2] it is described as constituting one of the eighteen traditional branches of knowledge. Elsewhere,[3] it is said to be an Upaveda of Yajur-veda, "by which one can be proficient in fighting, the use of arms and weapons and the use of battle-arrays." In the epics, it is often referred to in such a manner as to make us certain that it formed an essential part of a knight's education.[4] Further, it is described as having a *sūtra* like other Vedas, and as consisting of four branches (*catuṣpāda*) and ten divisions (*daśavidha*).[5] It is reasonable, therefore, to conclude that a literature on Dhanur-veda came into existence before the epics reached their present form.

Until recently it was generally believed that any work or works on Dhanur-veda that might have been composed in ancient times were lost beyond possibility of recovery.[6] In recent years, however, a number of treatises on Dhanur-veda have come to light, and a few of them have been printed and published.

So far as we know, the published manuals are the following:

1. Auśanasa Dhanurveda Saṅkalanam, edited by Paṇḍit Rājārām.
2. Kodaṇḍa-maṇḍana or Bāṇa-vidyā.
3. Dhanur-veda in the Bṛhat Śārṅgadhara Paddhati.
4. Dhanur-veda Saṁhitā of Vaśiṣṭha. It has twice been published, first in 1902 from Bombay, with a Hindi translation attributed on the title-page to Haradayālu Svāmī and in the colophon to Ramarakṣapāla; and a second time, in 1922, from Mymensingh (Bengal), with a Bengali translation by Paṇḍit Iśwar Chandra Śāstrī, Sāṅkhya-Vedānta-Nyāya-Darśaṇa-Tīrtha and Arun Chandra Sinha.

[1] Kathā-sarit-sāgara, VI, 22; Bhāgavata Purāṇa, I, 7, 44; 3, 12, 28; Mat. P. 220, 2, etc. The Ag. P. gives a dhanur-veda in ch. 249 ff. The account describes the names, lengths and methods of using various arms, with the proper employment of forces.

[2] Wilson, Works, VIII, 67.

[3] Śukra-nīti, ch. IV, sec. 3. Cf. also Madhusūdana Sarasvatī's *Sarvaśāstropalakṣaṇam*, pp. 13-14.

[4] Cf. Ayodhyā-kāṇḍa, 2, 28; Ādi-parva, 130, 3; Droṇa-parva, 22, 30 etc.

[5] Sabhāparva, 5, 121, mentions *dhanur-vedasya sūtram* along with *yantra-sūtram*. In the preceding verse mention is made of similar *sūtras* on elephants, horses and chariots. For *catuṣpāda* and *daśavidha*, compare Ādiparva 130, 21; 221, 72; Vanaparva 37, 4; Udyogaparva 157, 3. etc.

[6] Indo-Aryans I, 297.

In their present form, none of these manuals, however, can be referred to an early date. The *Auśanasa Dhanur-veda Saṅkalanam* has been extracted by the editor from the body of another work called *Vīramitrodaya*. Mitra Miśra, the author of this encyclopædic work, is known to have lived in the court of Vīrasiṁha Deva, the king of Orccha in Bundelkhand, and was, therefore, a contemporary of Akbar. The Dhanurveda in the Paddhati belongs to a slightly earlier age, in as much as Śārṅgadnara is believed to have flourished in the middle of the 14th century. The date of *Kodaṇḍa-maṇḍana* is more difficult to determine, but it is certainly later than Bhoja (11th century A.D.), to whose conquest of Koṅkan it refers (p. 2. v. 3). Nor is it possible to assign the *Dhanurveda Saṁhitā* of Vaśiṣṭha to any earlier epoch. It contains a clear reference (Bengal ed., p. 66; Bombay ed., p. 106) to the *Mitākṣarā* of Vijñāneśvara, who was a contemporary of the Cāḷukya king Vikramāditya VI (1076-1126 A.D.). In the relevant passage the Mitākṣarā is held up as a recognised authority on law, and its chapter on *vyavahāra* is recommended for study to warriors. It is reasonable to assume that a great number of years must have elapsed since the composition of the *Mitākṣarā* before it came to be recognised as an authoritative commentary on Hindu law. We may logically conclude, therefore, that the *Dhanur-veda Saṁhitā* of Vaśiṣṭha could not have been composed earlier than the 13th century A.D., and it may belong to an even later period. On p. 64 of the Bengal edition, (Bombay ed. p. 10), it mentions the title *Chatrapati*—a title which, so far as we know, was never used by any Hindu king or emperor before the time of the Maratha hero, Sivaji. The mention of this epithet, therefore, suggests that the manual did not reach its present form earlier than the 17th century of the Christian era.[1]

Yet there are good reasons to believe that all these manuals derive much of their materials from older works on archery and military science. The *Auśanasa Dhanur-veda Saṅkalanam*, for instance, is a collection of fragments from two older manuals on military science, quoted in the Vīramitrodaya and there ascribed to Uśanas and Traiyambaka (Śiva). It is probable that, like the Indika of Megasthenes, the old texts of Uśanas and Śiva are lost in oblivion, but they have partly survived in the form of quotations in later works. Like Mitra Miśra, Śārṅgadhara also admits that his work is merely a compilation from two older manuals on

[1] Mr Joges Chandra Roy (I. H. Q. VIII, 583) describes the Dhanurveda Saṁhitā of Vaśiṣṭha as "a work of the 12th century." But he has assigned no reasons for this assumption.

the subject, attributed to Śiva and Vyāsa, respectively.[1] Vaśiṣṭha is silent about the manual of Vyāsa, but he too frankly acknowledges his debt to an earlier work by Śiva or Sadāśiva.[2]

On their own admission, therefore, all these three authors had drawn upon an older manual on military science, alleged to have been composed by Śiva. The internal evidence of their works both justifies and strengthens this assumption. For, a large number of verses identical in meaning and in language occur in all the three. We may, therefore, designate the common original from which these works have drawn their teachings on military art as the Śiva-Dhanur-veda. The age of this half-lost manual cannot be determined with any approach to accuracy save within very wide limits. It seems clear, however, that this is not the Dhanur-veda to which the epics refer. The author's allusion to Śiva-yogis,[3] his seeming acquaintance with latter-day Tāntric phrases,[4] his adoption of the judicial astronomy based on the zodiac,[5] his calendarial use of the planetary names,[6] and last but not least his clear reference to the worship of the goddess Caṇḍī on the ninth day of the new moon in the month of Āśvina, accompanied with the sacrifice of goats,[7]—all point to the conclusion that the manual under discussion could not have been composed earlier than about the 5th or 6th century A.D.

The main theme of the Śiva-Dhanurveda is to provide an account of the training and tackle of an archer. The bow was one of the principal weapons of ancient India, and bowmen constituted an invariable concomitant of Hindu armies. In view of this importance of archery, an elaborate, thorough and regular course of training was prescribed for those who aspired to suitable positions in the military service of the state. For the bow was, as is the modern rifle, a weapon of precision, and the effective use of it was a fine art. It required a rare skill of eye and hand. It was, therefore, necessary to have the juvenile bowmen of the country adequately trained in the different modes and tactics of archery

[1] Cf. p. 263, no. 1714: *Iśvaroktād dhanur-vedād Vyāsasyāpi subhāṣitāt.* Cf. also colophon (p. 290); *Ete Śiva-dhanur-vedasya bhagavato Vyāsasya ca.*

[2] Cf. p. 1. (Bengal ed.): *Yāṁ sarahasyāṁ dhanur-vidyāṁ bhagavān Sadāśivaḥ Paraśu-rāmāyovāca, tāmeva sarahasyāṁ vacmi te hitāya.* Cf. also the remark on p. 11: *gaditaṁ Śambhunā purā.*

[3] Cf. Vaś. (Bengal ed.) p. 5, v. 16; Śār. p. 264, No. 1728.

[4] Vaś. p. 6. v. 21; Śār. p. 265, No. 1733.

[5] Vaś. p. 4, vv. 11-13; Śār. p. 264, No. 1723-1725.

[6] Vaś. p. 4, v. 4; Śār. p. 364, No. 1726. Comp. Fleet, J.R.A.S., 1912, p. 1044

[7] Vaś. p. 82; Śār. p. 282.

so that the state might count upon an abundant supply of skilful archers for the army. The Śiva-Dhanurveda primarily dwells on this course of training. But it also deals with archery tackle—how bows and bow-strings are to be prepared, what materials are best suited for the making of arrows, arrow-heads, quivers and arm-guards, and diverse cognate topics.

It will be a mistake to think, however, that the old manuals on Dhanurveda were concerned only with archery. They dealt with the preparation and use of other weapons also,[1] but the bow would appear to have been their primary subject as it was their primary interest.

Side by side with the literature on the bow, there had developed a similar literature on the sword. Some fragments of this literature are enshrined in the pages of the Bṛhat Saṁhitā (ch. IV) of Varāhamihira and the Yuktikalpataru (pp. 139-174) of Bhoja. The Sāraṅgadhara Paddhati also contains a lengthy section on "the examination of swords" (*khaḍga-parīkṣā*), which is avowedly extracted from a number of earlier works on the subject such as Lohārṇava, Khaḍga-kośa, Loha-ratnākara, etc.[2] This sword-literature, it may be noted, ranks far below the bow-literature in point of precision and scientific statement. It is often full of crudities and absurdities; but nonetheless it gives us valuable information concerning the methods followed in the manufacture and testing of swords.

Another class of literature, which throws some light on our subject of enquiry, are the ancient treatises on elephants and horses. These are plentiful in number, and available both in manuscript and print. The most noteworthy of the treatises on elephants are the Hastyāyurveda of Pālakāpya and the Mātaṅgalīlā of Nārāyaṇa,[3] the latter being comparatively modern in form. Among works dwelling on the treatment of horses, of special fame

[1] Compare, for instance, the Auśanasa-Dhanurveda-Saṅkalanam by Pandit Rajaram. Besides the bow, it describes swords of various kinds, spears and javelins, clubs, battle-axes and discs. It also enumerates different classes of forts and their distinguishing characteristics.

[2] There is also a chapter on the sword in the Nīti-prakāśikā (ch. 3). The published catalogues of Sanskrit manuscripts reveal the existence of a few manuscripts on the subject. Compare, e.g., Oppert's list of Sans. Mss. Vol. I. pp. 467 and 469. Edward Sachau in his preface to Al 'Berūnī's India (I, xxxiii) says that among Indian books which were translated into Arabic under the Abbasids, there is mention of one "On the signs of swords."

[3] Published in the Trivandrum Sanskrit Series, 1910.

are the Aśvacikitsā of Nakula,[1] Aśva-sāstra of Hemasūri and Aśva-vaidyaka of Jayadatta. The chief value of works, belonging to this category, lies in the fact that they testify to the esteem in which horses and elephants were held for military reasons, and the meticulous care with which they were classified, rationed and trained.

The foregoing paragraphs, it is hoped, will make it abundantly clear that there is an extensive military literature in Sanskrit, and this naturally constitutes the most copious source of information for the present study. It is, however, by no means the only source. One has to work his way through writings of an altogether different kind—the Purāṇas, Kāvyas, dramas and romances—and patiently collect the relevant information scattered through them. A sentence here and a clause there, a word here and a hint there, have to be picked up with care and fitted into the picture.

CHAPTER I

THE ARMY AND A GENERAL SKETCH OF ITS COMPOSITION

1. The Army in Hindu Political Thought

Ancient political thinkers of India conceived the state as consisting of seven essential elements (*prakṛtis*), of which the army was one. The conception dates from pre-Kauṭilyan times, and was accepted as an axiomatic truth by all later writers. The army was thus accorded a recognised position in the state-organism. But it is nowhere held up as the supreme element. In contemporary thought it usually takes rank as sixth in the order of gradation. There is a discussion in the Arthaśāstra (Bk. VIII. ch. 1) as to the relative importance of the army (*daṇḍa*) and the treasury (*kośa*), and Kauṭilya pronounces himself definitely in favour of the latter. "The army", he says, "may go to the enemy, or murder the king himself, and bring about every kind of trouble. But finance is the chief means of observing virtuous acts and of enjoying desires." Later writers, though adhering to the general principles of Kauṭilya, show a more positive inclination to idolise the army. Kāmandaka (XIII, 37), for instance, says that "even the foes of a king, possessing an efficient army, are turned into friends; a king with a strong army rules the earth unhampered." In the Śukranīti (ch. I, ll. 122-4), the relation of the army to the state has been compared with that of the mind to the man. As without the mind the human organism cannot work, so without the army the state-organism comes to a standstill. "Without the army," Śukra writes elsewhere (ch. IV, sec. ii, ll. 28-29), "there is neither kingdom, nor wealth, nor prowess. The treasury is the root of the army, and the army is the root of the treasury. It is by maintaining the army that the treasury and the kingdom prosper, and the enemy is destroyed."

2. 'Four-fold' division of the Army

In the Vedic period the army apears to have consisted of two divisions, viz. foot-soldiers (*patti*) and car-warriors (*rathin*). During the post-Vedic period, however, the horse and the elephant were incorporated in the fighting corps. Hence from the time of the Jātakas there came into vogue a new category in Hindu politico-military thought. It is the 'four-fold' army—*caturaṅga-bala* or *caturaṅga-camū*.[1] This 'four-fold' division of the army is a common feature throughout ancient literature. In course of time it was transformed into a literary convention, and the convention outlasted the extinction of one of the arms. As will be shown later, war chariots fell into total disuse about the 7th century A.D. But long after their abandonment as instruments of war, and long after the four-fold army had in actual practice become three-fold, the convention of *caturaṅga-bala* continued intact, and is referred to both in later literature and inscriptions. We shall here cite only two instances. In the Mānasollāsa (śl. 1176, p. 134) there is a mention of the epithet, though internal evidence proves beyond doubt that war-cars were no longer in use. So also the Jabalpur copper-plate of 1122 A.D. (Ep. Ind. 11, 3) refers to the army of Yaṣṭikarṇadeva as *caturaṅga*, notwithstanding the fact that chariots did not form part of the war-apparatus of that king.[2]

It should be noted here that the relative position of the four arms differed from age to age. Both Vedic and epic testimony prove that in the earliest period of our history, as in that of Greece, the chariots constituted the most important arm. The knights and nobles drove in chariots to the front line, and from them showered their missiles on the opposing knights and their masses of followers. But from the 4th century B.C. onwards, as already stated, the elephant occupied the first rank in the military service. The infantry and the cavalry seem to have always remained in a subsidiary position in the Hindu military system.

3. 'Six-fold' division of the Army

Besides the above classification of the army into four arms, there was also in vogue a six-fold division, presumably based on

[1] The Jātaka, tr. by Cowell, II, 66 153; III, 6, 298. Cf. also Ādi-parva 69, 4; Virāṭa-parva 68, 13; Udyoga-parva 5, 17; 19, 1, etc. Occasionally, too, the army is referred to as six-fold (*ṣaḍaṅginī*), where to the four arms are added the 'treasure' (*kośa*) and machines (*yantra*) brought to the camp. (Udyoga-parva 96, 16; Śānti-parva 103, 38; Manu VII, 185). Śānti-parva 121, 44 mentions an "eight-fold" division of the army, where in addition to the usual four, we have the workmen, officers, spies and military guides, (*daiśika-mukhyāḥ*).

[2] Cf. also Yukti-kalpataru, p. 6. A Hoysala Inscription, dated 1143 A.D, refers to the "army of elephants, horses, chariots and foot-soldiers." (Ep. Carn. VIII, 103). Another inscription (ib. VIII, 131) of 1302 A.D. mentions "*caturaṅga-balam*". Cf. also Ep. Ind. XX, 119; XXII, 155.

the area or source of recruitment. According to this conception, the army was supposed to consist of six 'limbs' (*ṣaḍaṅga*), these being the hereditary troops (*maula*), mercenaries (*bhṛta*), gild levies (*śreṇi*), soldiers supplied by feudatory chiefs or allies (*suhṛd-balam*), troops captured or won over from the enemy (*dviṣad-balam*), and forest tribes (*aṭavī-balam*). The earliest references to this six-fold division occur in the epics and the Arthaśāstra; but they may be traced in such late works as the Kāmandakīya and Mānasollāsa, and in inscriptions ranging from the 6th to the 11th century.[1]

Of the different classes of troops mentioned above, ancient military opinion appears to have attached the greatest importance to the *maulas* or hereditary troops. Graded qualitatively, the mercenaries came after the *maulas*, next came the gild levies, next the allied troops, while the forest tribes were placed at the bottom of the scale. In the Arthaśāstra (Bk. IX, ch. 2), Kauṭilya gives elaborate reasons in support of the above gradation. "A *maula* force," he says, "is more important than the *bhṛta* force in as much as it is dependent on the king for its existence, and is the recipient of constant favour from the latter." Mercenaries are better than gild levies because they are obedient to the king, stationed near at hand, and always ready to march. Similarly gild levies are better than allied troops on the ground that they belong to the same country as the king, have the same objects in view, the "same expectations of loss and gain," and are actuated by the same feelings of rivalry and anger. Kauṭilya proceeds in the same strain to show why he considers the allied troops superior to renegades from the hostile country, and the latter again to forest tribes. With regard to the two last, he says: "Both these are anxious for plunder. In the absence of plunder and in times of difficulty, they prove as dangerous as a lurking snake."[2] These views of Kauṭilya have been faithfully reproduced in the Nīti-sāra of Kāmandaka (XIX, 4-9); but they do not appear to have been universally shared. In the passage from the Mahābhārata, already referred to, the gild levies are considered as important as the mercenaries. In the Mānasollāsa (śl. 557-561), again, the hereditary, mercenary and allied troops are estimated as the best,

[1] Kauṭ. Bk. IX, ch. 2; Laṅkā-kāṇḍa, 17, 24; Āśrama-vāsika-parva, 7, 7-9 (here, however, *dviṣad-balam* is substituted by *cāra-balam* (spies); Raghu-vaṁśa, IV, 26; Kām. XIX, 3; Mānas. I, p. 79, śl. 557-61. For epigraphic references see. Ep. Ind. I, 235; III, 320, etc.

[2] Kauṭ. Bk. IX, ch. 2; Shām.'s translation (p. 401) of the passage appears to be faulty. Comp. Gan.'s ed. III, 55-56.

the gild levies as of medium quality, and the forest tribes as the worst, while troops from the hostile country (*amitraja-balam*) are declared to be absolutely untrustworthy.

The *maulas* appear to have resembled the personal retainers of the early German chieftains. Professor F. W. Thomas suggests that they were probably "connected by caste, and ultimately by race, with the king himself, such as in later times we find in the quasi-feudal states of Rajputana."[1] Most ancient writers emphasise their unfaltering loyalty to the king.[2] In the Arthaśāstra, (Bk. II, ch. 35) Kauṭilya speaks of villages which were exempted from taxation in lieu of the military services which they rendered to the state. It seems reasonable to believe that the *maulas* were endowed with rent-free lands, besides cash wages when on active service. Elsewhere, (Bk. IX, ch. 2), the author outlines the circumstances under which this class of troops should be mobilised against the enemy. "When the king," he writes, "thinks that the number of his *maula* troops is more than is necessary for the defence of his kingdom, or when he apprehends that his *maula* force is disaffected and may cause disturbance when he is away, or when the enemy has under command a large and loyal body of hereditary troops, and is therefore to be fought out with much skill on his part, or when it is expected that the journey would be so tedious and the duration of fight so long that a *maula* force can alone endure the wear and tear, or when the enemy is known to be in possession of a powerful secret service, in which case the mercenary and other kinds of troops cannot be relied upon lest they may lend their ears to the intrigues of the enemy, or when the king thinks that other kinds of troops are wanting in strength, then is the time for mobilising the *maula* force."[3] It is thus clear that this class of troops was not only considered as the most reliable (for they alone could be trusted in the face of a powerful secret service of the enemy), but as possessed of the greatest skill and fortitude. And this, in part, accounts for and perhaps justifies the special privileges which the state bestowed upon them. The Chinese pilgrim, Hiuen Tsiang, had perhaps these *maulas* in view, when he wrote about the so-called National Guard of India. This National Guard, he says, "are heroes of choice valour, and, as the profession is hereditary, they become adepts in military tactics. In peace they guard the

[1] Cambridge History of India, I, 489.

[2] References as before; also Kām. XIX, 4.

[3] Kauṭ. tr. pp. 398-9. The translation of the passage has been slightly altered to make the meaning clear. Cf. also Kām. XIX, 12-15.

sovereign's residence, and in war they become the intrepid vanguard."[1]

Two other classes of troops which require some explanation are the gild levies and the forest tribes. The former have provided the basis for a considerable amount of historical speculation in recent years. In his translation of the Artbaśāstra (pp. 398-401), Dr. Shamasastry renders the term *śreṇi-balam* as the "corporation of soldiers." Professor D. R. Bhandarkar takes it to mean "tribal bands of mercenaries."[2] In the opinion of Dr. R. C. Majumdar, again, the term refers to "a class of guilds which followed some industrial arts and carried on military profession at one and the same time."[3] On the other hand, Mr. Monahan makes the following observation on the point: "Probably the military *śreṇis* were special troops, composed of men of different fighting races, who enlisted in the royal army under their own chiefs. They would be called *śreṇi* from analogy to trade guilds, and, no doubt, served for pay, perhaps under a contract made between the king and the *śreṇi-mukhya*."[4] Lastly, Professor Thomas, writing in the Cambridge History of India (I, 480), says that the *śreṇis* probably refer to "ordinary trade-guilds, as an organisation for calling out the people for service in time of invasion, a sort of militia or *landwehr*."

On a close examination of the evidence at our disposal, it appears that there were two types of military *śreṇis* in existence in ancient India. First, there were those who like the Swiss Guard of medieval Europe, formed themselves into a quasi-military corporation and placed their services at the disposal of the highest bidder on the occasion of an armed conflict between two or more states. Such were probably the Vāhikas, Yaudheyas and certain other tribes in the time of Pāṇini, for he has referred to them as *āyudha-jīvi-saṁghāḥ*, i.e. guilds dependent on the profession of arms for their livelihood. The Kāśikā mentions more than sixty examples of corporations or clans as being included under the rules of Pāṇini (V. 3, 114-117).[5] It is, therefore, probable that at one time or another these military *śreṇis* were fairly widespread throughout the

[1] Watters, I, 171. It may be noted here that there is a close resemblance between the *maulas* of ancient and the *chelās* of Moghul India. For an account of the latter, see Irvine, *Army of the Indian Moghuls*, p. 11.

[2] The Carmichael Lectures, Calcutta University, 1919, p. 144.

[3] Corporate Life in Ancient India, 1922, pp. 30-31.

[4] The Early History of Bengal, Oxford, 1926, pp. 66-67.

[5] R. K. Mukherji, *Local Government in Ancient India*, 1920, p. 33.

country, and they may possibly have played the same part in the military history of India as the Condottieri in that of Italy.

There was, however, a second class of guilds which, as Dr. R C. Majumdar says, "followed some industrial arts and carried on military profession at one and the same time." Kauṭilya refers to guilds of this nature in his chapter on Saṁghavṛttam (Bk. XI, ch. 1). In the relevant passage, he speaks of Kṣatriya *śreṇis*, "who lived by agriculture, trade and wielding weapons" in Kāmboja and Surāṣṭra countries. Obviously these were trade and craft guilds, which, like the Arti Maggiori of Florence or the more well-known Hanseatic League of Northern Europe, had occasionally to resort to arms in defence of their commerce and industry. The conditions which brought these commercial-cum-military societies into being appear to have been the same in India as in Europe. Briefly, these conditions were the constant need of protection and the inability of the state to afford it to its citizens. The weakness of the central government, the internecine strifes, the still more dreadful barbarian invasions, and, last but not least, the frequency of brigandage on the highways and along river-routes—all these tended to create an atmosphere of insecurity, in which the industrial and commercial communities, being thrown on their private and local resources for protection, developed a defensive power of their own, which became at once a source of weakness and of strength to the state.

Ancient epigraphic records disclose a few instances of guilds of this nature. The best known case is that of the silkweavers' guild, referred to in the Mandasor Inscription of Kumāragupta and Bandhuvarman. The epigraph records that some members of the guild "became excessively well acquainted with the science of archery," and that the guild as a whole was "valorous in battle," and effected "by force the destruction of their enemies."[1] Another instance of this nature is provided by the Vīra-Vaḷañjiyas of the South. These were a great corporation of traders, whose centre was at Aiyāvoḷe (modern Aihole), and whose organisation seems to have spread over the greater part of southern India. The name denotes 'valiant merchants,' and is therefore similar to the 'Gentlemen Adventurers' of the East India Company. Like the silkweavers' guild of Daśapura, this great fraternity of traders frequently boasts of its prowess and heroism in contemporary inscriptions, and some of its records, to quote Dr. Barnett, "are couched in a tone of regal pomposity."[2] Closely associated with

[1] Fleet, C.I.I., III, No. 18.

[2] Rice, Mysore Inscriptions, pp. 8, 120 and 123; Ep. Carn. VII, 114 and 156;

the Vīra-Vaḷañjiyas were the Veḷaikkāras, a federation of working-class communities.[1] They figure prominently in a large number of South Indian inscriptions and in the Ceylonese chronicle, Mahāvaṁśa. It is clear from these records that they were an exceptionally powerful community, who wielded the sword with as much skill as the sickle. Sometimes they were entrusted with the protection of temples and shrines, with their property, lands and serfs. They supplied regiments to the Coḷa army, and also to the kings of Ceylon. At intervals in the history of the latter country, when the rulers were weak, they became the real power behind the throne; and repeated, on a smaller scale, the exploits of the Praetorian Guards in the Roman Empire.[2]

We have stated before that these commercial-cum-military guilds were at once a source of strength and of weakness to the state. They were a source of strength because they provided a means of local defence, when the state, for one reason or another, failed to discharge its normal functions. Moreover, in times of stress and need, without being a drain on the exchequer, they formed themselves into excellent battalions for the defence of the kingdom to which they owed their allegiance. In the Arthaśāstra, (Bk. V, ch. 3), dealing with the "subsistence to Government servants," the pay of *śreṇimukhyas* is set down as equal to that of the chiefs of elephants, horses and chariots. And then follows the significant remark: "With this amount they can have a good following in their communities." It is clear that in the age of Kauṭilya only the leaders of the guilds were paid from the royal treasury, while the rank and file served without pay. A statement in the Nītisāra of Kāmandaka (XIX, 5), proves that the same practice continued well into the last centuries of our period. In the passage, referred to, the author remarks that one of the reasons why the

Ep. Ind. IV, 296; Ibid. XIV, 332 ff.; A. Appodarai, *Economic Conditions in Southern India,* University of Madras, 1936, Vol. I, pp. 391. ff.

[1] In the Poḷannaruva Inscription of Vijaya-bāhu I, it is stated that the Veḷaikkāras consisted of three divisions, viz. the Mahātantra, the Vaḷañjiyar, and the Nāgarattār. Ep. Ind. XVIII, 331 ff.

[2] Madras Epigraphic Report, 1913, pp. 101-2; South Indian Inscriptions, Vol. II, Introd. p. 10; Ep. Ind. XVIII, 331 ff; Ep. Zeylonica, Vol. IV, no. 24; S. K. Aiyangar, *Hindu Administrative Institutions in South India* (Sir William Meyer Lectures, 1929-30), pp. 310-311.

Still another example of this nature is furnished by the Kaikkoḷars, a community of weavers in the Tamil country. Like the Veḷaikkāras, they too seem to have filled an important role in the military history of South India. Madras Ep. Rep. 1922-3, p. 14; 1923-4, pp. 15, 101; no. 627 of 1910 and 98 of 1915.

mercenary troops should be considered superior to the guild levies is that the former are dependent on the king for their wages.[1] In other words, the guild levies, though they might rally to the support of the king on occasions of grave danger to the state, did not receive any regular wages from the royal exchequer.

The military *śreṇis* were a source of weakness to the state because at times they became so powerful as to be able to defy the authority of the king. There are numerous indications in contemporary records to show that they were looked upon with ill-concealed suspicion and hostility by all advocates of absolutism. In the Nārada Smṛti (X,v.), for instance, it has been enjoined, with reference to guilds and other associations, that "confederacy in secret, resort to arms without due causes and mutual attacks will not be tolerated by the king."[2] The remark indirectly proves that the guilds sometimes betrayed a predilection for private warfare—a predilection, inherent in all feudalised communities, but antithetical to all conceptions of sovereignty, ancient or modern. In the Arthaśāstra, Kauṭilya makes no attempt to conceal his great distrust of these quasi-military fraternities. The whole of Bk. XI. is one long sermon against them. "Which is better", he asks elsewhere (Bk. VII, ch. 11), "the land with a scattered people, or that inhabited by guilds?" The reply is significant. "The former is better," he says, "in as much as it can be kept under control and is not susceptible to the intrigues of enemies, while the latter is intolerant of calamities and is susceptible of anger and other passions." The same distrust is implied in another passage (Bk. VII, ch. 16), where the author in course of a hypothetical discussion as to the methods that may be employed to keep down a hostile party or group, recommends that guild levies (*śreṇibala*) may be "provided with a piece of land, which is under constant troubles from an enemy." It is evident, therefore, that the guilds sometimes became so powerful as to constitute a state within the state. Both Nārada and Kauṭilya seem to imply that their distinguishing characteristics were turbulence, truculence and independence. The Mahāvaṁśa (Ch. LVII and LXXIV) proves that at least twice in the history of Ceylon the Veḷaikkāras rose in revolt against their legitimate sovereigns—first in the time of Vijayabāhu, and a second time in the reign of Parākramabāhu 1. It was a fight between the two fundamental forces of history, one centripetal and the other centrifugal.

[1] *Vṛtteśca svāmyadhīnatvād bhṛtam śreṇi-valād guru.*

[2] S. B. E. XXXIII, 154; R. C. Majumdar, *Corporate Life in Ancient India*, p. 30.

The mention of *aṭavī-balam* as a part of military establishment in the Arthaśāstra shows that the custom of associating predatory hordes with the army goes back to very early times. These predatory hordes used to live in vast forests and inaccessible mountains. They appear to have been most numerous in central and peninsular India, though they could also be found in other parts of the country. Both literary and epigraphic evidence prove that they were a constant source of danger to peaceful settlements in their neighbourhood.[1] In one place in the Arthaśāstra (Bk. VIII, ch. 4), Kauṭilya remarks: "Robbers carry off the property of the careless and can be put down as they are easily recognised and caught hold of, whereas wild tribes have their own strongholds, being numerous and brave, ready to fight in broad daylight, and seizing and destroying countries like kings."[2] In his Nītisāra (XIX, 8), Kāmandaka describes them as "wild and undisciplined, faithless, greedy and sinful."

Yet these wild tribes were often employed for military purposes by Hindu kings, in the same manner as the Red Indians were employed by the English and French in their wars in North America. They brought their own war-apparatus to the theatre of war, but they fought for pay and plunder. Their services were considered specially helpful when a king's army had to pass through forests and defiles, morasses or mountains,[3] or when it was the intention of the invader to ravage and devastate the enemy's country.[4]

It may be noted here that the same custom of associating predatory tribes with the army continued in later ages among the Marathas and the Moghuls. It is well-known that the Pindharis often accompanied a Maratha army in its expeditions, and were employed not so much for fighting as for plundering the country through which they passed. Describing the Moghul army, Manucci writes: "Along with the armies there marched privileged and recognised thieves called Bederia (Bidari); these are the first to invade the enemy's territory, where they plunder everything they find. The handsomest items are reserved for the general; the rest they sell on their own account. Prince Shah Alam, when he was

[1] References to these wild tribes in ancient literary and epigraphic records have been collected by Dr. B. A. Saletore in his book entitled *Wild Tribes in Indian History*, Lahore, 1935.

[2] Cf. also Bk. VIII, ch. 4 (tr. p. 389); Bk. IX, ch. 11 (tr. p. 401), etc.

[3] Kauṭ. Bk. IX, ch. 2; Kām. XIX, 23.

[4] Śānti-parva, 59, 48.

within the territories of Shivaji, near Goa, had in his army seven thousand such, whose orders were to ravage the lands of the Bardes." [1]

[1] Manucci, *Storia do Mogor,* II, 459.

CHAPTER II

STRENGTH OF ARMIES

Indian records do not give us any reliable information regarding the numerical strength of military forces maintained by Hindu states. The figures cited in the epics are poetic, fanciful and often self-contradictory. But this defect of Indian records is partly made good by foreign historians, who furnish us with some useful data on the question. The figures quoted in the following tables are gleaned entirely from this source.

Table A

According to the historians of Alexander, at the time of the Macedonian invasion some of the Indian states possessed military forces as shown below:

Name of the king, state or race.	Infantry.	Cavalry.	Chariots.	Elephants.	Page.[1]
Massaga ..	38,000	..	..	..	94
King Porus ..	30,000	4,000	300	200	102
	50,000	3,000	1,000	130	278
The Malloi and the Oxydrakai ..	90,000	10,000	900	..	234
	80,000	10,000	700	..	287
The Abastanoi ..	60,000	6,000	500	..	252
The Agalassoi ..	10,000	3,000	..	..	285
Agrammes, king of the Gangaridae and the Prasii ..	200,000	20,000	2,000	3,000	221-2
..	200,000	20,000	3,000	4,000	282
	200,000	80,000	8,000	6,000	310
The Assakenoi ..	30,000	20,000	..	30	66
The Ambri and Sigambri ..	80,000	60,000	..	..	324

[1] Reference is to McCrindle, *India and its Invasion by Alexander the Great.*

TABLE II

According to reports which had reached Megasthenes, when he was an ambassador in the Mauryan court at Pāṭaliputra, the military establishment of the various Indian states was as follows:

Name of the kingdom or race.	Infantry.	Cavalry.	Chariots.	Elephants.	Page.[1]
The Mauryan Empire	..	..	..	8,000, or	139
under Candragupta	600,000	30,000	..	9,000	156
The Calingae ..	60,000	1,000	..	700	136
The Modubae, the Molindae, the Uberae etc. ..	50,000	4,000	..	400	138
The Andarae ..	100,000	2,000	..	1,000	138
The Megallae	of unknown strength		..	500	142
The Chrysei, the Parasange and the Asangae ..	30,000	800	..	300	142
The Odomboerae, the Salabastrae and the Horatae ..	150,000	5,000	..	16,000	147
The Pandae ..	150,000	..	..	500	147
The Gangarides ..	60,000	1,000	..	700	147

TABLE III

The following figures are taken from the account of the Chinese pilgrim, Hiuen Tsiang, and a number of early Muhammadan historians. They relate to the period from the seventh to the twelfth century A.D.

1. On the eve of his famous campaigns of conquest, king Harṣa of Kanauj (606-647 A.D.) possessed an army which comprised 50,000 infantry, 20,000 cavalry and 5,000 elephants. When he had finished his task, the cavalry are said to have been increased to 100,000 and the elephants to 60,000. (Beal, *Buddhist Records* I, 213; Smith, *Early History of India,* p. 352).

2. Al Masudi (d. 956 A.D.) says that his contemporary Pratihāra (? Bauüra) king of Kanauj maintained four armies, "according to the four quarters of the wind." Each of them numbered 700,000 to 900,000 men. "The army of the north wars against the prince of Multan, and with the Musulmans, his subjects, on the frontier. The army of the south fights against the Balhara,

[1] Refer to the Indika of Megasthenes.

king of Mankir. The other two armies march to meet enemies in every direction." (Elliot. I, 23).

3. According to Al 'Utbi (Elliot. II, 25), Jaipal, the Raja of Bathindah, marshalled against Sultan Maḥmūd in 1001 A.D. a force consisting of 30,000 foot, 12,000 horse and 300 elephants.

4. Nizamuddin Aḥmad says (Tabqat-i-Akbari, Biblioth. Ind. p. 12) that when Maḥmūd invaded the Cāndella territory in 1019 A.D., he found king Gaṇḍa (995-1025 A.D.) ready for battle with an army which comprised 36,000 horse, 145,000 foot and 390 elephants. According to Firishta (Briggs. I, 64), however, the strength of the army amounted to 45,000 foot, 36,000 horse and 640 elephants.

5. The confederate host, which fought under the banners of Rai Pithora (Pṛthvīrāja) in 1191 A.D., is said to have included 200,000 horsemen, and 3,000 elephants, besides a countless mass of foot-soldiers. In the second battle of Tarain (1192 A.D.), Rai Pithora is stated to have had under his command a still larger army, of which the cavalry alone numbered 300,000. (Iswari Prasad, *History of Mediaeval India*, 1928, pp. 118-121).

It is to be noted, however, that figures in history, especially in ancient history, are often misleading. They are generally based on hearsay, and not on authentic scrutiny. There is also a tendency among ancient and mediaeval writers to make the hostile army look as big as possible; for, this heightened the glory of their victorious hero. The eyes of a youthful Macedonian or Ghaznavite must have shone in admiration when he read how Alexander and Maḥmūd, with only a handful of followers, inflicted crushing defeats on vast masses of barbarian, infidel armies in India.[1] Nevertheless, in the light of later history, the above figures do not seem to be entirely untrustworthy. The combined testimony of both Indian and foreign writers proves that similarly unwieldy armies were maintained in the empire of Vijayanagar. From the *Rāyavācakamu* we learn that Kṛṣṇa Deva Rāya, while fighting against the combined armies of Bijapur, Golkonda and Bidar, commanded an army which comprised 120 *ghaṭṭams* of elephants, 60,000 horse and 500,000 foot.[2]

[1] Professor Dalbrück has shown how unreliable are the figures given by Herodotus regarding the Persian forces who fought at Marathon and Plataea. Herodotus says that the army of Xerxes consisted of 5,100,000 men. "If it were true," retorts Dalbrück, "one may calculate that marching through paths, often very narrow, between the mountains, the last man could only have left Susa, beyond the Tigris, when the first arrived before Thermopylae."

[2] S. Krishnaswami Aiyangar, *The Sources of Vijayanagara History*, 1919, pp. 113 and 120.

Nuniz, the Portuguese chronicler, affirms that the same prince led against Raichūr an army consisting of 703,000 foot, 32,000 horse and 551 elephants, besides camp-followers, merchants, etc.,—"an infinitude of people."[1] Firishta says that in 1443 A.D. the Vijayanagar army consisted of 62,000 archers, 80,000 horsemen and 200,000 foot-soldiers.[2]

Many similar instances of the unwieldy size of Indian armies in the Middle Ages may be cited. The tables given above, however, indicate that the custom dates back from very early times. It is dangerous to be dogmatic; but we shall not be far from the truth if we assert that from the fourth century B.C. onwards the army in India has always been a major item of expenditure from the exchequer of the state. The above figures further prove that it is not always for want of numbers that the Indian armies failed in their resistance to Alexander, Sultan Maḥmūd or Muhammad Ghori. The causes of their successive failures lie elsewhere—in defective equipment and organisation, defective higher leadership, and to some extent, especially in the eleventh and twelfth centuries, in inferior morale. Napoleon used to say that in war the spiritual is more important than the material. It is not suggested that the Hindu armies who fought against the Turkish invaders were altogether lacking in moral qualities; but contemporary evidence proves that the morale in the ranks of the northern warriors was keyed higher. Moreover, in craft and resourcefulness, in tactics and strategy, Ānandapāl and Pṛthvīrāja were no better match for Sultan Maḥmūd and Muhammad Ghori than Porus was for Alexander.

1 Sewell, *A Forgotten Empire*, 1900, pp. 147, 326-8.

2 Briggs, II, 309.

CHAPTER III

THE INFANTRY

1. Historical outline

As everywhere else in the world, so in India, the original fighting-man was the foot-soldier. In Vedic times, the infantry (*patti*) fought along with the car-warriors. One of the epithets of Rudra in the Śatarudriya liturgy of the Vājasaneyi Saṁhitā (XVI. 19) is "lord of footmen" (*pattināṁ pati*). In the Atharva-Veda (VII. 62, 1) Agni is referred to as conquering the most powerful opponents, as a combatant on a chariot overcomes men fighting on foot.[1] The statement is important, because it shows that foot-soldiers in the Vedic period were looked upon as a helpless mass when pitted against car-warriors.

The same view of the relative inferiority of the footmen has been more graphically depicted in the epics. In the war-scenes of the Mahābhārata, for instance, they are described as a conglomerate mass, with hardly any individuality or initiative. They were mostly recruited from the lower classes, even from barbarians and foreigners. They followed the charioted knight as *padānugāḥ*, *anugāḥ* or *anucarāḥ*, but at the knight's death, they usually fled, and when they did not flee, were, as in the Iliad, slaughtered as a herd of sheep who had lost their shepherd.[2] In fact, the epic foot-soldiers seem to have been useful only in order to secure a decorous setting for the display of knightly prowess. They suffered the greatest number of casualties, but contributed little or nothing to the decision of battles. In this respect the early Indian infantry bears a remarkable affinity to European infantry in the feudal age. Early Indian tactics, as described in Vedic and epic literature, were, like feudal tactics in Europe, based principally on ideas of personal glory. Like their feudal counterparts, the early Indian foot-soldiers formed an unstable base of the knightly pyramid, and were not an arm, capable of offence and defence,

[1] *ayam Agniḥ saptatir vṛddha-vṛṣṇo rathiva pattin ajayat purahitaḥ.*

[2] J. A. O. S. XIII, 260-261.

having its own special organisation, functions in the line of battle and tactical method.

The evidence of the classical authors, the Arthaśāstra of Kauṭilya, later works on politics and military science, and early Muhammadan chronicles—all point to the conclusion that the infantry in ancient India never outgrew this subsidiary position in the military organisation of the country. There is a statement in the Śānti-parva (100, 24) that "an army, in which the infantry is numerically strong, is always victorious."[1] The figures cited in the preceding chapter show that facts tallied with the theory. From the 4th century B.C. till the close of the 12th century A.D., the combatants on foot continued to maintain their majority in Hindu armies. And yet it seems likely that during all these fifteen or sixteen centuries there was no continued or systematic attempt in any part of the country to use the infantry as the kernel of armies or develop in it that solidarity and defensive power, for which the Macedonian phalanx and the Roman legions became justly famous in the ancient world.

In the Arthaśāstra, Kauṭilya attaches much more importance to elephants, and even to horses than to foot-soldiers. In Bk. X. ch. 4, he gives a detailed analysis of the functions of the various arms, but referring to the infantry he simply says that its proper work is to carry weapons to all places and at all times, and drilling (*sarva-deśakāla-śastra-vahaṇaṁ vyāyāmaśca*). Elsewhere (Bk. X, ch. 6), he says: "Of infantry, cavalry, chariots and elephants, he should strike the first-mentioned with that which is subsequently mentioned," thus indicating clearly his views on the relative efficiency of the different arms. Somadeva in his Nīti-vākyāmṛta (pp. 82-85) waxes eloquent on the utility of elephants and horses, but says nothing concerning the utility of foot-soldiers. In the Agni Purāṇa, again, no distinction is made between the infantry as such and mere camp-followers. Describing the functions of the infantry, it says that they consisted in "carrying away the wounded and dead troops from the field of battle, offering resistance to elephants, supplying water and carrying arms and weapons."[2] The Nītiprakāśikā (VI, 57) provides us with a similar enumeration of the functions of the infantry. "The proper task of the foot-men," it says, "is to protect the granaries, arsenals and treasuries, and to make entrenchments for the army." It is clear, therefore, that no Hindu writer, not even Kauṭilya who has so often been

[1] The same statement is repeated in Ag. P. 288, 7.

[2] Ag. P. 236, 44-45; also ib. 242, 27.

compared to Machiavelli, possessed the latter's insight to recognise that the infantry was "the sinew and substance of the army."[1]

From the quotations cited above, it would seem that there probably existed no clear-marked line of demarcation between the infantry as such and mere camp-followers. V. A. Smith observes that in the time of emperor Akbar, porters, dāk runners or foot-men, gladiators, wrestlers, pālki bearers and water-carriers, were all classed as infantry.[2] Bernier says that in estimating the strength of the Moghul imperial infantry under Aurangzeb, servants, cutlers, tradesmen and all those individuals belonging to the bazars or markets, who accompanied the troops, were usually included.[3] This curious resemblance between the Hindu infantry of ancient India and the Moghul infantry of the 16th and 17th centuries shows how a change in a country's political destinies may take place without necessarily involving any change in its institutional life.

From the foregoing remarks it must not be thought that the infantry in ancient India was a mere 'residue'. As archers they seem to have been redoubtable fighters, and won the admiration of the Greeks. It is also probable that being the most numerous part of the army, they sometimes decided the fortunes of battles by the sheer weight of their numbers. Moreover, in certain special forms of warfare, their services must have been found of real importance. Most ancient writers emphasise the kind of ground on which the infantry could be employed to greatest advantage. In the Śāntiparva (100, 23) Bhīṣma says that "a region, which is full of inaccessible spots and which is overgrown with large trees and cane bushes, is the ground for the infantry." Kautilya (Bk. X. ch. 4) declares that the best ground for the infantry is one "which contains big stones and boulders, or is thickly planted with trees, green or dry." The Agni Purāṇa (236, 49) applauds uneven grounds as the most suitable for the employment of foot-soldiers.[4] It is clear, therefore, that in contemporary opinion, the infantry were of special value when the theatre of war lay, not in the open plains, but in forest and hilly regions. A striking confirmation of this fact is afforded by the Muruju-l Zahab of Al Mas'udi. "The greatest of the kings of India in our time," he writes, "is the Balharā sovereign of the city of Mānkīr...His troops and elephants

[1] We have, however, a contrary view in the Yukti-kalpataru, p. 7, where it is stated; *sarvaṁ patti-balādhīnaṁ tasmāt pattibalaṁ balaṁ.*

[2] Bernier, *Travels in the Mogul Empire* (A.D. 1656-1668), edited by Constable and revised by V. A. Smith, 1914, p. 220. f. n.

[3] Ibid. p. 219.

[4] *Pattibhūr-viṣamā jñeyā;* cf. also Ag. P. 242, 28.

are innumerable, but his troops are mostly infantry, because the seat of his government is among the mountains."[1]

In the defence of forts and strongholds, too, foot-soldiers were specially relied upon. The reason is simple. Elephants, chariots and horses could not be used when the enemy was hammering at the gates of a fort. Whatever resistance was offered at such times, was offered by footmen, standing on the walls, in the towers, or behind the parapets, and hurling their weapons and missiles on the besiegers. The classical chronicles provide us with a few instances of this nature;[2] but they must have occured in every century and in every part of the country.

2. Equipment and armament

The equipment of the infantry, like the dress of the common people, must have varied from age to age, and region to region. But our sources of information are so scanty that it is well-nigh impossible to throw any light on these local and periodic variations. Arrian, from whom we get a short description of the equipment of Indian foot-soldiers in the 4th century B.C., prefaces his account with the significant remark that "it is not to be regarded as the only one vogue." Evidently there were other modes of equipment, besides the one noticed and described by the Greek historian.

Arrian says that Indian foot-soldiers in the fourth century B.C. carried a bow made of equal length with the man who bore it. "This they rest upon the ground, and pressing against it their left foot thus discharge the arrow, having drawn the string far backwards;[3] for the shaft they use is little short of being three yards long, and there is nothing which can resist an Indian archer's shot,—neither shield, nor breast-plate, nor any stronger defence if such there be. In their left hand they carry bucklers made of undressed ox-hide, which are not so broad as those who carry them, but are about as long. Some are equipped with javelins instead of bows, but all wear a sword, which is broad in the blade, but not longer than three cubits; and this, when they engage in close fight (which they do with reluctance), they wield with both hands, to fetch down a lustier blow."[4]

[1] Elliot. I, 21.

[2] Cf. the story of the defence of Massaga, Aornos and the capital of the Malloi, as recorded by Arrian and Curtius Rufus.

[3] Kālidāsa's Raghuvaṁśa (XI, 14) shows that the same mode of archery continued in some parts of India as late as the Gupta period: *ninyatuḥ sthalaniveśitaṭanī līlayaiva dhanuṣī adhijyatām.*

[4] Arrian, Indika, XVI.

It will appear from the above quotation that the bow was the principal weapon of the infantry of this epoch; but the sword and javelin were also used. The bas-reliefs at Bhārhut and Sānchi, (assigned respectively to the second and first century B.C.), show that the same mode of equipment prevailed over wide regions of the country, and persisted till well-nigh the beginning of the Christian era. Nearly all the infantry in the scene depicting the "War of Relics" at Sānchi are represented as archers. But several of them are also furnished with broad, heavy swords, and javelins. In one of the bas-reliefs a soldier covered by a shield is shown holding a javelin horizontally ready to launch it forward.[1] There is, however, one great distinction between the foot-soldier's equipment as described by Arrian and that revealed by Sānchi and Bhārhut sculptures. The classical author seems to imply that all classes of infantry—archers, swordsmen and javelin-bearers—had shields to protect them. The bas-reliefs at Sānchi and Bhārhut, however, show that only the swordsmen and javelin-bearers were provided with shields, but the archers were without them, probably because they had their hands already full.[2] The evidence of Kauṭilya confirms what we learn from the sculptures. In Bk. X, ch. 5 of the Arthaśāstra, in course of a discussion about the formation of battle-arrays, he says that an array of pure infantry may be formed with the men with shields in front and archers in the rear.[3] This two-fold classification of infantry into *āvaraṇinaḥ* and *dhanvinaḥ* is noteworthy, and leads one to doubt the accuracy of Arrian's statement in this particular. It is, however, possible that the practice noticed by the classical historian was confined to the northwest, and did not obtain currency in other parts of the country.

The bas-reliefs at Sānchi and Bhārhut also shed some light on the soldiers' dress in the first and second centuries B.C. At Sānchi the typical archer has always a head-dress, very much like a modern *pugree,* with a large knot on the top. He wears a cotton cloth in the fashion of a kilt, and this is held by means of a belt. The belt is remarkably long and begins encircling just near the chest till it comes down below the navel and is then tied in a long bow. From the fact of tying, as also from the successive encirclements

[1] Sir Alexander Cunningham, *The Bhilsa Topes*, 1854, p. 217.

[2] Maisey, *Sanchi and its Remains*, London, 1892, Pl. XX; Cunningham, *The Stupa of Bharhut*, London, 1879, Pl. XXXII.

[3] *Patti-vyūhaḥ purastādāvaraṇinaḥ pṛṣṭhato dhanvino iti* For the meaning of *āvaraṇa* see Bk. II, ch. 18.

round the body, it may be inferred that the belt is made of linen. The upper part of the archer's body usually looks bare, but was probably, as Cunningham says, covered by a tight-fitting jacket of some kind.[1] The mode of fastening the quiver to the back is peculiar and picturesque. "The quiver is fastened to the right shoulder, and the fastenings, which are apparently leather straps, are passed over both shoulders, crossed in front, and carried to the back, where they were probably passed through a ring in the end of the quiver, and then carried to the front and again crossed, the ends being secured by loops to the upper straps."[2]

At Bhārhut there is a figure of a foot-soldier, nearly life-size, and in such fine preservation that all the details of his costume can be distinguished with ease. We cannot do better than describe it in the words of Cunningham. "His head is bare, and the short curly hair is bound with a broad band or ribbon, which is fastened at the back of the head in a bow, with its long ends streaming in the wind. His dress consists of a tunic with long sleeves, and reaching nearly to the mid-thigh. It is tied in two places by cords; at the throat by a cord with two tassels, and across the stomach by a double-looped bow. The loins and thighs are covered with a dhoti which reaches below the knees, with the ends hanging down to the ground in front of a series of extremely stiff and formal folds. On the feet are boots, which reach high up the legs, and are either fastened or finished by a cord with two tassels, like those on the neck of the tunic. In his left hand the soldier carries a flower, and in his right a monstrously broad straight sword, sheathed in a scabbard, which is suspended from the left shoulder by a long flat belt. The extreme breadth of the sword may be judged by comparing it with the thickness of the man's arm, which it exceeds, while its length may be about 2½ feet, or perhaps somewhat more. The belt of the sword is somewhat straight, and without a guard. The face of the scabbard is ornamented with the favourite Buddhist Omega symbol of *Tri-ratna*, or the triple gem. The sword belt, after being passed through a ring attached to the side of the scabbard, appears to be twice crossed over the scabbard downwards, and then fastened to a ring at the tip, below which the broad ends hang down like the ends of a scarf."[3]

[1] Cunningham, *The Bhilsa Topes*, p. 216. In some instances, the tunic worn by the archer is clearly visible. Compare Maisey, *Sanchi and its Remains*, Pl. XX.

[2] Cunningham, op. cit.

[3] Cunningham, *The Stupa of Bharhut*, pp. 32-33.

We hardly know anything about the equipment of foot-soldiers during the next few centuries. In the frescoes at Ajantā, which are usually assigned to the Gupta period, the footmen are generally depicted as carrying swords or spears in their right hand and shields in their left.[1] On the Begur Stone Sculpture we find the infantry equipped on similar lines.[2] In the same way, Māgha in his Śiśupālavadha (XVIII. 4, 19, 21; XIX, 55), describes the infantry as armed with swords and shields. But that these were not the only weapons used by the infantry of the Gupta and post-Gupta period is shown by the account of the Chinese pilgrim, Hiuen Tsiang. Describing the equipment of the Indian infantry in the 7th century A.D., the pilgrim says: "They carry a long spear and a great shield; sometimes they hold a sword or sabre, and advance to the front with impetuosity. All their weapons are sharp and pointed. Some of them are these—spears, shields, bows, arrows, swords, sabres, battle-axes, lances, halberds, long javelins and various kinds of slings." "These weapons," the pilgrim adds, "they have used for ages."[3]

1 Lady Herringham, *Ajanta Frescoes*, Pl. XVII and XXII.
2 Ep. Ind. VI, opp. p. 46.
3 Beal, *Buddhist Records*, I, 73.

CHAPTER IV

THE WAR CHARIOTS

1. Historical Outline

The use of chariots in warfare marks an important stage in the evolution of the world's military system. Man was, as stated before, originally a foot-soldier. But when tribes were fused into states, and distant marches became a necessity, it must have been found that a foot-soldier who, encumbered with arms and armour, had a long distance to march before coming to close quarters with his adversary, was at the disadvantage of being partly out of breath at the commencement of the conflict. It was then realised that the soldier who could be carried without fatigue and placed fresh upon the spot where he would be obliged to exert every energy in deadly conflict, would have a great advantage in a hand-to-hand struggle over one who had been obliged to march heavily laden for a long distance. This is probably one of the most important reasons which led to the use of chariots in ancient warfare. But there was possibly another equally important reason. The chariot-warrior could carry with him a larger number of weapons than an ordinary foot-soldier could do. Moreover, being elevated over his opponent, and partly protected from his weapons by the chariot-screen, he enjoyed the same advantage over a foot-soldier as the mail-clad feudal chivalry of mediaeval Europe enjoyed against the combatants on foot.

The use of war-chariots was not an isolated phenomenon in the history of India. They are known to have been in use throughout almost all the ancient world—China, Egypt, Assyria, Babylon, Greece and Persia. In India they were employed as early as the Vedic age. There are numerous references to war-chariots in the Ṛgveda (i. 20, 3 ; iii. 15, 5 ; iv. 4, 10 ; 16, 20 ; x. 103, 10 etc.)[1] In the epics they constitute the most important arm. The car-warrior is the main strength of the epic army, the stay and hope of contending hosts. So completely does he dominate

[1] The Atharva-veda (VI. 125) contains a beautiful hymn to the war-chariot, "compact with thongs of leather." It is described as the "bolt of Indra, vanguard of the Maruts, close knit to Varuṇa, and child of Mitra."

in the battle-scenes, so controlling is the rôle that he fills, that the period represented by the epics may well be designated as the veritable chariot-age of Indian history.

Both Vedic and epic evidence, however, prove that chariots were more or less a monopoly of warriors belonging to the noble classes. The rank and file fought on foot. Just as the knight in mediæval Europe was followed by his squires, or the Optimati attended by one or two personal retainers, the epic car-warrior in India was followed by two 'wheel-guards' (*cakra-rakṣau*), attended by a retinue of foot-men. These 'wheel-guards' were often younger members of the noble classes, who were thus "winning the name of hero by useful service under some renowned knight."[1] In the course of a brilliant analysis of the position of the epic car-warrior, Hopkins writes: "The knight's adversaries are generally of his own class. If he becomes *apratirathaḥ*, or has no foeman worthy of his steel, he rushes about the field till he meets one. Incidentally, as it were, he may shoot a few hundred common soldiers. He never makes a premeditated attack upon the foot-soldiers alone, but when their chief is killed, of whom they are, like the horses, an appendage, they ought to disperse; and if they do not, they are shot as nuisances, not as antagonists. Especially is this the case with the 'heel-catchers' or soldiers deputed to annoy the rear. These are legitimately shot as cowardly villains, though they never appear to do much harm."

"The knight in his chariot is equal to an army. Frequently we find thousands running from one mounted hero. In the case of a national hero, of course, no bounds are set in description. Through fear of Arjuna, everybody, even the knights ran away; the horse-riders abandoned their horses, the elephant-riders their elephants—falling from war-cars, elephants and horses."[2]

In dealing with the epics, we must, of course, make due allowance for poetic effusions. But there is always a grain of truth behind a mass of husks. And that grain of truth, in this case, seems to be that the car-warriors enjoyed unchallenged supremacy in the military organisation of post-Vedic India.

When we come down to the age of Alexander, we are, however, struck by a profound change in the Indian military situation. The chariots were still in use, but no longer as the most important arm. Unlike the average epic knight, king Porus came to the field of battle riding, not a chariot, but an elephant. A reference to Table

[1] J. A. O. S. XIII, 205. [2] Ibid. XIII, 261-2.

I in Chapter II will show that some of the Indian states of this epoch maintained no chariotry at all. Table II is even more significant. Though not perhaps wholly accurate, it shows the direction in which the wind was blowing. After his enumeration of the military forces maintained by various Indian states, Megasthenes makes the pregnant remark: "In fact, no one invested with kingly power ever keeps on foot a military force without a very great number of elephants and foot and cavalry."[1] The omission of war-chariots is noteworthy. The tables seem to have turned.

It is worth while recounting here the story of the part played by the Paurava chariot corps in the battle of the Hydaspes. We learn from the classical authors that in the preliminary encounter of the advance guard, which Porus had sent under his son to oppose the landing of Alexander on this side of the river, the chariots "proved to be of scarcely any service, for the storm of rain (which had raged during the night) had made the ground slippery and unfit for horses to ride over, while the chariots kept sticking in the muddy sloughs formed by the rain, and proved almost immovable from their great weight." Yet ignoring this strategic difficulty, the drivers rode at full speed into the midst of the battle, "thinking they could thus most effectively succour their friends." The idea probably was to use the momentum of the weight and speed of the horse and chariot as an offensive weapon. But it was not to be. The Macedonian foot-soldiers, who were exposed to the first shock of the onset, were no doubt trampled down; but the Paurava car-men themselves "were hurled from their seats, when the chariots in rushing into action, jolted over broken and slippery ground. Some again of the horses took fright and precipitated the carriages not only into the sloughs and pools of water, but even into the river itself."[2]

Even after this disaster, however, Porus had some 300 chariots left to his army.[3] When he found a place where he saw there was no clay, but that the ground from its sandy nature was all flat and firm, and suited for the movements of cavalry whether charging or falling back, he drew up his army in order of battle, and placed the chariots in front of the cavalry on the two wings.[4] But in the final action the chariots fared hardly better than in the preliminary skirmish. The first onset of the Macedonian cavalry threw them

[1] McCrindle, *The Indika of Megasthenes*, p. 155.
[2] McCrindle, *India and its Invasion by Alexander*, pp. 207-8.
[3] Ibid. p. 102. [4] Ibid. p. 108.

into confusion. Arrian says that the drivers of the chariots were all slain, and the chariots were broken to pieces.[1] Diodorus mentions that "the Macedonian cavalry began the action, and destroyed all the chariots of the Indians."[2] It may be added that the Greeks, even before they came down to India, had learnt the art of fighting chariots to the best advantage. In the battle of Arbela they had boldly faced the dreadful scythed chariots of the Persians, and crushed them by means of their superior cavalry.

This disastrous experience must have served as an eye-opener to contemporary military leaders; but it did not lead to the immediate rejection of chariots as an instrument of war. The evidence of Megasthenes, on the contrary, proves that they were maintained at considerable strength in the Mauryan empire, and one of the six boards in Candragupta's war-office was entrusted with the special duty of supervising this branch of the service. Dr. Krishnaswami Aiyangar has pointed out that ancient Tamil literature contains references to Mauryan war-chariots going out on an expedition to the distant south. Thus Māmulnār, an old Tamil author, speaks of the war-cars of the Mauryas as having penetrated as far as the Podiyil Hill in the Tinnevelly District. "The newly-installed Mauryas, whose army contained a very large number of elephants, marched down to attack them; and their beautifully decorated cars wore down hill sides, making dark passages through which clear water flowed in torrents." Elsewhere the poet refers to the same hill as "worn by the bright rolling-wheels of the cars of the Mauryas, who marched towards the south." Another ancient Tamil poet, called Paraṇar or Param Koṛṛanār, mentions the "cutting down of the hill to make a roadway for the war-chariots of the Mauryas."[3]

We do not know much about the history of war-chariots in the post-Mauryan epoch. It is reasonable to assume that they continued to be used in Indian warfare for several centuries yet. They are not only mentioned in the Junāgaḍh Inscription of Rudradāman (A.D. 151 or 152),[4] but occasionally, too, in the records of a much later period. In his preliminary description of the Indian army, Hiuen Tsiang says that it was composed of Foot,

[1] Ibid. p. 107. [2] Ibid. p. 275.

[3] Proceedings and Transactions of the Second Oriental Conference, pp. 310-322. It may be contended, however, that the Mauryas referred to in Tamil literature were the Mauryas of Koṅkan, not of Magadha.

[4] Ep. Ind. VIII, 48.

Horse, Chariot and Elephant soldiers. The chariot was occupied by an officer, was drawn by four horses, and was guarded on both sides by the infantry.[1] In the Daulatpur Plate of Bhojadeva I (706 A.D.), the camp (*skandhāvāra*) of this king is said to have been "furnished with many boats, elephants, chariots and foot-soldiers."[2] The Sāmnad copper-plate grant of Dantidurga or Dantivarma II (also called Khaḍgāvolaka), dated A.D. 753-4 (Śaka 675), tells us that this monarch "overcame the countless army of Karṇāṭaka", with a force "of chariots and horses which were not to be conquered."[3]

Yet the decline of chariots must have commenced many centuries earlier. Though they lingered on here and there, they appear to have been rejected as an arm by the more powerful states of the post-Kushan period. There is not an iota of evidence to prove that they were employed by the Guptas, and it is certain that they were not used in the empire of Harṣa. In the famous Madhuban copper-plate, there is no mention of chariots, though the other arms have been specifically referred to.[4] Bāṇa and Hiuen Tsiang describe, with an extraordinary wealth of detail, the military resources of their patron king. They speak of his foot-soldiers, cavalry and elephant corps, but are significantly silent about chariots.[5] The Chinese pilgrim also supplies us with a description of the military organisation of Pulakeśin II, whose court he had visited in the year 641 A.D., and here again he makes no mention of war-chariots.[6] Similarly the Gauḍavaho of Vākpati, though it gives interesting details regarding the military organisation of Yaśovarman, is characteristically silent about war-chariots. Finally, Muhammad bin Kāsim, who invaded and conquered Sindh early in the 8th century A.D., did not encounter war-chariots in any of the numerous armies with which he had to fight.

The final disappearance of chariots from India's military system probably came about in the eighth century A.D. The reasons which led to it are not difficult to guess. The doom of war-chariots had already been signalised many centuries earlier in the fateful field on the Hydaspes. Ancient military thinkers recognised that chariots needed a dry and plain soil for

[1] Watters. I, 171.
[2] Ind. Ant. XI, 108; XIII, 140.
[3] Ep. Ind. V, 211.
[4] Ep. Ind. I, 72.
[5] Beal, Records. I, 213; Harṣacarita, tr. by Cowell and Thomas, 1897, ch. VII.
[6] Watters. II, 239.

their use, that they could not be employed in hilly tracts or morasses, nor in the rainy season.[1] Such restricted employment must have reacted fatally upon their utility as instruments of war. With growing complexities in the texture of Indian political and military life, a premediated selection of soil and season became more and more difficult, and consequently war-chariots fell more and more into disuse.

Another important reason which conspired to bring about the same result appears to have been, as stated by Wilson, the infusion of Scythic tribes and manners about the commencement of the Christian era.[2] It is reasonable to believe that the influx of these foreign tribes with their traditions of superior horsemanship must have led to a re-orientation of military outlook, and to a recognition of the fact that the functions which a chariot corps was expected to perform in war could be discharged more efficiently by a trained and well-equipped cavalry.[3] Indeed, there are good reasons to think that as with the Greeks, so with the Hindus, the horse came to supersede the chariot.

2. Equipment, size, etc.

In the Vedic period the chariot was usually a small-sized, two-wheeled vehicle.[4] It was drawn by two horses, occasionally by three or even four.[5] The body of the car appears to have been exceedingly light, consisting of a wooden frame-work, fixed on an axle-tree (*akṣa*), fastened by cow-hide thongs. The framework consisted of a floor (*garta*) to stand on, and a guard of some sort round it. It was also provided with a seat (*vandhura*) where the warrior could sit when he wanted. The pole (*īṣā, praüga*) of the car was probably attached to the middle of the axle; and at the end of the pole was the yoke (*yuga*).

"Normally there was, it seems, one pole, on either side of which the horses were harnessed, a yoke (*yuga*) being laid across their

[1] Kauṭ. Bk. X. ch. 4; Śānti-parva 100, 22; Ag. P. 242, 29-30; Yukti. Kalpataru p. 7, v. 45.

[2] Wilson, Works. IV, 207.

[3] These functions are enumerated in many ancient texts. Cf. Kauṭ. Bk. X. ch. 4 and 5; Kām. XX, 4; Ag. P. 242, 23 ff., etc.

[4] Chāndogya Upaniṣad, IV. 16, 5; Jaiminīya Upaniṣad Brāhmaṇa, III, 16, 7; Kauṣītakī Upaniṣad, I, 4.

[5] There horses in Ṛv. X. 33, 5; four in ib. II. 31, 1; Kāṭhaka Saṁhitā (XV. 2) refers to even five stallions as yoked to a chariot: *ratha-pañcavāhī*.

necks; the pole was passed through the hole in the yoke (called *kha* or *tardman*), the yoke and the pole being then tied together."[1]

"The horses were tied by the neck (*grīvā*) where the yoke was placed, and also at the shoulder, presumably by traces fastened to a bar of wood at right angles to the pole, or fastened to the ends of the pole, if that is to be regarded as it probably should be, as of triangular shape, wide at the foot and coming to a point at the tip. The traces seem to be denoted by *raśmi* and *raśanā*. These words also denote the reins, which were fastened to the bit (perhaps *śiprā*) in the horse's mouth. The driver controlled the horses by the reins, and urged them on with a whip (*kaśā*). The girths of the horse were called *kakṣyā*".[2]

The wheels, like the body of the chariot, were of wood. It is probable that originally solid wheels were used, but gradually these were replaced by those with spokes (*ara*).[3] Besides the spokes, a wheel consisted of a rim (*pavi*), a felly (*pradhi*), and a nave (*nabhya*). The rim and the felly together constituted the tire (*nemi*).[4]

The dimensions of a Vedic chariot may be inferred from the following passage in the Śulba Sūtra of Āpastamba (VI. 75): "The masters of the cartwright profession say that the *īṣā* (the pole of the chariot, which lies in the middle lengthwise—this has been compared with the centre line, the *pṛṣṭhya* or back-bone of a *vedī*) measures 188 (*aṅgulis*),[5] perpendicular (*tiryak*) to which (*īṣā*) are *akṣa* (hind part of the car) equal to 104 (*aṅgulis*) and *yuga* (the forepart) equal to 86 (*aṅgulis*); such is the chariot (constructed according to the rules of the gild). These are the measures of the car." This quotation has been given by Āpastamba as an authority for certain measures he proposes for the *nirūḍha-paśubandha-vedī*. It is evident, however, that the pole of a standard chariot measured 188 *aṅgulis* (finger-breadths), the axle 104 *aṅgulis* and the yoke 86 *aṅgulis*. The Baudhāyana and Kātyāyana Śulba Sūtras (Baudh. I, 10-12; Kāt. II, 1-4) mention the same dimensions for a chariot.

Passing over to the epics, we notice two types of chariots being employed in contemporary warfare. The first of these was a

[1] Vedic Index, II, 202.
[2] Ibid.
[3] Ibid. II, 201.
[4] Ibid.
[5] Karavindaswāmī says in his commentary: '*munibhiraṅgulisaṁkhyoktam rathaparimāṇam*'.

vehicle of small size, two-wheeled and two-horsed, very much like its Vedic fore-runner. The second variety, however, was of comparatively larger and thicker build, occasionally resting on four wheels, and generally drawn by four horses. Mr. C. V. Vaidya's assertion that the epic war-chariot was "always a four-wheeled construction"[1] is not justified by evidence. Epic testimony, on the contrary, tends to show that in spite of the development of four-wheelers, the two-wheelers still continued to hold their ground. Thus in the Droṇaparva (83, 15), Kṛṣṇa's chariot is expressly said to have had "two wheels like the sun and the moon." Elsewhere (ib. 188, 54), it is stated that a wheel came off a car, and then "the horses dragged the car with one wheel only." In another passage we read: "The one yoke, the one pole, the two wheels and the one axle were broken, cut to pieces by arrows."[2] Instances like these may be multiplied; but it is clear that the epic war-chariot was not always a four-wheeled construction. The bas-reliefs at Sānchi prove beyond doubt that two-wheeled, small-sized chariots were still in vogue as late as the first century B.C.[3]

And yet it is true that in the post-Vedic period, chariots with increasing size and weight and provided with four wheels were coming more and more into fashion. In both the Rāmāyaṇa and the Mahābhārata, there are occasional references to four-wheeled and even eight-wheeled cars.[4] There are references, too, to chariots being drawn by four horses. In the opening scene of battle in the Udyoga-parva (155, 13 ff.), we are told that "all the cars were drawn by four horses (*caturyuj*), and equipped with arrows and spears, and a hundred bows apiece; for each car were two pole-horses, directed by one driver (*dhuryayor hayayor ekaḥ . . . rathī*), and two outside horses fastened to the axle-end (*pārṣṇi*), and driven by one driver apiece (*pārṣṇisārathi*)."[5] It must be remembered, however, that four horses do not necessarily imply four wheels; the one has no connection with the other. Kṛṣṇa's two-wheeled chariot, to which reference has been made, is expressly stated to have been drawn by four horses.[6]

[1] Epic India, p. 257.

[2] J. A. O. S. XIII, 250.

[3] Maisey, *Sanchi and its Remains*, Pl. XX. Two-wheeled chariots are also implied as the regular form in the Sūtra period. Comp., e.g., Āśv. Gṛhyasūtra. III. 12, 1 ff; Pār. Gṛhyasūtra. III. 14, 2.

[4] Cf. Rām. Laṅkā. 44, 27: *aṣṭacakrasamāyukto mahārathaḥ*; Droṇaparva 165, 38; ibid. 173, 13 etc.

[5] J. A. O. S. XIII, 251.

[6] op. cit. In Rām. Laṅkā. 90, 39 (also ib. 48, 49) Indrajit's car is described as drawn by four black horses with gilded trappings.

The number of charioteers, however, depended on the number of horses. "When two horses are sufficient, one *sārathi* or charioteer is sufficient also. In the case of four horses, (two fastened to the pole, two by straps outside, not tandem: *dhur* and *pārṣṇi*), we have one charioteer in the middle, who guides the pole-horses, and on each side of him the two drivers of the outer steeds, *pārṣṇisārathi*."[1]

The Vedic car-warrior usually stood on the left hand of the charioteer, on whose skill he so largely depended.[2] In the epics, however, the charioteer is generally represented as standing in front of the chariot, and never in a line with the knight. It is probable that the floor of the chariot was a little elongated so as to consist of two parts, viz. the *upastha* ('the chariot lap'), where the knight usually took his stand, and the *nīḍa* ('the chariot nest'), "the little shelf in front where the charioteers stood."[3] The use of such terms as *vandhura* and *ativandhura* suggests that the charioteer was provided with a seat.[4] Whether the knight was similarly provided with a seat is not quite clear, although it is not impossible that he had one, called *talpa*.[5]

The epic war-car, like its Vedic fore-runner, appears to have been provided with a sort of 'guard' or fence-rim (*varūtha*) to prevent the warrior from falling down while engaged in action. One verse in the Udyogaparva (155, 8) suggests that the fence-rim was made of tiger-skins and other stiff leather.[6]

A few additional details in regard to the construction of the epic chariot are also available. For instance, it was provided with a pole (*ratha-īṣā*), which was "fastened to the box of the car (*kāṣṭha*) and to the double yoke (*yuga*) that crosses it, and rests in turn on the necks of the steeds."[7] It was, moreover, embellished with standards and flags with the distinctive devices of each knight.[8] Another noteworthy part of the car's furniture was the *chattra* (umbrella). Whether it served merely the purpose of a sun-screen or approached anything in the nature of a real protector cannot, however, be ascertained. Hopkins says: "Inspite of its frequent occurence in the descriptions of spoils, it does not seem to play any

[1] J. A. O. S. XIII, 237.
[2] Cambridge History of India I, 98.
[3] J. A. O. S. XIII, 236.
[4] Comp. Vanaparva 240, 31; Droṇaparva 35, 31.
[5] Comp. Droṇaparva 191, 68.
[6] *Vyāghra-carma-parīvārā dvīpi-carmāvṛtāśca te.*
[7] J A. O. S. XIII, 240.
[8] Ibid. XIII, 243-4.

part in the action, and I fancy it does not really come into the poem until a later age, but properly is to be associated with the mass of effeminate luxuries depicted long after the original."[1] Still another apparatus of the war-car was the *anukarṣa* ('drag'), which has been explained by the commentator as a "piece of additional wood fastened beneath the car for the purpose of quickly repairing damages done in battle."[2]

On the size and construction of war-chariots in the age of Alexander and the Mauryas, the classical authors supply us with a few hints. Megasthenes, perhaps referring to Magadhan practice, says that each war-car carried two men, who sat beside the charioteer.[3] We learn from Curtius Rufus that after their subjugation, the Malloi and the Sudracae sent some presents to Alexander, which included, *inter alia*, one thousand and thirty chariots, "each drawn by four horses."[4] Describing the chariotry of king Porus, the same writer observes that each car "was drawn by four horses and carried six men, of whom two were shield-bearers, two archers posted on each of the sides of the chariot, and the other two, charioteers as well as men-at-arms, for when the fighting was at close quarters they dropped the reins and hurled dart after dart against the enemy."[5]

Both Wilson and Hopkins maintain that Curtius' account of the Paurava war-chariot "does not seem to be correct," on the ground that it is so radically different from the "native account." A reference to the Arthaśāstra (Bk. II. ch. 33) will, however, show that the Indian account is not so divergent as it might appear at first sight. Kauṭilya is here describing the different kinds of chariots, used both for peaceful and warlike purposes. Of the latter, he especially specifies three, viz. the *sāṁgrāmika* (battle chariots), the *parapurābhiyānika* (chariots used in assaulting the enemy's strongholds), and the *vainayika* (training chariots). Regarding the size of chariots, he says: "The best chariots should accomodate ten persons, and in extreme cases twelve. After this there should be six more varieties of chariots with gradually decreasing weight and size till we come down to one which might contain four persons ordinarily, and six in exceptional cases."[6]

[1] Ibid. XIII, 246.

[2] Udyogaparva 15, 8; Bhiṣmaparva 80, 38.

[3] Indika. Fragm. XXXIV.

[4] McCrindle, *India and its Invasion by Alexander*, p. 251.

[5] Ibid. p. 207.

[6] The original runs thus: *Daśapuruṣo dvādaśāntaro rathaḥ. Tasmādekāntarāvarā ṣaḍantarāditi sapta rathāḥ.* Scholars differ in their interpretation of this passage. Shām. and Gap. have taken *puruṣa* in the

There is no discrepancy between the above statement and the account given by Curtius. It may be inferred, therefore, that with the passage of time, the old, light, two-horsed chariots were gradually superseded by bulkier prototypes.[1]

sense of measurement. See Shām.'s tr. p. 170; Gaṇ. I, 337. Meyer has however shown that Kauṭ. always uses the term *pauruṣa* and not *puruṣa* in the sense of measurement. *Das Altindische Buch Vom Welt-Und Staatsleben*, 1926, pp. 223-4. I have accepted Meyer's interpretation.

[1] The Purāṇas often mention chariots and their ornaments. "But their descriptions," says Rajendralal Mitra, "lead me to suppose that their idea of the car was the ratha of the modern times, a tower-like structure of many storeys, a cumbrous apparatus altogether," and "utterly unfit for warlike purposes." *The Antiquities of Orissa, Calcutta*, 1875, Vol. I. p. 131.

CHAPTER V

THE CAVALRY

1. Historical Outline

It is difficult to fix the period at which cavalry in the proper sense of the word were first used in India. Horse-riding was known as early as the Vedic age,[1] but there is no satisfactory record of the use of cavalry in battles of that period.[2]

In the epics the cavalry is recognised as a separate arm, but it is of no real value and is wholly unorganised. "The mounted soldiers," says Hopkins, "are recognised as a body (*kulam*) apart from others, of course, but do not act together. They appear as concomitants of the war-cars, dependent groups; but separate horsemen appear everywhere. Their employment was much influenced by that of the elephants. A body of horsemen is routed by an elephant. They were therefore detailed in small numbers to guard the war-cars and keep on the flanks of their own elephants. To the latter, indeed, they are formally assigned, but seem generally to be circling about the chariots."[3]

Hopkins adds that they were generally grouped with the *hasti-sādinaḥ* or elephant-riders, as a force antithetical to the main strength of the army, the car-men, and that in the battle scenes they are conspicuous through falling off their horses, quite often

[1] Cf. Ṛv. I. 162, 17; 163, 9; V, 61, 1-3 mention horses, the reins and the whip "laid upon the flank". In riding horses "the heroes stretch their thighs apart like women when the babe is born." Aśva-sāda or horse-rider is also mentioned in Vājasaneyi Saṁhitā, XXX, 13; Taittirīya Brāhmaṇa, III, 4, 7, 1 etc.

[2] Zimmer, *Altindisches Leben*, p. 295; Macdonell and Keith, *Vedic Index* I, 42, says: "No mention is made of riding in battle." Cf. also Cambridge History of India I, 98, 137. On the other hand, Dr. A. C. Das (Ṛgvedic Culture, 1925, pp. 222-226) maintains the opposite view that 'war-horses' were actually employed in battles of that period. But the quotations he has cited in support of his view do not seem to be convincingly clear on the point.

[3] J. A. O. S. XIII, 262-3.

from fear alone. "Their most efficient aid was given when they were hurled against the foes after the elephants had become useless, and the throng was too dense and mixed for the employment of war-cars. Then the agile and single horsemen could do good work on the herd of frightened foot-soldiers, unimpeded by fear of heavier foes."[1]

The classical chronicles show that the Indian cavalry in the age of Alexander were no longer as inefficient and unskilful as in the epic age. They were gradually out-growing the impotence of infancy, and winning recognition as an arm of real value. Aelian says that the Indians of this epoch held the horses in high esteem because of their "great use in arms and warfare."[2] The tables, given in Chapter II prove that most of the Indian states in the fourth and third century B.C. maintained large cavalry forces.

In the battle of the Hydaspes, the cavalry in the service of king Porus were posted in the two flanks of the Indian army. Alexander despatched against their left wing a contingent of 1,000 mounted archers, brought from the steppes of Central Asia, to throw the enemy in that part of the field into confusion with storms of arrows and charges of their horses. "He marched rapidly forward himself with the companion cavalry against the left wing of the barbarians, making haste to attack their cavalry in a state of disorder while they were still in columns and before they could deploy into line. The Indians meanwhile had collected their horsemen from every quarter, and were riding forward to repulse Alexander's onset, when Koinos, in accordance with his orders, appeared with his cavalry upon the rear. Seeing this the Indians had to make their cavalry face both to front and rear—the largest and best part to oppose Alexander, and the remainder to wheel round against Koinos and his squadrons. This, therefore, at once threw their ranks into confusion, and disconcerted their plan of operations; and Alexander, seeing that now was his opportunity while their cavalry was in the very act of forming to front and rear, fell upon those opposed to him with such vigour that the Indians, unable to withstand the charge of his cavalry, broke from their ranks, and fled for shelter to the elephants as a friendly wall."[3] Arrian, from whom the above quotation has been extracted, adds that shortly afterwards the Indian cavalry, when they saw their own infantry men engaged in action, once again wheeled round and charged the Macedonian cavalry. But the Macedonian horsemen,

[1] Ibid. XIII, 264. [2] McCrindle, *Ancient India*, p. 142.
[3] McCrindle, *India and its Invasion by Alexander*, pp. 104-6.

being far superior in skill and discipline, again routed them, and drove them back upon the elephants.

If we compare the foregoing account with that found in the epics, we shall hardly fail to recognise that the Indian cavalry of the age of Alexander were decidedly an improvement upon their epic fore-runners. It is true that they could not withstand the cleverly-planned attack of Alexander; but that was because of two reasons. First, the Macedonian cavalry were better-trained, better-disciplined and better-equipped; and second, Alexander himself was a cavalry commander of superb genius. As at Granicus, Issus and Arbela, so here on the bank of the Hydaspes, he showed all the best qualities of a great cavalry leader. Like Hannibal, he understood the advantage of hurling masses upon the enemy and breaking through them by the mere momentum; he demonstrated the efficacy of using the horse and the rider as a projectile weapon. "Military critics," writes McCrindle, "cannot point to a single strategical error in the whole series of operations conducted by Alexander himself, or his generals acting under his orders, from the time he encamped on the bank of the Hydaspes till the overthrow and surrender of Poros."

The gradual emergence of the cavalry as an efficient arm is further attested by the nature and variety of functions assigned to them in the Arthaśāstra. In one place (Bk. X. ch. 5) Kauṭilya says: "Running against; running round; running beyond; running back; disturbing the enemy's halt; gathering the troops; curving, circling, miscellaneous operations; removal of the rear; pursuit of the line from the front, flanks and rear; protection of the broken army; and falling upon the broken army—these are the forms of waging war with the horses." Elsewhere (Bk. X. ch. 4) he defines the principal tasks of the cavalry as consisting in cutting off the provisions and reinforcements of the enemy, screening and protecting the strategic front of the armies, outpost and detached service, occupying advanced positions, delivering a charge, scouting and reconnoitring, gaining the flanks and rear of an enemy, covering an advance and pursuing a retreating foe. In other words, in the opinion of Kauṭilya, they were expected to intervene in the prologue, in the principal act, and in the dénoûement.[1]

Our knowledge of the Hindu cavalry in the Gupta and post-Gupta period is extremely meagre. A few facts, however, are

[1] The functions of the cavalry are also dwelt upon in later works. Cf. Kām. XX, 5-6; Ag. P. 242, 25-26; Nīti-p. VI, 64-65.

worth noting. In the first place, it will be evident from a comparison of the tables given in Chapter II that there was a gradual increase in the ratio of cavalry in relation to other branches of service. It is not improbable that this increase was a direct sequel of the growing importance of this arm in contemporary military estimation. Secondly, it is noteworthy that on certain types of their coins, the Gupta emperors are depicted as full-dressed cavaliers. Whether the Guptas issued these coins merely in slavish imitation of the Indo-Bactrian and Indo-Parthian rulers, or were imbued with the idea of making the cavalry the most honourable form of service, is more than we can say. For reasons given in the preceding chapter, it seems reasonable, however, to believe that the early centuries of the Christian era witnessed a general improvement in the standard of cavalry service in India and a better recognition of the genius and utility of this arm. Certain remarks, contained in later works on polity, perhaps prove that this change in military outlook persisted till well-nigh the close of our period. Writing in the tenth century A.D., Somadeva says: "The cavalry represents the mobility of the army. With a king, having a strong cavalry force, war becomes almost a sport. On him fortune smiles, and even enemies at a distance easily come within his grasp."[1] In the same strain Someśvara (twelfth century A.D.) observes: "The cavalry is the key to fame; a king in possession of a strong cavalry need entertain no apprehension regarding his territory."[2]

Nevertheless it must be noted that the cavalry never came to occupy the front rank in the army organisation of ancient India. It never in fact came to form the core of a Hindu army. As in the time of Porus, so in the time of Pṛthvīrāj much greater reliance appears to have been placed upon the elephant than upon the horse. And as in the 4th century B.C., so in the 11th and 12th century A.D., the superiority of foreign horsemen once again decided the fate of India. There is ample evidence in the early Muhammadan chronicles to show that both Maḥmūd of Ghazna and Muhammad Ghori won some of their most brilliant military triumphs in India by the skilful use of a numerous and well-trained cavalry.[3]

One of the reasons why the Hindus never did or could evolve a cavalry system comparable in strength and efficiency to that of the Greeks or Muhammadans was the lack of good horses in India. Ancient writers are singularly unanimous in regarding the horses of

[1] Nītiv. pp. 83-4. [2] Mānas. I, 81, v. 574.
[3] Elliot. II, 38, 51, 181, 248, 295-6.

the north and west as better than those of India proper. In the Mahābhārata, the most famous horses come from the Sindhu country, or Bāhlika, or Kāmboja. The Sauptika-parva (118, 13) speaks of the people of the latter country as among the finest horsemen.[1] In the Sumaṅgalavilāsinī (I, 124) Kāmboja is referred to as the home of horses—*Kāmboja assānaṁ āyatanaṁ*. The Jaina Uttarādhyayana Sūtra (Jaina Sūtras. S. B. E., II, 47) tells us that a trained Kāmbojan horse exceeded other horses in speed, and that no noise could frighten it. Kālidāsa in his Raghuvaṁśa (IV. 70) makes Raghu exact a tribute of horses from the Kāmbojan kings. In the Gauḍavaho (p. 78, v. 261), Vākpati refers to the tradition that the horse was a product of the Himalayan regions—*hima selanta-saṁbhavā*. In the Rājataraṅgiṇī (IV, 165), Kalhaṇa eulogistically speaks of the stables of the Kāmbojas. Finally, according to Someśvara, horses from Sindh, Arabia and the Kāmboja countries were by far the best.[2]

This paucity of good horses within India proper often compelled powerful monarchs both in the north and in the south to get their supply of horses from foreign countries. Bāṇa tells us that the royal stable of emperor Harṣa was filled with horses "from Vanāyu, Āraṭṭa, Kāmboja, Bharadvāja, Sindh and Persia."[3] The Khālimpur copper-plate of Dharmapāla speaks of his "unlimited troops of horses presented by many kings of the north."[4] The Monghyr copper-plate of Devapāla indicates that this king of Bengal got his supply of horses from the Kāmboja country.[5] The Arab merchant, Sulaiman, says that his contemporary king of Jurz (who has been identified with Bhoja of the Gurjara-pratihāra dynasty) possessed the finest cavalry in India. "This king maintains numerous forces," he says, "and no other Indian prince has so fine a cavalry."[6] It is reasonable to believe that he could get together such a strong and efficient cavalry because his kingdom lay in close proximity to the regions mentioned above.

The Deccan states seem to have suffered from this handicap even more than the northern states; and contemporary authorities affirm that they had to secure their supply of horses "from distant

[1] *Syandaneṣu ca kambojā yuktā parama-vājinaḥ*. Cf. also Karṇaparva 38, 13.

[2] Mānas. I, 81, v. 573: *Saindhavair-yavanadbhūtaiḥ kāmboja-prabhavairapi*. It is probable that by *yavanodbhūta* Arabian horses are meant.

[3] Harṣacarita, tr. by Cowell and Thomas, p. 70.

[4] Ep. Ind. IV, 243 ff.

[5] R. D. Banerji, *Vāṅglār Itihāsa*, pp. 179 ff.

[6] Elliot. I, 4. For identification see R. C. Majumdar, *The Gurjara-Pratihāras*, p. 57.

lands beyond the seas."[1] Referring to the Malabar coast, Rashid-uddin says that there were no horses there, or rather those which were there were weak, and "it was therefore agreed that every year Jamālu-ddin Ibrāhim should send to the Dewār 14,000 strong Arab horses obtained from the island of Kīs, and 10,000 horses from all the islands of Fars such as Katif, Lahsa, Bahrein, Hurmuz and Kilahat, etc. Each horse is reckoned 220 dinars of red gold current."[2] Describing the same region, Marco Polo says that "there is no possibility of breeding horses in this country."[3]

This lack of good horses of indigenous breed must have proved a serious obstacle to the development of a first-rate cavalry system in ancient India. It was indeed a fatal lack.

2. Equipment and Armament

It is difficult to decide when and how the bridle and the saddle came to form a part of the horse's equipment. Arrian says that in the fourth century B.C. the Indians had a bit but no curb bit, and directed the horse by a spike outside, that is, behind the jaw.[4] Hopkins points out that in the multifarious heaps of articles described as abandoned on the battle-field, the Mahābhārata makes no mention of bits or saddles.[5] Fergusson states that the presence of the bit in the sculptures at Sanchi is extremely doubtful.[6]

It is probable that the great architect considered the subject too trivial to require sufficient attention. For, a closer examination of the Sanchi sculptures will reveal the presence of both bitted and unbitted horses. The former are specially noticeable in the South and West *toraṇa*, the latter in the North. Where bits are used, the horses have but two bands in their head-stall. But when the spike (behind the jaw) is intended, the head-stall has three bands, one passing over the nostrils, another beneath and a third above the eyes.

1 Kanakasabhai, *The Tamils 1800 Years Ago*, p. 27; S. K. Aiyangar, *The Beginnings of South Indian History*, p. 126.

2 Elliot. I, 69.

3 Yule, *Marco Polo*, II, 342. This ill success in breeding horses was sometimes exaggerated to impossibility and made to extend to all India. Thus a Persian historian, speaking of an elephant that was born in the stables of Khosru Parviz, observes that "never till then had a she-elephant borne young in Iran, any more than a lioness in Rūm, a tabby cat in China (!), or a mare in India."

4 Indika. Fragm. XVI.

5 J. A. O. S. XIII, 285 ff.

6 Tree and Serpent Worship. p. 134.

The same curious phenomenon is also noticed at Ajantā. In cave No. 17, usually ascribed to the 4th century A.D., there are some finely painted horses, wearing bits, which plainly enter the mouth. On the other hand, in the procession of cave No. I horses are represented as without bits. Similarly, in a large slab from Belur, now deposited in the Museum at Bangalore, there are two horses having the reins going plainly to the back of the jaw and not to the mouth. The stone is ascribed to the middle of the ninth century A.D.[1] This representation of unbitted horses long after bits had become well-known in the country may be due to the conservatism of religious art. It is not impossible, however, that two different modes of guiding the horse, with and without bit, continued side by side for centuries.

The question as to when the saddle first came into use in India is equally difficult to decide. In the Mahābhārata we find frequent mention of such epithets as the *pīṭhaka*,[2] *pīṭhamarda*,[3] *khalīna*,[4] *aśvāstara*, *paristoma*, *rāṅkava*,[5] etc., indicating thereby the existence of some covering for the horse's back. Hopkins suggests that these probably consisted of only blankets (*kambola*), which are often stated to be found on the field after a day's fight.[6] But the saddle, along with stirrups, is clearly perceptible on some of the horses at Sanchi.[7] Sir John Marshall says that this "is the earliest example by some five centuries of the use of stirrups in any part of the world."[8] The saddle is also represented on the Aśvamedha type of Kumāragupta I.'s coins. The Kurram plates of the Pallava king Parameśvaravarman I mention that the royal horse "bore a saddle set with jewels."[9] In the procession of the first cave of Ajantā, already referred to, the horses are provided with saddles. These are of the chārjāma type with short stirrups. "There are leather straps round the throat and across the fore-head, and embroidered bands round the nose and across the muzzle."[10] As against this, however, we have the statement of Al 'Beruni that as late as the eleventh century A.D. the Indians "ride without a

[1] J. A. O. S., 1898, 29 ff.
[2] Ādiparva, 84, 21.
[3] Virāṭaparva, 21, 33.
[4] Bhīṣmaparva, 54, 59 ff.
[5] Ibid. 96, 74.
[6] J. A. O. S. XIII, 264-5.
[7] Maisey, *Sanchi and its Remains*, Pl. VI, fig. 2; Pl. IX, fig. 2; Pl. XV, XX, XXVII; Cunningham, *The Stupa of Bharhut*, p. 42; Pl. XXXII.
[8] Sir John Marshall, *A Guide to Sanchi*, p. 138, n. 3.
[9] Ep. Ind. XVII, 344.
[10] G. Yazdani, *Ajanta*, Pt. i, p. 19, n. 3; Ind. Ant., 1930, p. 170; Mrs. Herringham's Ajanta Frescoes, Pl. 57.

saddle, but if they put on a saddle, they mount the horse from its right side."[1] The only way in which we can harmonise these two rival sets of evidence is on the supposition that though the use of the saddle was well-known in the country, the mass of the people rode their horses without one. It is not impossible that the use of the saddle was regarded as a mark of distinction, and was consequently confined to the higher aristocratic classes.

Horses were occasionally provided with a kind of armour. The Mulaipāṭṭu, a Tamil Idyll, mentions "shields of protection for horses." The Rājataraṅgiṇī (VIII, 728) refers to 'armour-clad horses.' The Mānasollāsa (p. 135, v. 1187) speaks of horses 'well-protected by means of body-armour'—*gātra-trāṇa surakṣitaiḥ aśvaiḥ*.[2] Representations of horsemen on certain coins of the Guptas and the Hindu kings of Ohind (c. 875 to 1000 A.D.) further confirm the above view.[3]

The riders themselves generally appear as wearing ordinary tunics, but sometimes they wore breast-plates or coats of mail and strong helmets. In the Arthaśāstra (Bk. X. ch. 5) Kauṭilya contemplates an array of pure cavalry, in which, he says, the centre is to be occupied by heavy armoured horsemen, and the flanks and wings by those without armour.[4] Representations of mailed horsemen may be seen on some Gupta coins and the "Bull and Horseman" type of the kings of Ohind.[5]

For weapons they generally carried long lances for the charge and swords for the mêlée. Concerning the equipment of the Indian horsemen in the 4th century B.C., Arrian says that it consisted of two lances and a short buckler—"shorter than that carried by the infantry".[6] The Mahābhārata usually describes them as armed with spears (*śakti*), lances (*prāsa*) and short swords (*ṛṣṭi*).[7] In the Rāmāyaṇa, besides the above, they are assigned battle-axes (*paraśvadha*), maces (*gadā*), and hammers (*mudgara*).[8] The 'Horseman' type of Gupta coins depict the mounted kings as armed with swords and bows. In some of the frescoes at Ajantā

[1] Sachau. I, 181.

[2] Cf. also. Karṇaparva 24, 63-64; Mahā-assāroha Jātaka, Cowell's ed. III, 6, etc.

[3] Allan, *Gupta Coins*, Pl. XXII; Smith, *Catalogue of the Coins in the Indian Museum*, Pl. XXVI, fig. I.

[4] *Aśva-vyūha varmiṇāmurasyaṁ śuddhānāṁ kakṣa-pakṣāviti.*

[5] Allan, *Gupta Coins*, Pl. XXII; Smith, op. cit.

[6] Indika. Fragm. XVI.

[7] Cf. Bhīṣmaparva 57, 11, 19; Droṇaparva 165, 21, etc.

[8] Laṅkā-kāṇḍa 52, 11.

(Pl. XVII) horsemen are equipped with spears. The Kurram Plates mention "squadrons of horsemen connected by their swords that had struck each other's heads."[1] The Śiśupālavadha (XVIII, 23) speaks of mounted troops as armed with *kuntas* (spears). Similarly, the kings of Ohind are found on their coins as carrying heavy spears in their right hand.[2] The Rājataraṅgiṇī (VIII. 947-53) contains a reference to "horsemen whose drawn sabres formed a line." The Jainad Stone Inscription of the Paramāra Jagaddeva (king of Mālava in the latter part of the 11th century) attributes lances, swords and nooses to horse-riders.[3]

A close scrutiny of old records would appear to reveal, however, a grave defect in the equipment of the Indian horseman. He does not seem to have ever developed any marked proficiency in mounted archery. The bow was indeed held in high esteem, but it was the weapon *par excellence* of the infantry and chariot-men, not of the cavalry. The epics with all their wealth of details regarding military matters are hardly cognisant of such a thing as horse-archery. The historians of Alexander make no mention of Indian horse-bowmen.[4] The Śiva-Dhanurveda, which gives detailed rules regarding the practice of archery in its different branches, is curiously silent about the training of horse-archers.

But the Scythian and Parthian satraps, who invaded and conquered north-western India in the first century B. C., appear to have been well-acquainted with the art of horse-archery. This is shown by certain types of their coins. King Azes I, Azilises and Azes II, and the satrap Jihunia or Zeionises are depicted on their coins as horsemen equipped with bows.[5] It is not preposterous to think that superiority of cavalry in general, and of horse-archery in particular, was one of the causes which facilitated their military success in India.

The testimony of numismatics further indicates that the art thus introduced by the Scythian and Parthian invaders long outlived

[1] Ep. Ind. XVII, 364. [2] Op. cit.

[3] Ep. Ind. XX, 63.

[4] Herodotus, indeed, refers to Indian mounted archers in the army of Xerxes, but the statement of the 'father of history' must always be taken with a grain of salt. Moreover, there is nothing to show whether by mounted archers he meant horse-archers or chariot-archers.

[5] Smith, *Catalogue of the Coins in the Indian Museum*, Calcutta, pp. 43-4, Percy Gardner, *The Coins of the Greek and Scythic Kings of Bactria and India in the British Museum*, Pl. XX, 2; XIX, 4; Whitehead, *Catalogue of the Coins in the Punjab Museum*, Pl. XVI, 32.

their political domination in India. It seems even probable that it survived to the time of the Guptas. On certain types of their coins, Candragupta II, Kumāragupta and Prakāśāditya are represented as horse-archers. Candragupta and Kumāragupta are seen riding fully caparisoned horses and holding their bows in their hands.[1] Prakāśāditya is portrayed as seated on his horse, with a sword in his right hand which he thrusts at a leaping lion, and a bow round his body with its string resting on his left shoulder.[2] It is not impossible that these coins were merely the products of a servile imitative tendency on the part of the Guptas; but the more probable hypothesis seems to be that they bear on them the imprint of a military custom which was well known to, and practised in, Gupta India.

Nevertheless, the art of mounted archery did not strike deep roots in the Indian soil. Introduced by the Parthians and continuing for a time as a sickly exotic, it withered away shortly after the Gupta period. This is the impression that one gathers from a study of the records of post-Gupta India. Whether we ransack the valuable works left to us by the Chinese pilgrims and Muhammadan chroniclers, or examine the indigenous literature, inscriptions, sculptures and coins of the later Hindu period, we will scarcely find a reference to Indian horse-archers. The conclusion is, therefore, irresistible that after a short endeavour to learn this important branch of the art of war, the Hindus fell back into their old grooves and relapsed into their traditional tactics.[3]

This lack of horse-archery was another fatal lack in the military system of ancient India. It was especially so, because the Turks, who invaded India in the 11th and 12th centuries, were past-masters in that art. They had inherited it as a legacy from the old Parthians, and had demonstrated its effectiveness on many a field in the West. The battles of Manzikert and Dorylaeum had proclaimed to the world the excellent fighting skill of the Turkish horse-archers; and India proved as easy a victim to their onslaught as the Byzantine empire after the extinction of the Basilian dynasty.

[1] Allan, *Gupta Coins*, Pl. XIII, 11-19. [2] Ibid. Pl. XXII, 1-6.

[3] The hypothesis set forth above receives curious confirmation from the history of the ancient Hindu colony of Campā. The Cāms, who derived their political and military ideas and institutions from the mother country, appear to have been ignorant of the art of horse-archery till the later half of the twelfth century. It was in the reign of Jaya Indravarman that they first learnt the art from a Chinese officer, ship-wrecked on the coast of Campā. R. C. Majumdar, *Ancient Indian Colonies in the Far East*. I, 103, 152.

The Indian foot-archers, with their formal drill and slow traditional tactics, were no match for the swift-moving, light Turkish horse-bowmen.

3. Classification and Training of Horses

Most ancient writers, dealing with the art of war, have emphasised the careful selection of horses for the army. Horses were accordingly classified in a variety of ways. One of these was based on their breed. Thus according to the Arthaśāstra (Bk. II. ch. 30) : "The breed of Kāmboja, Sindhu, Āraṭṭa and Vanāyu countries are the best; those of Bāhlīka, Pāpeya, Sauvīra, and Taitala are of middle quality; and the rest ordinary (*avarāḥ*)".[1] Another method of classifying horses was by means of their physical proportions. "The face of the best horse", says Kauṭilya, "measures 32 aṅgulas; its length is five times its face; its shank is 20 aṅgulas; and its height is 4 times its shank. Horses of medium and lower sizes fall short of the above measurement by two and three aṅgulas respectively. The circumference (*pariṇāha*) of the best horse measures 100 aṅgulas, and horses of medium and lower sizes fall short of the above measurement by five parts (*pañcabhāgavarman*)."[2] A comparison of the above figures with those given in the Garuḍa Purāṇa (207, 4-5) and the Śukranīti (Ch. IV. sec. vii, 11. 85-144) will show that the standard of measurement was not rigidly fixed, but differed from age to age.

It may be noted further that horses were considered auspicious and inauspicious according to the colour of their body and the location of twists in the hair (*āvartas*).[3] And this again led to further divisions and subdivisions. The Bṛhat Saṁhitā (66, 12 ff) and the Agni Purāṇa (289, 1 ff.) give ten good and ten bad *āvartas*. The Yukti-kalpataru (pp. 182 ff.) divides horses into four castes in accordance with their distinguishing characteristics, and gives an exhaustive analysis of their colour and hair-rings. In the Aśva-śāstra of Hemasūri, a Jain author of the 14th century A.D., horses have been classified into as many as one hundred and fifty-three varieties. The classification is based on their curls, marks, colours and qualities.[4]

[1] Cf. also Yuktikalpataru, pp. 181-182.

[2] Kauṭ. tr. pp. 160-161.

[3] Cf. Vanaparva 71, 14: *Śuddhān daśabhirāvartteḥ* . . . The Siśupālavadha (V, 4) has: *āvartinaḥ śubhaphala-prada-śukti-yuktāḥ.*

[4] Aśva-śāstra (Science of Horses), by Hemasūri, tr. into English by Pandit V. Vijayaraghavacharya, 1928.

Great care was bestowed on the training of horses for war. Megasthenes says that in the 4th century B.C. there was a class of professional horse-trainers in India, who were trained from boyhood to manage horses. It was their practice to make the horses move at a measured pace and in a straight course. They did not gall the tongue of their horses by the use of spiked muzzles, nor did they torture the roof of their mouth, but broke them in by forcing them to gallop round and round in a ring, especially when they saw them refractory. "Such as undertake this work," adds the Greek ambassador, "require to have a strong hand as well as a thorough knowledge of horses."[1]

The Arthaśāstra of Kauṭilya (Bk. II. ch. 30) provides us with a detailed account of the various movements employed for the training of horses. The author begins his description with the statement that "the regular training of the horse is its preparation for war". This, according to him, involved the mastery of five principal movements, viz.,

(1) *valgana* (circular movement).

(2) *nīcairgata* (slow movement with the head and ears kept erect).

(3) *laṅghana* (jumping).

(4) *dhoraṇa* (gallop).

(5) *nāroṣṭra* (movement following signals).

Most of these, again, consisted of several varieties. Thus *valgana* was of the following kinds :

(*a*) *aupaveṇuka* (turning in a circle of a cubit in diameter).

(*b*) *vardhamānaka* (advancing, and yet turning in a circle as above).

(*c*) *yamaka* (running the figure-of-eight).

(*d*) *ālīḍha-pluta* (running and jumping simultaneously).

(*e*) *vṛthāṭṭa* (movement only of the forepart of the body).

and (*f*) *tṛvacālī* (movement of only the hinder portion of the body).

Similarly *nīcairgata* consisted of the following sixteen varieties :

(*a*) *prakīrṇaka* (a combination of all kinds of movements).

(*b*) *prakīrṇottara* (the same as above, but with one kind of movement kept prominent).

[1] McCrindle, *Ancient India*, pp. 89-90.

(c) *niṣaṇṇa* (a movement in which the hinder part of the body is kept steady).

(d) *pārśvānuvṛtta* (movement sideways).

(e) *ūrmimārga* (movement up and down like a wave).

(f) *śarabha-krīḍita* (playing like a *śarabha*, a kind of deer).

(g) *śarabha-pluta* (leaping like a deer).

(h) *tritāla* (movement using only three legs).

(i) *vāhyānuvṛtta* (moving right and left).

(j) *pañcapāṇi* (movement by using two and three legs alternately).

(k) *siṁhāyata* (pacing like a lion).

(l) *svādhūta* (long strides).

(m) *kliṣṭa* (moving straight without a rider).

(n) *ślāghita* (moving with the forepart of the body bent).

(o) *bṛṁhita* (moving with the hinder part of the body bent).

and (p) *puṣpābhikīrṇa* (zig-zag motion).

The several forms of *laṅghana* were as follows:

(a) *kapipluta* (jumping like a monkey).

(b) *bhekapluta* (jumping like a frog).

(c) *ekapluta* (sudden jump).

(d) *ekapādapluta* (jumping with one leg).

(e) *kokila-saṁcāri* (leaping like a cuckoo).

(f) *urasya* (dashing with the breast almost touching the ground).

and (g) *bakasaṁcāri* (leaping like a crane).

In the same way, *dhoraṇa* included the following movements:

(a) *kāṅka* (flying like a vulture).

(b) *vārikāṅka* (dashing like a water-duck).

(c) *māyūra* (running like a peacock).

(d) *ardha-māyūra* (half the speed of a peacock).

(e) *nākula* (dashing like a mungoose).

(f) *ardha-nākula* (half the speed of a mungoose).

(g) *vārāha* (running like a hog).

and (h) *ardha-vārāha* (half the speed of a hog).

Besides the above, a few kinds of trot are also enumerated in the Arthaśāstra. One of these is called *mārga* (trot). "Trotting according to strength (*vikrama*), trotting with good breathing (*bhadraśvāsa*), and trotting with a good load on the back (*bhāravāhya*) are the three forms of *mārga*." Another kind of trot is designated *dhārā*. This consisted of five movements, viz., trotting according to strength (*vikrama*), trot combined with circular movement (*valgita*), pacing with gallops (*upakanṭha*), medium speed (*upajava*), and low speed (*java*).

It is difficult for us, especially after the lapse of so many centuries, to understand the full meaning of all the technical terms mentioned in the Arthaśāstra. Words and phrases, which once appeared obvious in the context of daily life, have now become obscure. Yet the above list of technical terms, each signifying a special kind of movement, testifies to the extreme care with which horses were trained in ancient India. We do not know how long this elaborate system of horse-training continued in actual practice. Casual references in literature and inscriptions show that the five movements styled *dhārā* by Kauṭilya were well-known to the horse-trainers of later epochs. Thus in the Śiśupālavadha (V, 60) we read of a horse being actually taken out to practise these movements.[1] The Anamkoṇḍa Inscription, (dated śaka 1084), referring to Rudradeva's cavalry force, says: "His horses are of the most pleasing shape,—of low-sounding neighings,—possessed of all the excellent characteristics that are made famous by the writings that treat of horses,—adapted in their make for speed and weight,—very long-lived,—and trained in the five kinds of paces (*pañcadhārāḥ*)."[2] In the Bednagar Praśasti of the reign of Kumārapāla (1151 A.D.), Bhīmadeva's horses are referred to as "supremely skilled in accomplishing the five kinds of trot called dhārā."[3]

The Agni Purāṇa (288, 60-62) and the Dhanurveda Saṁhitā of Vaśiṣṭha (p. 66) supply us with a new list of technical terms in connection with horse-training, but it is difficult to make out their full import.[4]

[1] *dhārāḥ prasādhayitum . . . navasu vīthisu kaścidaśvaṁ valgā-vibhāga-kuśalo gamayāmvabhūva.*

[2] Ind. Ant. XI, 20; J. B. B. R. A. S. X, 53.

[3] Ep. Ind. I, 302, v. 9.

[4] It may be mentioned here that ancient writers have also laid down detailed rules for the stabling and rationing of horses. Cf. Kauṭ. Bk. II. ch. 30; Mānas. p. 87; Śukranīti, ch. IV. sec. vii. 11. 270-286.

CHAPTER VI

ELEPHANTS

1. Historical Outline

Elephants are mentioned in the Ṛgveda probably under the designation of *mṛga vāraṇa* (viii. 33, 8; x. 40, 4), certainly under that of *mṛga hastin*. They are usually spoken of as wild, terrible beasts, and Roth suggests that the compound name is a proof of the newness of the animal to the Vedic Indians.[1] This may well have been so, but there are good reasons to think that before the period closed, elephants had been both tamed and domesticated. The Yajur-veda uses the term *hastipa* to denote an elephant-trainer.[2] In the Atharva-veda (ix. 3, 17) we read: "Thou hall (or house) standest on the earth with feet like a female elephant." The passage suggests that its author must have been accustomed to look familiarly at the animal close at hand. Elsewhere (ib. iii. 22) there is a verse which pointedly says that the elephant "hath now become chief of all pleasant beasts to ride."

There is, however, no reference in any of the Vedas to the use of elephants in war. But once they were tamed and domesticated, it did not take long to realise that their extraordinary strength might be profitably utilised for military purposes. The initial steps in this direction were probably taken in the post-Vedic period. In both the Jātakas and the epics the elephants are represented as taking part in military operations.[3] But they were not yet the most important arm. They became the most important arm about the time of the Macedonian invasion. The classical chronicles make it abundantly clear that in his titanic struggle against Alexander, Porus pinned all his hopes on the elephants in his army. In the battle-array that he drew up on that fateful day, he posted the elephants along the front like bastions in a wall. He seems to have thought that these monsters would terrify the foreign soldiers, and render the Macedonian cavalry unmanageable. In

[1] Vedic Index. II, 171-172.

[2] Vājasaneyi Saṁhitā. xxx. 11; Taittiriya Saṁhitā. iii. 4, 9, 1.

[3] J. A. O. S. XIII, 265.

fact, he counted without his host. Alexander, a shrewder judge of military affairs, instinctively realised the grave danger involved in such extensive employment of elephants in war.[1] But neither Porus nor any other Indian prince did. Everywhere there was the same demand for elephants, the same implicit faith in their military effectiveness. In the eastern kingdom of Magadha, Mahāpadma Nanda had collected a huge contingent of elephants, numbering about four thousand, "all trained and equipped for war."[2] Shortly afterwards Candragupta Maurya increased the strength of the Magadhan elephant corps to nine thousand.[3] The age of chariots had passed, that of elephants had begun.

In the succeeding centuries, the importance of elephants went on mounting higher and higher in Indian military estimation. In the Arthaśāstra (Bk. VII. ch. 2) Kauṭilya provides us with an inkling into the military thought of his age when he writes that "it is on elephants that the destruction of an enemy's army depends." "The victory of kings in battles", he remarks elsewhere, "depends mainly upon elephants; for elephants, being of large bodily frame, are able not only to destroy the arrayed army of the enemy, his fortifications and encampments, but also to undertake works that are dangerous to life."[4] Where Kauṭilya is merely affirmative, his successors are superlative. For instance, Pālakāpya, the famous author of Hastyāyur-veda, says: "The Sumeru is the ornament of the world, the moon of the night; learning is the ornament of the man, and the elephant of the army." Again, "where there is truth, there is religion; where there is religion, there is prosperity; where there is beauty, there is nobility; and where there are elephants, there is victory."[5] Kāmandaka (XVI, 10-12) says that "the kingdoms of kings depend on elephants," and that "one elephant, duly equipped and trained in the methods of war, is capable of slaying six thousand well-caparisoned horses."[6] The Nīti-vākyāmṛta (pp. 82-83) and the Agni Purāṇa (287, 5-6)

[1] McCrindle, *India and its Invasion by Alexander*, pp. 209 and 224. Alexander is said to have remarked to Coenus that the assistance of elephants "is not of a kind to be depended on," and that he was "fully convinced that they occasion more harm to their own side than to the enemy."

[2] McCrindle, *Indika of Megasthenes*, p. 34.

[3] Cf. tables given in Ch. 2.

[4] Bk. II. ch. 2.

[5] Hastyāyur-veda, published in the Ānandāśram Sanskrit Series, 1894, ch. I. sec. v. śl. 23 and 29.

[6] Cf. also Kām. XX, 61.

join their voice to this general chorus of tribute. A mediæval author goes so far as to declare that an army without elephants is as despicable as a forest without a lion, a kingdom without a king or as valour unaided by weapons.[1]

There is no ground to think that the theory was divorced from practice. In a previous chapter we have cited a few figures bearing on the military strength of some post-Guptan states. A comparison of these figures will show that wherever possible elephants were maintained at enormous strength. Referring to the king of Ruhmi, the Arab traveller, Sulaiman, says: "When he goes out to battle, he is followed by 50,000 elephants. He takes the field only in winter because elephants cannot endure thirst, and can only go out in the cold season."[2] Ibn Khurdadba says that "the kings of Hind take great delight in maintaining elephants, and pay largely for them in gold."[3] The elephants continued to fill an important rôle in the Indian military system long after the conquest of India by the Muhammadans. It was only after the introduction of fire-arms and the gradual extension of their use that they ceased to be of any value in the fighting line of battle.[4]

It may be pointed out here that it was not in India alone that elephants were used in war. The same practice was in vogue among the Greeks and the Romans, the Turks and the Mongols. Classical authors tell us that after his conflict with Candragupta Maurya, Seleucas Nikator ceded to the Indian emperor the three satrapies of Aria (Herat), Arachosia (Kandahar) and Paropanisadai (Kabul) and received in exchange a gift of five hundred war-elephants. A few years later (301 B.C.), when fighting against Antigonus, the Syrian king brought these elephants into the field, and it is to their instrumentality that contemporary opinion ascribed his resounding victory at Ipsos. Many centuries later, Sultan Maḥmūd carried off from India a large number of trained elephants, and used them in his wars against the Turks in Transoxiana. As a matter of fact, elephants, though dangerous, were of real value in ancient and mediæval warfare. Used with caution, and as a subordinate arm, they sometimes turned the scale of victory at the decisive moment. The Hindus erred not in the use of elephants but in the emphasis they put upon that use.

[1] Śārṅgadhara Paddhati, ed. by Peterson, p. 249.

[2] Elliot. I, 5, 25.

[3] Ibid. I, 13.

[4] Irvine, *The Army of the Indian Moghuls*, p. 179.

2. Merits and Defects

Most ancient politico-military writers have attempted to formulate the functions which a trained elephant corps was expected to perform in war. According to Kauṭilya, the most important of these functions were (a) acting as the vanguard of a marching army (*puroyānam*), (b) preparing roads, camping grounds, and landing ghats in rivers (*akṛtamārga-vāsa-tīrtha-karma*), (c) clearing away such impediments as small trees and shrubs (*viṣama-sambādha-praveśa*), (d) battering down walls, gates and towers of a fortress (*sāladvārāṭṭālaka-bhañjanam*), and (e) breaking up, scattering or trampling down the hostile force.[1] Kāmandaka adds that "breaking into forest forts" (*vana-durga-praveśanam*) was another important function of war-elephants.[2] In the Agni Purāṇa (242, 37) it is stated that elephants were specially useful in all confused battles.

But, as hinted before, elephants were sometimes of more harm than benefit. If wounded, they were liable to get beyond control and escape at the top of their speed. It also happened that once taken by terror, they turned round and trampled their own men under their feet. The earliest known instance of this kind occured in the battle of the Hydaspes.[3] Maddened by the wounds received from the enemy's missiles, the elephants in the Paurava army "attacked friend and foe quite indiscriminately, pushed them, trampled them down, and killed them in all manner of ways", and being at last spent with wounds, "spread havoc in their own ranks."[4] Another example of this nature recorded is Kalhaṇa's Rājataraṅgiṇī (VII. 1551-55). King Harṣa was fighting for his very life and throne against the Ḍāmaras and Khāśikas, headed by Uccala near the bridge on the stream called Kṣiptikā. "Then Janakacandra and others shot arrows at the king's fighting elephant, which stood in front of the bridge and had thrown off its armour. Hit in the joints by the arrows, the elephant raised a trumpeting roar, and turning back trampled with his feet his own force. Attacked by the elephant which had turned hostile, as fate (had done), the foot and horse of the army were routed."

In other ways, too, elephants sometimes proved to be a source of immense danger. With the growing importance of elephants,

[1] Kauṭ. Bk. X. ch. 4; for a slightly different account of the same see Bk. X. ch. 5.

[2] Kām. XX, 1-3.

[3] There is, however, a similar example recorded in the Bhīṣmaparva 46, 26-27.

[4] McCrindle, *India and its Invasion by Alexander*, pp. 106 and 211.

kings and generals began to appear in the fighting line mounted on these ponderous beasts. They apparently thought that being thus easily visible, they would be a source of inspiration to all the troops. But there was one grave risk attending the practice, for they were thereby making themselves a target of attack by the enemy. In those days battles were nearly always decided by the fate of the leader; and it was believed that if the king or general were killed, his army would give up the contest and in a very short space of time melt away altogether. An instance of this nature occured when Muhammad bin Kasim invaded the kingdom of Dāhir. The Chachnāma relates how Dāhir was observed seated on a lofty elephant by the enemy. "Muhammad Kasim told the naphtha throwers that the opportunity was theirs, and a powerful man in obedience to this direction, shot his naphtha arrow into Dāhir's howdah and set it on fire." This produced immediate confusion in the Hindu army and decided the day.[1] A similar incident took place in 1008 A.D., when the confederate Hindu army under Ānandapāla met the Ghaznavide troops under Sultan Mahmud on the plains of Chach (lying between Attock and Hazro). Here the Hindu and Muslim armies lay in front of each other in entrenched camps for forty days, each watching for an opportunity to gain advantage of the other. Then the Gekkhars, impatient of further delay, began the action by rushing the entrenched Ghazni camp, and slaying a few thousand Muhammadan soldiers. The two armies thus became grappled in deadly conflict, and for a time it seemed that the Hindus would win the day.[2] But all on a sudden, says Firishta, "the elephant, upon which the prince who commanded the Hindus rode, becoming unruly from the effects of the naphtha balls and the flights of arrows...turned and fled. This circumstance produced a panic among the Hindus, who seeing themselves deserted by the general, gave way and fled also."[3] Still another instance of this nature occured towards the close of the twelfth century A.D., when the Rājā of Benares was attacked by Kutb-ud din Aibak. The Rājā, we are told, prided himself on the number of his troops and war-elephants. He came to the field seated on a lofty howdah; but within a short time received a deadly wound from an arrow, and "fell from his exalted seat to the earth." Thereupon his army lost heart and fled in confusion.[4]

[1] Elliot. I, 170.
[2] C. V. Vaidya, *History of Medieval Hindu India*, III, 45-46.
[3] Briggs, Firishta, I, 47.
[4] Elliot. II, 223.

3. Equipment and Armament

Unlike the horse, the elephant was usually ridden by several warriors. Megasthenes says that in his time the usual practice was for a war-elephant to carry three fighting men, of whom two shot from the side, while the third shot from behind. "There is also a fourth man, who carries in his hand the goad wherewith he guides the animal, much in the same way as the pilot and captain of a ship direct its course with the helm."[1] Wilson remarks that this account agrees well with what may be gleaned from incidental notices of Sanskrit writers.[2] In the sculptures at Sānchi, however, we find three, instead of four, riders seated on each war-elephant. The same is the case in the frescoes at Ajantā.[3] The Mānasollāsa, on the contrary, speaks of two warriors as riding an elephant,[4] whereas the Agni Purāṇa (252, 31) enjoins that every war-elephant should carry two hook-bearers, two archers and two swordsmen.

The elephantry fought with both missile and short-arm weapons. In the Mahābhārata, the *gajārohāḥ* or *hasti-sādinaḥ*, (who, by the way, were generally low-born soldiers, not knights),[5] are described as armed with knives, daggers, pots of oil, stones and other weapons and missiles.[6] But from the Gupta period onwards, their principal weapons appear to have been bows and arrows. At Ajantā, they are usually depicted as equipped with quivers.[7] In one instance, we find an elephant-warrior actually shooting from his bow.[8] In the Begur stone sculpture, the leader on the elephant is shown as wielding a spear, but he is attended by an archer in the howdah.[9] Māgha in his Śiśupālavadha (XVIII, 9, 24, 30) speaks of bowmen discharging their arrows from the back of elephants. While describing Yaśovarman's contest with the Cedi king, the author of the Khajuraho Inscription (no. 11) says that the latter "tried to protect himself by showers of enraged irresistible archers, standing

[1] Aelian, *History of Animals*, XIII, 10.

[2] Wilson, *Works*, IV, 295.

[3] Lady Herringham. Ajantā Frescoes, Pl. XLII.

[4] Mānas. p. 135, śl. 1182: *nāgaṁ . . . yodhadvaya-samanvitam*.

[5] But there are exceptions. Cf., e.g., Virāṭaparva 65, 6 where we find a prince on an elephant; also Bhīṣmaparva 20, 7, where Duryodhana enters the field riding an elephant. See also ibid. 95, 38 ff.; Droṇaparva 26, 19 ff.

[6] J. A. O. S. XIII, 265.

[7] op. cit. Pl. XLII.

[8] Ibid. Pl. XII.

[9] Ep. Ind. VI, 46.

on mighty infuriated elephants, that were marching along like towering Añjana mountains."[1] The Kurram plates of Pallava Parameśvara-varman I mention "heroes holding bows and riding mighty elephants."[2]

Besides the warriors, the elephant carried a driver called *aṅkuśadhara*,[3] because he always carried an *aṅkuśa* or hook to guide and direct the beast. In the Droṇaparva (148, 46) the hook is described as 'gilded' like the whip; and so does the Tamil poet Kapilar (Puram 14). There are beautiful sculptural representations of the hook at Bhārhut and Sānchi.[4] Māgha (XVIII, 30) says that the *aṅkuśa* had peacock feathers attached to it. According to Śukra, again, the hook had one point for driving on and another for drawing back.[5] The *tottra*, mentioned in the Mahābhārata and the Arthaśāstra,[6] appears to have been another instrument used for the same purpose.

The elephants themselves appear to have been elaborately equipped from very early times. In the Vessantara-Jātaka they are described as wearing ornaments on the four feet and on their sides, a blanket under their belley, a rug on their back and ornaments on the frontal globes.[7] In the Mahābhārata, they are referred to as armed with spikes and iron harness, and wearing a *kakṣyā* or girth about the middle, "neckchains, bells, wreaths, nets, umbrellas, and blankets, possibly with rings about the feet."[8] Kauṭilya gives the following account about the war accoutrement of elephants: "A hook, a bamboo staff and machines (*yantra*) are instruments. Necklaces, such as *vaijayanti* and *kṣurapramālā*, and litter and housings are the ornaments of elephants. Mail armour (*varma*), *tottra*, arrow bags and machines are war instruments."[9] At Bhārhut and Sānchi, the elephant is provided with a housing on its back, which is sometimes plain but more often ornamented. The head of the animal is usually encircled by a string of pearls with pendant symbols. Two bells are attached to the front corners of the housing; but when the housing is very

1 Ibid. I, 132.

2 Ibid. XVIII, 343.

3 Ag. P. 252, 31.

4 Maisey, *Sanchi and its Remains*, Pl. VI, fig. 1; Pl. XVI, XX, XXVII; Cunningham, Pl. XI, XII and XXXIV.

5 Śukranīti, Ch. IV, sec. vii, 11. 339-40.

6 Cf. Droṇaparva 134, 6; Śalyaparva 20, 15; Kauṭ. Bk. II. ch. 32.

7 Cowell, *The Jātaka*, VI 253.

8 J. A. O. S. XIII, 268.

9 Kauṭ. Bk. II. ch. 32.

small, the bells are hung down the elephant's body by means of short ropes, fixed to the howdah itself.[1] Round the elephant's body a twisted cord is firmly tied, and people mounting the beast probably did so with its help.

In his Harṣacarita, Bāṇa refers to "gaudy housings on elephants," "kept tight on their back by means of girth-bands," to "bells tied to their necks", and, again, to "girths", which "confining on either side the ends of the saddle, kept their cloth cushions motionless and gave a firm seat."[2] From the account of Hiuen Tsiang and the Śiśupālavadha of Māgha, it may be inferred that two important additions were made to the equipment of war-elephants in the last centuries of our period. One of these, referred to by the Chinese pilgrim, was that the tusks of elephants came to be provided with sharp barbs.[3] The other, spoken of by Māgha, was the adoption of a practice of covering the eyes of elephants by means of cloths, which were not removed until the commencement of the conflict.[4]

The howdah on the back of elephants is also often referred to in early Muhammadan chronicles, but the easy manner in which they were set on fire by naphtha balls thrown by the enemy, shows that they were not, as in the Middle Ages, covered with iron or brass plates.[5]

4. Classification and Training

Elephants, like horses, were usually classified either according to their breed or according to their physical characteristics.[6] In the Arthaśāstra (Bk. XX. ch. 2), Kauṭilya says that "elephants

[1] Maisey, op. cit., Pl. XVI, fig. 1.

[2] Harṣacarita, tr. by Cowell and Thomas, pp. 202-3.

[3] Watters, I, 171. There is probably a reference to the same fact in the Kām. XX, 60: *saloha-jālaiḥ dṛḍha-vandha-dantaiḥ.*

[4] Śiśupālavadha XVIII, 28-30. For other details about the accoutrement of war-elephants in the same work, see XVIII, 6; XIX, 36; XIX, 66, 80 etc. Comp. also Raghuvaṁśa VII, 41; Kām. XX, 59. Mānasollāsa (p. 135, śl. 1182) has: *nāgaṁ tanutrāṇa-samopetam.*

[5] Elliot. I, 170; II, 223 etc. The Agni Purāṇa says that the howdah "should be made of wood cut out of trees that emit a milky sap when wounded; it should be fifty fingers broad, and three cubits long, painted and decorated with gold."

[6] Often this classification according to characteristics is carried to an absurd length. Cf. Yukti-kalpataru, pp. 200-205; Ag. P. ch. 287; Mānas. pp. 51-54.

bred in countries such as Kaliṅga, Aṅga, Karūśa, and the east are the best; those of Daśārṇa and Western countries are of middle quality; and those of Surāṣṭra and Pañcajana countries are of low quality." It may be mentioned here that just as ancient writers have ascribed, with surprising unanimity, the pre-eminence in horse-breeding to the north-west, they have attributed the pre-eminence in elephant-breeding to the east. For instance, it is noted in the Śāntiparva (101, 4) as a distinguishing characteristic of the easterners that they could fight skilfully with elephants (*prācyā mātaṅga-yuddheṣu kuśalāḥ*). In the Raghuvaṁśa (IV. 40, 83; VI. 27, 54), while describing the campaigns of Raghu, Kālidāsa speaks of the mighty elephant forces of the Kaliga and Aṅga kings. Similarly, Vākpati refers to the king of the Vaṅgas as "powerful in the possession of a large number of war-like elephants."[1] Referring to Kāmarūpa, the Chinese pilgrim, Hiuen Tsiang, says that there were "wild elephants which ravaged in herds, and so there was a good supply of elephants for war purposes."[2] Elsewhere, he mentions that the military establishment of the contemporary king of Kāmarūpa included a contingent of 20,000 war-elephants.[3] This peculiarity of fauna may have been an important factor, as Rhys Davids has suggested, in the gradual rise of Magadha to supreme power.

The training of elephants for war must have involved a more laborious process than the training of horses. Of the methods employed to capture wild elephants, some have stood the test of time and are well known in modern India.[4] Captured elephants were first carefully tamed. Megasthenes says that this was usually done by tying their feet one to another, their necks to a pillar firmly fixed in the ground, and leaving them without food. According to the Ārthaśāstra, the training of elephants consisted of several

[1] Gauḍavaho, Introd. XXVI.

[2] Watters. II, 186.

[3] Beal, *Life*, p. 172. It may be noted further that the Hastyāyurveda of Pālakāpya, the earliest extant work on elephants in Sanskrit, is in the form of an interlocution between Romapāda, the king of Aṅga, and the sage Pālakāpya. That elephants bred in eastern forests are the best in quality is also stated in the Gajalakṣaṇa. J. B. O. R. S. X, 323.

[4] These methods are described by Megasthenes (McCrindle, *Ancient India*, pp. 49-50), Kauṭilya (Bk. II. ch. 2), and Someśvara (Mānas. pp. 45-49). The mode of capturing elephants, as noticed by the Greek ambassador, is still employed in India and has not been much improved upon. Of the five contrivances described by Someśvara, the *vāribandha* corresponds to the modern kheddāh operations.

clearly marked stages. "The process began when the animal was brought to attach itself to a herd of tamed elephants, and lost its wildness by contact with them; this was called the *yūthagata* stage of training. Then the animal was cleverly thrown into a pit, specially dug to subdue its ferocity; this was the *apapāta* stage. The next step in the training (*vārigata*) was to keep the animal confined within a particular area of the forest instead of allowing it to roam at large. The next disciplinary measure was to tie the animal to a post when it was found to be sufficiently gentle for the purpose (*stambhagata*). The taming was completed when the animal became so gentle that it allowed its driver or trainer to sit on its withers without protest; this was the *skandhagata* stage."[1]

When sufficiently tamed, elephants were divided into two groups, viz., those meant for peaceful traffic and those for warlike services. According to Kauṭilya, the military training of elephants comprised two successive stages. In the first, they were accustomed to girths (*kakṣyākarma*), collars (*graiveya karma*), and to co-operation with a herd of trained elephants in a joint work (*yūthakarma*). In the second, they were trained in the following manœuvres :—

(*a*) *upasthāna* (drill, such as riding, bending, jumping over fences, ropes etc.)

(*b*) *saṁvartana* (lying down, sitting and leaping over pits and lines drawn)

(*c*) *saṁyāna* (moving forward straight or transverse, or making serpentine movements)

(*d*) *vadhāvadha* (trampling down and killing)

(*e*) *hastiyuddha* (fighting with other elephants)

(*f*) *nāgarāyaṇa* (assailing forts and cities)

and (*g*) *sāṁgrāmika* (other cognate movements relating to war.)[2]

Bāṇa informs us that in the 7th century A.D. leathern figures were used to train elephants in military manœuvres.[3] There is an elaborate description of this method of training in the Māṇasollāsa.[4] It may be further noted that elephant-trainers developed a code of technical terms in various parts of the country. Māgha has a

[1] N. N. Law, *Studies in Ancient Hindu Polity*, pp. 62-63.

[2] Kauṭ. Bk. II. ch. 32.

[3] Harṣacarita, tr. by Cowell and Thomas, p. 190.

[4] Mānas, vv. 307 ff.

reference to drivers speaking words of encouragement to the elephants.[1] Someśvara supplies us with a list of these technical terms as used in Mahārāṣṭra and Guzerat in the eleventh and twelfth century A.D.[2]

The elaborate training thus given to elephants often produced amazing results. The Greeks in the fourth century B. C., and the Muhammadan invaders in the eleventh and twelfth century A.D., were equally amazed by the astonishing feats of Indian elephants.[3] It is no wonder, therefore, that the elephant drivers of ancient India acquired a reputation, which spread beyond the borders of the country. It is probable that the war-elephants in the Sassanian army were mostly managed by Indian drivers;[4] it is certain that the elephant trainers in the army of Sultan Maḥmūd and Sultan Mas'ūd were mostly Hindus.[5]

[1] Śiśupālavadha, XVIII, 10.

[2] Mānas. pp. 55-56. These included the following: *ehi ehi, heḍe heḍe, phāpa, hijja hijja, bhale bhale, de de, he haiya, curu cula, mā mā, higa, hā hū, leca leca, dhe dhe* etc.

[3] McCrindle, *Ancient India*, p. 50; *India and its Invasion by Alexander*, p. 213; Aelian, Hist. Anim. c. XXXVII; Elliot. II, 251.

[4] The chief of the Sassanian elephant corps was called Zendkapet or "commander of the Indians." Rawlinson, *The Seventh Monarchy*, p. 649.

[5] Elliot. II, 143; Muhammad Nazim, *The Life and Times of Sultan Mahmud of Ghazna*, 1931, p. 130. It may be mentioned here that besides horses and elephants, camels are also sometimes mentioned in ancient records as constituting a part of the army. These were probably employed when the theatre of hostilities lay in deserts. For references to camels as a part of the army, see Kauṭ. Bk. IX, ch. 1; Bk. X, ch. 4; Harṣacarita, tr. by Cowell and Thomas, p. 47; South Ind. Inscr. Vol. II, pt. iii, p. 307; Ep. Ind. XIV, 327, ll. 37-38, etc. An Arab traveller tells us that in the middle of the ninth century the Gurjara-Pratīhāra king, Bhoja, commanded a powerful army, including a large force of camels. The territories of Rajputana have always been famous for their breed of camels, which is still maintained. Smith, *Oxford History*, p. 184.

CHAPTER VII

NAVAL WARFARE

I

The old notion that the Hindus were essentially a land-locked people, lacking in a spirit of adventure and the heart to brave the seas, is now dispelled. The researches of a generation of scholars have proved that from very early times the people of India were distinguished by nautical skill and enterprise, that they went out on trading voyages to distant shores across the seas, and even established settlements and colonies in numerous lands and islands, skirting the Indian Ocean. But the question as to whether they ever developed a navy to fight battles on rivers and seas is a more baffling one.

There are, however, reasons for thinking that naval warfare, though not widely practised, was not unknown in ancient India. Ancient writers sometimes speak of fighting galleys as constituting a part of the royal military establishment. In the Arthaśāstra (Bk. II. ch. 28), while describing the functions of the Superintendent of Ships (*Nāvadhyakṣa*), Kauṭilya remarks: "Pirate ships (*hiṁsrikā*), boats from an enemy's country when they cross its territorial limits,[1] as well as vessels violating the customs and rules enforced in port towns, should be pursued and destroyed." It is obvious that the task set forth above could only be performed by armed vessels belonging to the state. There are, however, more direct literary references to ships employed as instruments of war. For instance, in the Śānti-parva (59, 41), there is a verse which mentions the navy as one of the 'limbs' (*aṅgas*) of a complete army.[2] In the Manusaṁhitā (VII, 192), it is laid down that boats should be employed for military purposes when the theatre of hostilities abounded in water. Kāmandaka (XVI, 50) alludes

[1] Here the original is '*amitra-viṣayātigāḥ*'. Shām. takes it to mean "vessels which were bound for the country of an enemy". (Kauṭ. tr. p. 153). Gan. (I, 308), suggests the same interpretation: "*amitra-viṣāyātigāḥ śatrude-śayāyinīḥ*". But *atiga* means "going beyond limits". We should have had *abhigāḥ* instead of *atigāḥ* to mean "bound for the country of an enemy."

[2] *Rathā-nāgā-hayāścaiva padātās-caiva Pāṇḍava*
Viṣṭir nāvas carās caiva deśikā iti cāṣṭamam.

to naval warfare when he says: "By regular practice one becomes an adept in fighting from chariots, horses, elephants and boats, and a past-master in archery."[1] Finally, describing the various classes of boats, the Yukti-kalpataru (p. 228) specifies one class called *agramandira* (because they had their cabins towards the prows) as eminently adapted for naval warfare (*raṇe kāle ghanātyaye*). It is clear, therefore, that there was a continuity of naval tradition in the country from the days of Kauṭilya till the age of Bhoja.

Actual instances of the use of the navy as a part of the military machine are not altogether lacking. The earliest known case belongs to the time of Candragupta Maurya. Megasthenes informs us that the Mauryan War-Office had a naval department, with an admiral at its head and a committee of five to assist him. We learn from the XIIIth Rock Edict of Aśoka that the great emperor maintained diplomatic relations not only with Ceylon, but with the Hellenistic monarchies of Syria, Egypt, Cyrene, Macedonia and Epirus. It is probable, as V. A. Smith has suggested, that diplomatic relations with such distant countries presuppose the existence of a "sea-going fleet as well as an army."[2]

The naval traditions thus created by the Mauryas did not die with them. Certain pieces of Andhra or Sātavāhana coins, belonging to the reign of Puḷumāyi, bear the figure of a two-masted sailing ship.[3] It is not fanciful to assume that these coins, found mostly in Toṇḍaimaṇḍala, were issued by Puḷumāyi to commemorate a naval victory, which he won over the people of that region. This inference gains additional strength from the fact that the coast region in question was from time immemorial inhabited by a sea-faring people, known to Tamil literature as the Tiraiyar (lit. sea-people).

It is probable also that a flotilla of ships continued as an important weapon during the Gupta period. The Allahabad

[1] Comp. also Kām. XVI, 39.

[2] Edicts of Aśoka, Introd. p. viii.

[3] In his article in the Z. D. M. G. (1903, p. 613), as well as in his Early History of India, (4th ed., p. 223), V. A. Smith refers these "ship" type coins to the reign of Yajña Śrī. But in the *Catalogue of Indian Coins* (Introd. xxxi-xxxii), Professor Rapson says that on the solitary specimen on which the traces of the coin-legend admit of any probable restoration, "the inscr. appears to be intended for *Siri pu* (*ḷumā*) *visa* (No. 95, p. 22, Pl. V). This restoration is not altogether satisfactory; but there is no doubt about the first syllable of the name *Pu*-, and, as the next syllable may well be -*ḷu*-, it is almost certain that the coin was struck by Puḷumāyi."

Praśasti mentions Samudragupta's suzerainty being extended over "the people of Siṁhala and all other dwellers in islands."[1] The statement may be merely a covert allusion to the embassy sent by Meghavarṇa, the Buddhist king of Ceylon, to the court of the Gupta emperor. But if Samudragupta's sovereignty had really extended over the island-dwellers, we may well credit him with the possession of a naval force. Moreover, some contemporary or semi-contemporary inscriptions ocasionally refer to ships as forming part of the royal camp. The Deo-Baraṇārk Inscription, for instance, speaks of the "victorious camp" of Jīvita Gupta II as "invincible through (its) equipment of great ships and elephants and horses and footsoldiers."[2] Similarly, the inscriptions of Harṣa always refer to his camp as "furnished with ships," besides elephants and horses. The Aphsaḍ Inscription probably contains a veiled reference to a naval victory won by Mahāsena Gupta over the contemporary Kāmarūpa monarch, Susthitavarman. This victory, says the epigraph, "is still constantly sung on the banks of the river Lohitya, the surfaces of which are (so) cool, by the Siddhas in pairs." The scene of the engagement was obviously the Brahmaputra river. Occasionally also the fleet was employed as transports to carry soldiers across. For instance, in the Nilguṇḍa Plates of Vikramāditya VI, it is stated that king Maṅgalīsa prepared a grand bridge of boats (*nau-setu*), crossed over to Revatī, and captured the island.[3] From the Aihole Inscription we learn that with a flotilla of a hundred vessels Pulakeśin II attacked Puri, which was the mistress of the sea, and reduced it to submission.[4] The Kendur Plates of Kīrtivarman II tell us that Pulakeśin's grandson, Vinayāditya, sailed out to Ceylon, humbled its king and compelled him to pay tribute.[5]

II

History is oftener than not the creation of geographical environments. The peculiarities of the terrain have a tremendous influence on the growth of national and regional characteristics. It is an axiomatic truth of history that a people living along the sea-coast, with opportunities of harbourage, or in inland territories intersected by large and navigable rivers, naturally develops an

[1] C. I. I. III, 14.
[2] C. I. I., III, 217.
[3] Ep. Ind. XII, 151.
[4] Sir R. G. Bhandarkar says that Puri was probably the capital of the Maurya kings of Koṅkan and afterwards of the Silāhāras. *Early History of the Deccan,* 3rd ed., p. 88, f.n.
[5] Ep. Ind. IX, 205.

aptitude in the art of plying boats. The sea and the river become a part of their life and blood.

In ancient India, owing to this geographical influence, nautical skill and enterprise seem to have been best developed in three widely separated regions of the country. These were Bengal, the valley and delta of the Indus, and the extreme south of the Deccan peninsula, called Tamilagam. Each of these regions possessed all those natural and physical advantages which promote naval and maritime activities.

The people of Bengal seem to have become famous for their nautical resources very early in history. In his Raghuvaṁśa (IV, 36), Kālidāsa characterises the Vaṅgas as expert in the art of plying boats (*nausādhanodyatān*). Epigraphic evidence proves that harbours and dock-yards were well-known in the 6th century A.D. A copper-plate grant of Dharmāditya (dated 531 A.D.) refers to a *nāvāta-kṣeṇī* or ship-building harbour, though we do not know where exactly it was located.[1] Another grant of the same monarch speaks of *nau-daṇḍaka* or ship's mast. A few centuries later, when the Pālas became the rulers of Bengal, they seem to have utilised this nautical aptitude of the people in building up a regular fleet for fighting purposes. Contemporary records refer to this fleet as *nau-vāṭa* or *nau-vāṭaka,* and to the admiral in command as the *Naukādhyakṣa.* The Khālimpur copper-plate of Dharmapāla describes this royal fleet as "proceeding on the path of the Bhāgīrathī," and thus making it "seem as if a series of mountain tops had been sunk to build another causeway for Rāma's passage."[2] The Kamauli Grant speaks of a glorious naval victory which Vaidyadeva, the minister of Kumārapāla, won over an unknown enemy in southern Vaṅga, near the mouths of the Ganges.[3]

The naval power of Bengal seems to have long outlived the collapse of the Pāla dynasty. The epigraphic records of the Candras, the Varmans and the Senas prove that the river-flotilla continued as an important instrument of offence and defence under them. As in the Khālimpur copper-plate of Dharmapāla, so in the Deopārā Inscription of Vijayasena, the

[1] Ind. Ant. XIX, 198.

[2] Ep. Ind. I, 299 ff.; ibid. XIV, 326 ff.

[3] Ibid. II, 351. Mr. R. D. Banerji suggests that this naval encounter took place with Anantavarman, king of Utkala and Kaliṅga. *The Pālas of Bengal,* Mem. of the Asiatic Society of Bengal, vol. V., no. 3, p. 101.

Bengal fleet is described as proceeding on a conquering expedition "up the whole course of the Ganges."[1] There was however a change in the nomenclature of the admiral. The naukādhyakṣa of the Pāla period was replaced by the *nau-vyāpṛtaka* or *nau-bala-vyāpṛtaka* of the Sena period.[2] The use of the term *bala* after *nau* brings out the real character of the fleet.

It may be noted here that Bengal's reputation as a naval power continued even in the mediæval period. Husain Shāh (1498-1520), the most prominent of the independent Pathan rulers of Bengal, maintained a powerful fleet, with which he once invaded Assam.[3] Pratāpāditya is also credited with a fleet of seven hundred fighting vessels, equipped with all the instruments of war.[4] Shaistah Khān, the Nawab of Bengal, is said to have gathered a numerous fleet of armed galleys to check the depredations of the Arakan pirates, both Mangh and Feringi.

III

While in Bengal the nautical aptitude of the people was organised by the state into a pillar of strength, in the Indus basin it seems to have found expression chiefly in piracy. The people living in the territory adjoining the mouth of the Indus had acquired notoriety for bringandage on the high seas even before the invasion of India by Alexander the Great. Issuing in their 'keels,' these sturdy sea-rovers captured what they could find afloat, and carried fire and sword into the countries which they visited. It was the great Persian monarchy which seems to have been the worst sufferer from their depredations. Both Strabo and Arrian inform us that in order to protect their cities against piratical attacks the Persians made the Tigris entirely inaccessible to navigation. The course of the stream was obstructed by masses of stone, which Alexander on his return from India caused to be removed for the furtherance of commercial intercourse.[5]

But the pirates did not give up their profession. Many centuries later, when Berūnī wrote his account of India, he noted that the people of this region were still notorious for "their robberies on sea in ships called *bīra*."[6] Balādhurī says that the immediate cause of the first Muhammadan invasion of India in the

[1] Nanigopal Majumdar, *Inscriptions of Bengal*, III, 48: Ep. Ind., I, 305 ff.
[2] Ep. Ind. XII, 40, 11. 33-34; p. 139, 1. 20; p. 9 etc.
[3] Blochmann, J. A. S. B., 1872, Pt. I, no. 1.
[4] Prabāsī, Āśvin, 1326 B.S., p. 552.
[5] Strabo, *Geography*, XVI, 1; Arrian. VII, 7; Elliot. I, 552.
[6] Sachau. I, 208.

8th century A.D. was a piratical attack committed "by some of the Meds of ad-Daibul" on a ship carrying some Muslim women from Ceylon. When tidings of this mishap reached Hajjāj, the governor of Iraq, he sent envoys to Dāhir asking him to set the women free. Dāhir replied : "Pirates, over whom I have no control, captured." Not satisfied with the reply, Hajjāj sent the first Muslim army across the frontiers to punish the Sindhians.[1]

The Indus and its tributaries, however, provided the scene for at least two naval encounters during the last centuries of our period. The first of these was waged between Dāhir's son, Hullishāh, and Junaid. Balādhurī says that "Hullishāh was taken prisoner, his ship having missed the way."[2] The second engagement took place between the Jats and Sultan Maḥmūd. Nizāmuddīn Ahmad informs us that when Maḥmūd arrived at Multan, "he ordered fourteen hundred boats to be built, each of which was armed with three firm iron pikes, projecting one from the prow and two from the sides, so that everything which came in contact with them would infallibly be destroyed. In each boat were twenty archers, with bows and arrows, grenades and naphtha; and in this way he proceeded to attack the Jats, who, having intelligence of the armament, sent their families into the islands and prepared themselves for the conflict. They launched, according to some, four, according to others, eight thousand boats, manned and armed, ready to engage the Muhammadans. Both fleets met and a desperate conflict ensued. Every boat of the Jats that approached the Muslim fleet was broken and overturned. Thus most of the Jats were drowned, and those who were not destroyed, were put to the sword."[3]

IV

If Bengal and the Indus valley played an important rôle in naval affairs, it was in the extreme south of the Deccan peninsula that naval power reached its climax. The people of the southern promontory seem to have learnt the art and craft of the sea long before the beginning of the Christian era. Literary evidence, both indigenous and foreign, proves that from very early times they carried on oversea trade with Western Asia, Egypt, and later with the Greek and Roman Empires.[4] But there is no trace of any

[1] Futūḥ al-Buldān, tr. by Clark Murgotten, pp. 215-16.
[2] Ibid. p. 226.
[3] Elliot. II, 478.
[4] Cambridge History of India. I, 594.

naval operations in southern waters till about the time of Ceṅguṭṭuvan.

Of the three Tamil states, it is the Ceras who seem to have first developed a sort of naval power. According to Tamil authors, the early Cera king, Ceṅguṭṭuvan, led an expedition to the Gangetic valley, and in that expedition the "journey from the Cera kingdom to Orissa was performed by sea."[1] It is obvious that the fleet on this occasion was merely used for purposes of transport; but on another occasion it is said to have fought a naval engagement with the Yavanas at sea and won a complete victory.[2] Centuries later in the reign of the Coḷa king, Rājarāja I, we hear once again of the Cera fleet fighting with the Coḷa navy in the "Roads of Kāṇḍalūr". This time, however, it was routed; but it survived the shock. And once again in the time of Rājādhirāja (1042-1052 A.D.) it met its Coḷa rival at Kāṇḍalūrśālai, "on the never-decreasing ocean." This second venture, however, was attended with no better fate than the first. The Cera fleet was again defeated and probably destroyed.[3]

The Coḷas seem to have begun their naval career later than the Ceras, but they attained to a much higher point of achievement. Their age-long hostility with the kings of Ceylon necessitated the creation of a fleet of ships. The first historical or semi-historical Coḷa monarch, Karikāla, is represented by the early Tamil poets as having invaded Ceylon and carried off three thousand captives to work on the embankments of the Kaveri river, which he constructed.[4] In the fourth decade of the 10th century, Parāntaka I once again crossed the narrow channel between the two countries, and carried out a raid on Ceylon. An Ukkal (Viṣṇu temple) Tamil inscription tells us that Rāja-rāja I not only subjugated Ceylon, but conquered "twelve thousand ancient islands of the sea."[5] It has been already noted that the same monarch inflicted a crushing defeat on the Cera navy at Kāṇḍalūr.

Emboldened by these early triumphs, the Coḷa navy under Rājendra Gaṅgaikoṇḍacoḷa pushed out on longer and bolder enterprises. About the thirteenth year of his reign, Rājendra equipped

[1] Kanakasabhai, *The Tamils 1800 years ago*, p. 95. Ceṅguṭṭuvan is quite historical but his northern expedition seems mostly mythical.

[2] S. K. Aiyangar, *Hindu Administrative Institutions*, p. 314. *Beginnings of South Indian History*, p. 151.

[3] South Ind. Inscr. vol. II, p. 241, n. 1; Vol. III, Pt. I, pp. 4-6.

[4] V. A. Smith, *Early History of India*, 4th ed., p. 481.

[5] Kielhorn's List, No. 719.

and floated a grand armada, which sailing 'across the middle of the sea lashing with waves,' conquered extensive districts in the Far East. An inscription found on the Rājarājeśvara Temple at Tanjavur, and belonging to the nineteenth year of Rājendra's reign, says that the fleet first proceeded against Saṁgrāmavijayottuṅgavarman, the king of Kaḍāram, captured him with all his fighting elephants and carried off huge treasures. It then took possession of Śrī Vijaya, 'in the midst of which was set the *vidyādharatcṛaṇa*'; Pannai, 'watered by the river'; Malaiyūr 'of ancient fame having for its ramparts many hills'; Māyiruḍingam, 'surrounded by the deep sea as a moat'; Ilaṅgā-śogam, 'undaunted in fierce battles'; Māppappālam, 'surrounded by deep waters let in for defence'; Mevilimbaṅgam 'with well-defended fortress walls'; Vaḷaippandūru, 'possessing both cultivated land and jungle'; Talaittakkolam, 'praised by great men versed in the sciences'; Mudammāliṅgam, 'firm in great and fierce battles'; Ilāmurideśam 'defended by a strong fleet of ship'; Mānakkavāram 'whose flower-gardens resembled the girdle of the nymph of the southern ocean'; and Kaḍāram, 'defended in great strength by the sea which touches it.'[1]

This was the climax of Coḷa naval achievement. The countries conquered by Rājendra included the Nicobar (Nakkavaram) Islands, the Isthmus of Kra, and parts of the Malay Peninsula and Sumatra.[2] Gaṅgaikoṇḍacoḷa thus came into possession of one of the great strategic keys of the world. The Bay of Bengal was converted into a Coḷa Lake, and the old movement of colonisation was given a new impetus.

The naval supremacy of the Coḷas seems to have continued under the immediate successors of Rājendra. Rājādhirāja, (1018-1035 A.D.) is recorded to have sent out an expedition against Ceylon, and defeated and destroyed the Cera fleet at Kāṇḍalūr. The Tirumūkkuḍal Inscription has it that Vīrarājendra Coḷa continued this traditional hostility against Ceylon, and despatched against the latter "a number of ships laden with excessively large forces in the ever-swelling and highly protected sea."[3] The Kaliṅgattuparaṇi proves that Kulottuṅgacoḷadeva (1070-1118 A.D.)

[1] These over-sea conquests of Rājendra have been recorded in many of his inscriptions. Comp. e.g., South Indian Inscr., Vol. II, Pt. I., no. 20.

[2] For identification of the place-names mentioned in the fore-going list, comp. *Sir Asutosh Mukherji Silver Jubilee Volume*, Orientalia, Part II, pp. 568-576; M. Coedes' article in the *Bulletin de l'Ecole Francaise d'Extreme-Orient*", 1918.

[3] Ep. Ind. XXI, 243.

repeated some of the naval adventures of Rājendra and reconquered Kaḍāram.[1]

It will thus be evident that naval warfare was not unknown in ancient India. But it was certainly not as widely practised as land warfare. Boats were indeed used in war, but probably more often as transports than as a fighting line of ships. Naval battles were fought, but only when the theatre of hostilities made it impossible to fight on land. It is a singular misfortune that our records do not throw any light on how our ancient galleys were constructed, equipped or manned.[2]

[1] The small Leyden Grant also refers to an unnamed king of Kaḍāram as a vassal of Kulottuṅga. *South Ind. Inscr.* Vol. II, Pt. I, p. 106, f. n. 1.

It was probably the Eastern or Coromandel coast that formed the chief vantage-ground of Coḷa naval power. The Western or Konkan coast was often infested with pirates. Comp. Mc.Crindle, *Ptolemy*, p. 45; Yule, *Marco Polo*, 2nd ed., II, 378. It is not improbable, however, that the Rāṣṭrakūṭas, and later the Kādambas maintained some sort of a fleet in Koṅkan waters. Comp. Ind. Ant. XII, 18; Ep. Ind. XIII, 309, ff.

[2] For some indirect light (very faint) see J. R. A. S. 1937, p. 469.

CHAPTER VIII

MILITARY ESPIONAGE

I

Spies filled an important rôle in both the civil and military affairs of ancient India. They were employed as early as the Vedic age. The Ṛgveda often speaks of the spies (*spaśah*) of Varuṇa. They sit down around him (I. 24, 13) ; they behold the two worlds (VIII. 87, 3); they are undeceived and wise (VI. 67, 5). In the Artharva-veda (VI. 16, 4) it is stated that Varuṇa's spies, descending from heaven, traverse the world; "thousand-eyed they look over the earth." Besides Varuṇa, spies are also attributed to Mitra (VIII. 61, 3), to Agni (VI. 4, 3), to Soma (IX. 73, 4, 7), to demons combated by Indra (I. 33, 8) and to the gods in general (X.10, 8).[1]

The Institute of Viṣṇu (III, 35) enjoins that "the king must explore, by means of spies, both the state of his own kingdom and of his foes." Manu speaks of five classes of spies (VII, 154), and of their "various disguises" (IX, 261). They were to detect crime (IX, 256), keep watch on the conduct of officials in the districts (VII, 122), and constantly ascertain the king's and his enemy's strength (IX, 298).

In the epics and post-epic literature in general, spies have been described as the "eyes of the king" in the same sense as Hobbes describes them in his Leviathan (II, 23). Before long the metaphor passed into an axiomatic formula in the politico-military thought of India.[2] In the Udyoga-parva (33, 34) it is stated that "cows see by smell, priests by knowledge, kings by spies, and other men through eyes." A preceding verse (33, 32) inculcates that "a king may learn wisdom from a fool, as one gets gold from a

[1] Macdonell, *Vedic Mythology*, 1897, pp. 23-24.

[2] Cf. Śāntiparva 96, 21; Manu IX. 256; Kauṭ. p. 12; Rām. Araṇya. 33, 10; Kām. XII, 28, 30; Nītiv. p. 53: *cārāḥ khalu cakṣūṁṣi kṣitipatīnām;* Ag. P. 220, 20; Mat. P. 215, 89: *rājānaścāracakṣuṣaḥ;* Mṛcchakaṭikā (VII. 8) has *paśyeyuḥ kṣitipatayo hi cāradṛṣṭayā.*

rock......, and should glean information from spies, as a gleaner gets ears of corn." The king must, therefore, employ spies in every district and every fort.[1] Like the 'Mysterious Thread' of China, the spies were to overspread the entire country. They were to keep watch on the conduct of officials, guard against conspiracy, and especially haunt the assemblies of priests, public meetings, cross-roads, and market-places.[2] Under various disguises they were also to roam about in foreign states and collect reliable information about them.[3] In the Rāmāyaṇa, Rāma enquires of Bharata if he was keeping an eye on the eighteen *tīrthas* of foreign countries through spies (*cāraṇaiḥ*).[4] We meet with the same inquiry in the Mahābhārata coming from a sage.[5] In the Virāṭaparva we notice Duryodhana's spies returning from neighbouring states to submit reports to the king.[6]

In military affairs also, the spies played an important part. In the Rāmāyaṇa, a king mentions the wise adage that "the enemy, whose secrets have been known through espionage, can be conquered without much effort."[7] One verse in the Śānti-parva, quoted before, regards the spies as a regular part of the army. In the war-scenes of the Mahābhārata they are always taken for granted as forming part of a camp. They are frequently sent across from one side to another and bring news of one another's plans and objectives. In the Udyoga-parva (196, 2), Yudhiṣṭhira says: "The spies I had placed in the army of Dhṛtarāṣṭra's son brought me this news in the morning." In the Droṇaparva (73, 27) Kṛṣṇa says; "I had sent some spies into the camp of Dhṛtarāṣṭra's son. These spies, quickly returning, gave me this information." They bring the news of the formidable military array to be formed next day by the Kurus. The news of Arjuna's vow is likewise carried across by spies to the other camp (Droṇaparva 74, 1). In the Rāmāyaṇa, the king of Laṅkā, time and again, sends spies to the opposite camp to discover the exact military resources and plans of the enemy.[8]

II

During the Maurya period, a complete system of espionage was established in the country. Arrian refers to a class of men

[1] Vanaparva 150, 37-8; 42, 43.
[2] Śāntiparva 69, 8-12.
[3] Śāntiparva 86, 20-21; 93, 19.
[4] Rām. Ayodhyā. 100, 36.
[5] Sabhāparva 5, 38; also comp. Ādiparva 140, 63-65.
[6] Virāṭaparva 25, 5-6, 9-13.
[7] Rām. Laṅkā. 29, 21.
[8] Rām. Laṅkā. ch. 25, 29 and 30.

called Overseers (Episkopoi) who "overlook what is done throughout the country and in the cities, and make report to the king where the Indians are ruled by a king, or the magistrates where the people have a democratic Government." Strabo calls this class of men the Ephori or Inspectors. "They are," he says, "entrusted with the superintendence of all that is going on, and it is their duty to report privately to the king. Some are entrusted with the inspection of the city, and others with that of the camp. The former employ as their co-adjutors the courtesans of the city, and the latter the courtesans of the camp. The ablest and the most trustworthy are appointed to all these offices." The number of spies appointed by the king was apparently so large as to mislead the Greek ambassador into thinking that they constituted one of the seven classes of the Indian people.

III

The Arthaśāstra of Kauṭilya provides us with a graphic account of the activities of spies in Mauryan and post-Mauryan polity. Spies, according to the author, were primarily divided into two classes, viz. local agents (*saṁsthāḥ*) and wandering or travelling supervisors (*saṁçarāḥ*). To the former category belonged spies under the guise of a 'fraudulent disciple' (*Kāpaṭika-chātra*), recluse (*udāsthita*), householder (*gṛhapatika*) merchant (*vaidehaka*), and ascetic practising austerities (*tāpasa*); while under the latter group came spies called 'class-mate' (*satri*), 'fire-brand' (*tīkṣṇa*), poisoner (*rasada*), and 'mendicant woman' (*bhikṣukī*). The mention of monks, ascetics and mendicant women as spies provides an eloquent commentary on Kauṭilya's religious attitude.[1] Though a Brahman, and certainly a believer in the established order of society, he feels no hesitation in advocating an unscrupulous exploitation of the religious susceptibilities of the people. But the spies were to put on an unlimited variety of disguises. Moreover, as far as practicable, they were not to be known to each other; and the king must, on no account, rely upon the report of a single spy. There were to be five Institutes of Espionage, controlling the entire intelligence department, and checking and verifying the reports coming from different sources. Cipher writing was to be used by the spies, and carrier pigeons were to carry secret intelligence.[2]

[1] Besides the above, Kauṭilya mentions a few other kinds of ascetic spies, e.g., *muṇḍa* (a man with a shaved head), *jaṭila* (a man with braided hair), *parivrājikā* (a woman ascetic), etc.

[2] Kauṭ. Bk. I. ch. 11 and 12.

There were numerous duties which the spies had to perform. They were to watch the conduct of government officials of all ranks, from the highest to the lowest. They were to keep the king informed about the trend of public feeling in the kingdom. They were to detect sedition and crime, and assist in the administration of justice. And, last but not least, they had to collect accurate information regarding the state of affairs in neighbouring kingdoms, discover and foil the ruses of the other side and neutralise its successes.[1]

Broadly speaking, in relation to foreign states espionage took three forms, viz., political, diplomatic and military. The first involved an attempt to get into touch through secret emissaries with the discontented or disloyal elements in the hostile state, and utilize their services for the destruction of the latter. Various forms of political espionage of this kind have been elaborated by Kauṭilya in Bk. I, ch. 14, Bk. VII and Bk. XII. Strangely enough, some of these have a curious resemblance to methods employed by Hitler and Mussolini on the eve of the Spanish Civil War.

Diplomatic espionage was carried on by ambassadors and diplomatic agents in foreign courts. The duties of these officers in peace-time included not merely the carrying out of negotiations, but also observation of what went on in the kingdoms to which they were accredited. They were specially expected to keep an eye on all matters which, directly or indirectly, affected the interests of the state they represented. While discussing the duties of the ambassador (*dūta*), Kauṭilya lays down: "The envoy shall make friendship with the enemy's officers such as those in charge of wild tracts, of boundaries, of cities, and of country parts. He shall also contrast the military stations, sinews of war, and strongholds of the enemy with those of his own master. He shall ascertain the size and area of forts and of the state, as well as strong-holds of precious things, and assailable and unassailable points." Further, "he shall through the agency of ascetic and merchant spies or through his disciples, or through spies under the guise of physicians and heretics or through the recipients of salaries from two states (*ubhayavetana*) ascertain the nature of the intrigue prevalent among parties favourably disposed to his own master, as well as the conspiracy of hostile factions, and understand the loyalty or disloyalty of the people to the enemy, besides any assailable points. If there is no possibility of carrying on such conversation, he may try to

[1] Kaut. Bk. I, ch. 11 and 12.

gather such information by observing the talk of beggars, intoxicated and insane persons, or of persons babbling in sleep, or by observing the signs made in places of pilgrimage and temples, or by deciphering paintings and secret writings (*citra-gūḍha-lekhya-saṁjñābhiḥ*).[1] It is thus clear that an ambassador in ancient India, like his modern prototype, was nothing more than an honourable spy acting under the protection of the customary law.[2]

Military espionage consisted in the employment of secret agents to procure accurate information regarding the military resources of the hostile state, plans and movements of the hostile army, and safe-guarding one's own camp and army from the poisonous contamination of enemy's spies. In Bk. XII, ch. 4 of the Arthaśāstra, Kauṭilya speaks of "spies who are residing as traders in the enemy's forts, and those that are living as cultivators in the enemy's villages, as well as those who are living as cow-herds or ascetics in the district borders of the enemy's country." Like the German agents in the eastern departments of France during the Great War, these were apparently expected to transmit news of military importance to the king. Further, Kauṭilya advocates the employment of spies along with the marching army, in the camp, and also in the fighting line. They were to keep up the morale of the troops "by declaring the success of their own operations and the failure of those of the enemy."[3] They were also to harass the enemy, create divisions in their ranks, and demoralise the hostile king "by telling him that his own fort was burnt, stormed or that some one of his family or an enemy or wild chief rose in rebellion."[4] In the work of espionage, all methods were admissible—spying, lying, bribing, poisoning, woman's wiles and the assassin's knife.

To a weak king, menaced by a strong neighbour, Kauṭilya's advice is to rely chiefly on spies, and wage what he describes as

[1] Kauṭ. Bk. I, ch. 16.

[2] Some later writers on *nīti* state in unequivocal terms that an ambassador was but a spy in disguise. Comp. Ag. P. 241, 11-13. The Yukti-kalpataru (p. 10, v. 71) has the following interesting couplet:

Prakāśaścā-prakāśaśca cārastu dvividho mataḥ
Aprakāśo-yamuddiṣṭaḥ prakāśo dūta-saṁjñakaḥ.

[3] Kauṭ. tr. p. 427. Cf. also p. 300, where it is laid down that "spies, prostitutes, artisans, singers, and aged military officers shall vigilantly examine the pure or impure conduct of military men."

[4] Ibid. Bk. X, ch. 6.

'battle of intrigue' (*mantra-yuddha*) and 'secret war' (*kūṭa-yuddha*). The spies were to practise all kinds of fraud, artifice, incendiarism and robbery. They were to demoralise the enemy's troops by circulating false news, and seduce the allegiance of his ministers and commanders. The underlying idea seems to have been to keep the strong neighbour so preoccupied with domestic troubles as to make it impossible for him to launch upon a foreign expedition.[1]

In capturing a fort, Kauṭilya advises the invading king to "infuse enthusiastic spirit among his own men and frighten the enemy's people by giving publicity to his power of omniscience and close association with gods."[2] The circulation of this precious information was to be entrusted to spies disguised as "astrologers, sooth-sayers, horologists, story-tellers (*paurāṇika*), as well as those who read the fore-bodings of every moment." To induce credence in the story, the spies were to perform certain religious and magical tricks such as "the shower of fire-brand (*ulkā*) with the noise of drums (from the sky) on the day of the birth-star of the enemy."[3] They were also to spread rumours about the justice and magnanimity of the invading king. "When the people of the enemy were convinced of this, they may be sent to the conqueror to receive wealth and honour. Those of the enemy who were in need of money and food should be supplied with an abundance of those things. Those who do not like to receive such things may be presented with ornaments for their wives and children."[4] By methods such as these, the invading king was to create a party favourable to his interests in the enemy's fort, and later to capture it through their help.

IV

Our knowledge of espionage in the Gupta and post-Gupta period is extremely meagre. Yet it is only reasonable to assume that there was no sudden reversal of the old strategy and that spies continued as an important feature of Indian civil and military administration through succeeding ages. The activities of spies in both the internal and external affairs of the state are graphically described in some of the dramas and kāvyas composed from the

[1] Kauṭ. Bk. XII. [2] Ibid. tr. p. 457. [3] Ibid. p. 458.
[4] Ibid. p. 459.

Gupta period onwards.[1] Moreover, in later works on arthaśāstra and nīti the functions and disguises of spies are delineated more or less on the pattern of Kauṭilya.[2] In the *Lalita-Vigraharāja-nāṭaka*, a Sanskrit play composed about the middle of the twelfth century A.D. in honour of King Vigraharājadeva of Śākambharī (only a portion of which has been preserved as an inscription at Ajmere), it is stated that the king's spy went to the camp of Hammīra,[3] and returning later informed his master of what he had been able to gather regarding the enemy's forces and plans.[4] The Anamkoṇḍa Inscription of the Kākatīya king, Rudradeva (dated 1162-63 A.D.) speaks of the spies through whom Rudradeva got all necessary information about the kingdom of Bhīma, which he was bent upon invading.[5] The Rājataraṅgiṇī makes frequent mention of *tīkṣṇa* spies. They were often employed for the secret assassination of the enemy. In one place (IV. 323) it is said that Lalitāditya-Muktāpīḍa employed these "firebrands" for the treacherous assassination of the king of Gauḍa; in another (VIII, 3311) they are found conspiring to kill a rebel chief. Elsewhere (VII, 627) we read that prince Harṣa made an abortive attempt to kill his father with the help of these desperadoes.[6]

V

Ancient writers repeatedly enjoin that the king must not merely employ spies to find out the secrets of the enemy, but simultaneously safeguard his own secrets against foreign spies.

[1] Of these special mention may be made of the *Mṛcchakaṭika* VII, 8 (cf. also Wilson, *Theatre of the Hindus*, I, 121), the *Mudrārākṣasa* of Viśākhadatta, Bhavabhūti's *Uttara-Rāmacarita*, Bhāravi's *Kirātārjjunīya* I, 19, and Māgha's Śiśupālavadha (II, 82, 113; XX, 23). Daṇḍi in his Daśakumāracarita relates how a spy wandered about in the guise of an ascetic, and ultimately returning to Rājahaṁsa, the Magadhan king, supplies him with all necessary information regarding the Mālava kingdom.

[2] Kām. XII, 25-49; Yukti-kalpataru, pp. 9-10; Nītiv. pp. 53-55; Ag. P. 220, 20-22; 241, 11-13; Jolly, Z.D.M.G. 69, 374.

[3] Hammīra or Hamvīra is probably the Indian adaptation of the Arabic title al-amīr. See Thomas, *Chronicles of the Pathan kings of Delhi*, 50, n.; Lane-Poole, *Coins of the Sultans of Delhi*, XXV.

[4] Ind. Ant. XX, 201 et seq.

[5] Ibid. XI, 18. A similar instance of spies ascertaining the movements of the enemy is furnished by the Wani Copper-plate grant of Govinda III, dated A.D. 806-7. Ind. Ant. XI, 162.

[6] Comp. also Rājat; VI, 171; VII. 629, 1016, 1045; VIII. 1326, 2085, 2200, etc. The *tīkṣṇas*, it would appear, were something like modern gangsters.

Consequently, penal measures were taken against foreign espionage, especially when it was of a military character.

It has already been mentioned that the king of Laṅkā repeatedly sent spies into Râma's camp with a view to discovering the latter's military plans. The story has it that while Râma was on the mainland of India, Rāvaṇa sent an ambassador (*dūta*) to Sugrīva imploring him to keep away from the conflict. But, unfortunately, the *dūta* was suspected of being a spy. Aṅgada, one of the chief followers of Rāma, said: "Methinks he is not an ambassador, but a spy, sent to examine our forces and plans. He should, therefore, be immediately arrested and on no account be permitted to go back to Laṅkā."[1] And immediately, we are told, he was arrested and mercilessly beaten. Later, however, he was released by Rāma on the ground that he was really a *dūta*, not a spy (*mucyatāṁ dūta āgataḥ*).[2] A few chapters later, we read that Rāvaṇa again sent two spies into Rāma's camp to make an accurate estimate of the strength, weapons and armaments of the enemy. They were, however, discovered and brought before Rāma; and then we have the significant statement that "they gave up all hopes of their life" (*nirāśau jīvite tathā*).[3] Thus baffled, Rāvaṇa once again sent spies into the invading army. Once again they were discovered, maltreated, belaboured, but ultimately set free. On their return to the city, they reported to the king on the kind of treatment that was meted out to them by the enemy. One of them said: "As soon as I entered, and was scanning that host, I was discovered. I was furiously assaulted by the monkeys with thighs, clenched fists, teeth and palms. I was dragged by them in the midst of the army. When at length I was taken before Rāma, my limbs were bleeding, and my senses benumbed."[4] No comment is needed. Though a story, it speaks a volume.

The Maṇimekhalai records another instance of the treatment of spies. The story runs that there was a war between two princes, named Vasu and Kumāra, cousins by birth, and ruling respectively Siṁhapura and Kapila in the fertile country of Kaliṅga. The war led to much desolation and bloodshed. A merchant, named Saṅgama, went to Siṁhapura to sell jewellery and other articles. "In course of his business, he was arrested by Bharata, a police official of the state, and was shown up before the monarch as a spy. Under royal orders he was beheaded."[5] But sometimes a

[1] Rām. Laṅkā, 20, 29-30.
[2] Ibid. 20, 34.
[3] Ibid. 25, 15.
[4] Ibid. 29, 16 ff.
[5] S. K. Aiyangar, *Manimekhalai in its Historical Setting*, p. 187.

more cruel punishment was in store for spies. The Rājataraṅgiṇī (VIII. 2200) mentions the eyes of *tīkṣṇa* spies being torn out by the enemy against whom they were employed.

It is abundantly clear from the above account that penal measures, often of an extreme nature, were taken against spies or suspected spies. The severity of penalties probably depended, in a large measure, on the character of the monarch or the authorities inflicting them. The story of the Rāmāyaṇa further proves that suspicion of espionage often led to violent reactions of public opinion; and that spy-mania led in ancient times, as it does even today, to terrible scenes of brutality, and perhaps to gross miscarriage of justice as well.

CHAPTER IX

SOME ASPECTS OF MILITARY ADMINISTRATION

In the preceding chapters we have been mainly concerned with the history and evolution of the various branches of the service. In the following we propose to deal with certain aspects of military administration, in so far as our materials throw any light upon them.

1. Recruitment of Troops

In early Vedic times the king probably maintained no standing army. He had a small retinue of personal attendants, who acted as his body-guard, served him in hall and bower, and went out on his errands. When any expedition for offensive or defensive purposes was necessary, local levies were raised from the people-caste (*viśaḥ* or *vaiśyas*). These brought their own arms and weapons, and were probably captained by their own chiefs.[1]

It was from the nucleus of a body of king's personal retainers that there grew up a standing army of the state. We do not know when this great change took place. It is certain, however, that in the fourth century B.C., when Alexander invaded India, standing armies had become a normal feature of Indian military life.[2] The causes which led to this development seem to have been mainly two—first, the increasing unwillingness on the part of cultivators to leave their plough for an indefinite length of time, and second, the ambition of rulers to conquer more territories and absorb them in their growing empires. A strong standing army was the very *sine qua non* for an activist, expansionist policy. It is worthy of note that Magadha, which had been consistently following a policy of expansion since about the 6th century B.C., was in possession of the strongest standing army in the last quarter of the fourth century B.C.

[1] A. C. Das, *Ṛgvedic Culture*, 1925, pp. 340-41. [2] Cf. chapter II.

Classical authors offer us a glimpse of the sort of life led by the army of Candragupta Maurya. Megasthenes says that when not engaged in active service, the soldiers passed their time in idleness and drinking. "They are maintained at the king's expense, and hence are always ready, when occasion calls, to take the field, for they carry nothing of their own with them but their bodies."[1] Arrian reports that they lived a life of supreme freedom and enjoyment. "They have only military duties to perform. Others make their arms, others supply them with horses, and they have others to attend on them in the camp, who take care of their horses, clean their arms, drive their elephants, prepare their chariots and act as their charioteers. As long as they are required to fight, they fight; and when peace returns, they abandon themselves to enjoyment,—the pay which they receive from the state being so liberal that they can with ease maintain themselves and others besides."[2]

It may be assumed that most of the post-Mauryan dynasties maintained standing armies of their own, the number and strength of which, of course, depended upon the extent of territory they controlled and their economic resources. But simultaneously with this maintenance of standing armies, the old Vedic custom of raising local levies on the occasion of a grave emergency seems to have continued. Describing the military usages prevailing in the 7th century A.D., Hiuen Tsiang says: "The soldiers are levied according to the requirements of service; they are promised certain payments and are publicly enrolled."[3] Elsewhere he writes: "The summonses are issued according to circumstance, and after proclamation of the reward the enrolment is awaited."[4]

Both literary and epigraphic records prove that the army was not always composed of local recruits alone, but was strengthened by the enlistment of foreign adventurers. To this latter category probably belonged the *bhṛtas* or mercenaries mentioned in the Arthaśāstra and other politico-military manuals. Ancient Tamil authors sometimes speak of the Yavana body-guard of Pāṇḍya kings.[5] We learn from the Chachnāma that in the 8th century A.D. king Dāhir of Sindh had in his employ as many as 500 Arab troopers under the leadership of Muḥammad 'Allāfī.[6] The Kaṇaswa

[1] McCrindle, *Ancient India as described by Megasthenes and Arrian*, p. 85.
[2] Arrian, *Indika*, XI. [3] Beal. I, 77-8. [4] Watters. I, 177.
[5] Kanakasabhai, *The Tamils 1800 Years ago*, pp. 37-38.
[6] Elliot. I, 156.

Inscription of Śivagaṇa, dated 738-739 A.D., says that the rulers of the Maurya race were "served by armies from afar" : *dūr-ābhyāgata-vāhinī-parikara.*[1] The Bhagalpur plate of Nārāyaṇapāla informs us that the Bengal army, during the period of Pāla supremacy, was composed of troops not merely from Gauḍa, but also from Mālava, Khaśa, Hūna, Kulika, Karṇāṭa and Lāṭa countries.[2] From the Rājataraṅgiṇī we learn that the kings of Kasmir recruited mercenaries not only from Rajputana, the Salt Range (Saindhava),[3] in the Punjab and distant Rājagṛha in Magadha,[4] but also from the Yavanas[5] and the Turuṣkas.[6] The Rajputs, who in later times appear to have acquired a reputation similar to that of the Swiss Guards in medieval Europe, found a hospitable market in every state, and Kalhaṇa's narrative makes it abundantly clear that they, along with other foreigners, constituted the mainstay of the Kasmirian rulers. Time and again, the chronicler speaks of the bravery and fidelity of the Rājaputras and other mercenaries in sad contrast with the inveterate cowardice and empty bragging of the indigenous troops of Kasmir.[7]

The popular notion that the military profession was the exclusive monopoly of the Kṣatriya caste is wholly without foundation.[8] Equally erroneous is the assertion made by Wheeler that "except in some wildly supernatural legends, the Brāhmaṇs are not represented as warriors."[9] We need not recount here the formal law according to which any priest might serve as a soldier if unable to support himself as a priest.[10] It is well-known that some of the most celebrated warriors in the Mahābhārata such as Droṇa, Aśvatthāman and Paraśu-Rāma were born in the priestly class. The Śarabhaṅga Jātaka relates the story of a Brāhman priest of Benares sending his son to Taxila for training in archery.[11] It is stated in the classical chronicles that Alexander in the course of his campaigns in India met with the most stubborn resistance from the Brāhman confederacy of the Indus valley. They

1 Ind. Ant. XIX, 58.
2 Ibid. XV, 306.
3 Rājat. VII. 1868.
4 Rājat VII. 1501.
5 Ibid. VIII. 2264.
6 Ibid. VII. 1149.
7 Ibid. VIII. 1047, 1148, 1082-86, etc.

8 See Dr. N. K. Bhattasali's article in the Modern Review, August 1930, p. 158. The writer attributes the downfall of the Hindus to this cause.

9 Wheeler, *History of India,* I, 77.

10 Gautama Dharmaśāstra. VII, 6; Vāś. II, 22; Manu, X, 81; Yājñ. III, 35.

11 Cowell, *The Jātaka,* No. 522.

denounced those princes who submitted to the Macedonian,[1] and goaded the free tribes into open revolt.[2] Arrian mentions a "city of the Brachmanas", to which Alexander laid siege. For sometime the inhabitants beat back his onslaughts with vigour and determination. But at length considering the situation desperate, they "set fire to their houses, in which they were sought and killed, but most part fell fighting. About 5,000 in all were killed, and as they were men of spirit, a few only were taken prisoners."[3] Alexander regarded the Brāhmans as his worst enemies, and his hand fell heavily upon them. As the Greek historian says: "They were put to death whole-sale; their bodies were hung up for the kites and vultures by the roads—to the unspeakable horror, we may believe, of the people of the land."

The records of succeeding centuries point definitely to the conclusion that the Brāhmans continued to serve as soldiers and commanders of armies throughout our period. The names and exploits of Puṣyamitra, the Brāhman commander-in-chief of the last Mauryan monarch, Bṛhadratha, and of Mayūraśarman, the founder of the Kadamba dynasty of Banavāsī, are too well-known to need recapitulation. Epigraphic records disclose the names of a host of other Brahman generals, who figured prominently in the military history of Gupta and post-Gupta India. A few instances are cited below:

1. Pṛthivīṣena. In the Karamḍāṇḍa Inscription of the reign of Kumāragupta, he has been described as the mantrin, kumārāmātya and mahā-balādhikṛta (commander-in-chief) of the emperor. That he was a Brāhman by birth will be apparent from the fact that his grandfather has been referred to as "a teacher of the Chāndogya (veda), of the gotras Aśva and Vājin."[4]
2. Maṇḍalika Vanapati. He was a Brāhman of the *ātreya* gotra, and a general of Rājarāja of the Gaṅga dynasty. The Dirghasi Inscription, dated 1075-76 A.D., says that he led the king's forces, won a victory over the contemporary Coḷa king (Rājendra-coḷa or Kulottuṅga-coḷa I), and subjugated the kings of Veṅgi, Kimidi (now a zamindari in the Ganjan district), Kośala (corresponding to the upper valley of the Mahānadī and its tributaries), Giḍrisingi and Oḍḍa (Orissa):[5]

[1] Sabbas, for instance. [2] For example, the Mousikanos.
[3] McCrindle, *India and its Invasion by Alexander*, pp. 143-4.
[4] Ep. Ind. X, 72. [5] Ibid. IV, 314 ff.

3. Gopāla. He was a Brāhman general of the Cāndella king Kīrtivarman. A Cāndella Inscription from Mahoba says that he vanquished the Cedi monarch, Karṇa, and re-instated his master on his rightful throne.[1]

4. Madanapālaśarman. He was a general under the Cāndella king, Paramardideva. We learn from the Icchāwar plates, dated 1171 A.D., that his father Ṭhākkura Maheśvara was "a Brāhman of the Kṛṣṇātreya gotra, who studied the śākhā of the Chāndogyas."

5. Meḍamārya, a commander in the army of Vīra-coḍa-deva (also known as Viṣṇuvardhana).[2]

6. Kṛṣṇa Rāma, the great commander-in-chief of Rāja-rāja the Great and Rājendra-coḷa. That he was a Brāhman by birth is apparent from his title Mummaḍi-śora-brahma-nārāyan.[3]

7. Vaidyadeva, the minister of Kumārapāladeva. He is credited with having won two notable victories for his master—one in the southern part of Vaṅga and the other 'in the East.'[4]

8. Guravamiśra, the minister of Nārāyaṇapāla. In the Badal Pillar Inscription, he is referred to as follows: "In the assemblies of the learned he at once confounded the pride of self-conceit of opponents by his speeches to which the constant study of the śāstras imparted deep meaning, just as, possessed of boundless wealth of valour, he did in battle the conceit of bravery of enemies."[5]

9. Brahma or Brahman, the Brāhman general of the last Cālukya emperor, Someśvara IV. In an inscription of 1175 A.D., he is described as the mahā-pradhāna, daṇḍa-nāyaka and senādhipati of the king.

10. Kholeśvara. He was a minister-general of the Yādava king Siṅghana (c. 1210-47 A.D.). The Ambā Inscription says that he "humbled the Gurjaras and the Mālavas, and destroyed the race of the 'heroic Ābhīra king'." His worthy son, Rāma, is also said to have led an expedition against the Gurjaras, but was slain.[6]

[1] Ibid. I, 220.
[2] South Ind. Inscr. I, 61.
[3] Ibid. Vol. II, pt. i, 130.
[4] Ep. Ind. I, 348; II, 84, f. n.
[5] Ep. Ind. II, 106.
[6] Archeological Survey of Western India, Vol. III, p. 86. Upendra, the first historical person in the Paramāra dynasty, is described in the Udaipur

Moreover, there are a few passages in the Rājataraṅgiṇī which go to show that Brāhman troops were often enlisted in the Kasmirian army. It is noteworthy that Kalhaṇa sometimes eulogises the fidelity and resoluteness of Brāhman troops in contradistinction with the treachery and fickleness of other classes of soldiers. After Sussala's murder, for instance, the relatives of the king, as well as his troops, broke away pell-mell. But "the Brāhmanas Lavanarāja and Yasorāja, who were skilled in military exercises, and the chief of Kānda were the only three who fell bravely fighting."[1] Elsewhere we read: "The whole force ran away, and only the Brāhman Kalyānarāja, who was well versed in military exercises, was killed fighting with his face to (the enemy)."[2] In the kingdom of Orissa during the period of Keśarī and Gaṅga dynasties, the Mahāsthāna Brāhmans used to contribute a substantial number of military recruits to the peasant militia of the state. To this day some of their descendants bear the family title of *senāpati,* meaning commanders of armies.[3]

Nor were the lower classes of the community—the Vaiśyas and Śūdras—excluded from military service. The truth, on the contrary, seems to be that they constituted the rank and file of the army, in spite of the formal law that men might follow the profession of a lower caste, if unable to sustain themselves by what appertained to their own, but must never follow the profession of a higher caste. We have already seen that castle-less forest tribes were often employed by Hindu kings for military purposes. Hopkins says that the mass of the epic army was composed of the lowest classes, mixed with barbarians and foreigners. "Among these too fought men of the people-caste, when necessity called them into the field."[4] In the Arthaśāstra (Bk. IX, ch. 2), Kauṭilya approves of the employment of Vaiśya and Śūdra troops in the army. The Agni Purāṇa specifically lays down that the Śūdras have a right to the art of war and that they, along with the mixed castes, are expected to contribute to the défence of the state.[5]

In southern India, caste-less indigenous tribes such as the Maravar formed the best recruiting ground for the Coḷa army in

Praśasti as "a jewel among the twice-born (*dvija-varga-ratna*)," who gained "high honour of kingship by his valour." H. C. Ray, *Dynastic History of Northern India,* II. 844-5.

[1] Rājat. VIII. 1345. [2] Ibid. VIII. 1071.

[3] J. B. O. R. S. XIV. [4] J. A. O. S. XIII, 185.

[5] Ag. P. 249, 8:

Yuddhādhikāraḥ śūdrasya svayaṁ vyāpadi śikṣayā

Deśasthaiḥ saṁkaraiḥ rājñaḥ kāryā yuddhe sahāyatā.

the early centuries of the Christian era.[1] Epigraphic evidence proves that in the 10th and 11th centuries the Coḷa army was largely recruited from the Left hand and Right hand (*Iḍaṅkaiyar* and *Valaṅkaiyar*) castes.[2] Similarly the Hoysoḷa army consisted, among others, of gold-smiths, barbers and a large number of Beḍas. These last are described in contemporary inscriptions as "the confidential agents of the Hoysaḷa camp."[3] We notice the same phenomenon in the north-western state of Kasmir. Kalhaṇa mentions that there were occasions in the history of this kingdom when cultivators, artisans, and even carters were recruited for the army.[4] Occasionally we hear of men of even lower castes pushing their way to positions of importance in the army. The Drākṣārāma Inscription of Kulottuṅga I records the meritorious services rendered to that monarch by one of his generals, variously named Vaṇḍurāja, Pallavarāja and Timvaraṅga, and described as the "the crest-jewel of the Śūdra family."[5] It is also well-known that the Reḍḍis began their career in history as generals of the Kākatīyas.

The facts and examples cited above totally disprove the contention that the military profession was the exclusive monopoly of any one caste. And yet it is probable that captains and leaders of armies were, oftener than not, members of the higher castes. "Career according to talent" was not an ideal of the social or political system. In discussing the qualifications of the *senāpati*, most ancient writers have emphasised that he must be a man of high social standing, not one from the gutter.[6]

2. Units of the Army

We know very little about the organization of the army in ancient Hindu states. There is evidence, however, to show that in the interest of administrative efficiency the army was divided into sections, platoons, brigades, etc. There is a verse in the Vaśiṣṭha-Saṁhitā (XIX, 17), which says: "On the march against the enemy the army, which consists of companies of ten, shall be able to perform a double duty." In the following verse (XIX, 18) the author speaks of a division of a hundred as the next higher unit

[1] Kanakasabhai, *The Tamils 1800 Years ago*, p. 37.
[2] South Ind. Inscr, Vol. II, Pt. v., Introd. p. 9.
[3] The Half-yearly Journal of the Mysore University, Vol. III, no. I.
[4] Rājat. VIII, 727, 2518 etc.
[5] Ep. Ind. XXVII, 139.
[6] Sabhāparva 5, 46; Rām. Ayodhyā, 100, 30; Śāntiparva 85, 30 ff; Kām. XIX, 27 ff; Nītiv. pp. 48-50; Ag. P. 220, 1-2; Nīti-p. VI. 72-73.

in the army-organisation. In the Arthaśāstra (Bk. X. ch. 6), Kauṭilya says: "For every ten members of each of the constituents of the army, there must be one commander, called padika; ten padikas under a senāpati; ten senāpatis under a nāyaka." Thus according to Kauṭilya, the smallest unit of the army was a squad of ten, which was commanded by an officer called *padika*. Ten such squads formed a platoon of a hundred, officered by a *senāpati*. Ten platoons constituted a regiment under the command of a general, called *nāyaka*. The Śāntiparva (100, 31) recommends that in the event of meritorious service the master of ten (*daśādhipati*) should be promoted to the headship of a hundred (*śatādhipati*), and the latter to the next higher grade.

Besides the above, ancient works mention another method of distributing troops into units. According to this scheme of distribution, the smallest unit of the army was a *patti*, described as consisting of 1 chariot, 1 elephant, 3 horses and 5 men. The next higher units in the ascending order were the *senāmukha*, *gulma*, *gaṇa*, *vāhini*, *pṛtanā*, *camū*, *anīkinī* and *akṣauhiṇī*. Each of these was three times as big as the corps preceding it; but the ninth formation (called *akṣauhiṇī*), which was considered to represent a complete army, was ten times as numerous as the preceding *anīkinī*. The following table will more clearly explain the nature of these formations:

Unit	Chariot	Elephant	Horse	Foot
Patti ..	1	1	3	5
Senāmukha ..	3	3	9	15
Gulma ..	9	9	27	45
Gaṇa ..	27	27	81	135
Vāhinī ..	81	81	243	405
Pṛtanā ..	243	243	729	1,215
Camū ..	729	729	2,187	3,645
Anīkinī ..	2,187	2,187	6,561	10,935
Akṣauhiṇī ..	21,870	21,870	65,610	109,350

The above account of the distribution of troops is given in the Ādiparva (2, 19 ff.) of the Mahābhārata and in the lexicography of Amara (Kṣatriyavarga. vv. 80-81). How far the scheme was based upon actual military usage we cannot say, but that it was of comparatively later origin is clear enough. The epics themselves do not show any intimate acquaintance with it. In the Udyogaparva (154, 24) it is stated that "a *senā* consists of five hundred war-cars and the same number of war-elephants; while ten of these constitute a *pṛtanā;* and ten of these a *vāhinī.*" Moreover, in the following verses (28-29) we are told that "a *patti* has five times fifty men, the *gulma* seven hundred and fifty, three *gulmas* make a *gaṇa*, and there is no difference between a *gulma* and a *senāmukha.*" But more important is verse 25, where it is categorically stated that "in common parlance the words *senā, vāhinī, pṛtanā, dhvajinī , camū, akṣauhiṇī* and *varuthinī* are used in the same sense." It is clear, therefore, that the Ādiparva scheme of military formations was neither fully understood in the epic age, nor based upon epic military practice.

In certain inscriptions of a much later date we find mention of such epithets as *mahāgaṇastha* and *gaulmika.*[1] These have been interpreted by scholars as meaning officers in charge of a *gaṇa* and *gulma* squadron.[2] If the suggested interpretation be correct, we may well believe that the scheme of military formations outlined above was actually put into operation in eastern India, perhaps in a mutilated form. We say in a mutilated form because chariots by then had dropped out of the military machinery of the country.

Gustav Oppert in his now out-of-date work on the Weapons and Army Organisation of the Hindus has given a third scheme of military formation, based on the Nītiprakāśikā of Vaiśampāyana.[3] The names of the units are as before, but the number of constituents of each unit has been enormously increased, as will be evident from the following table :

Unit		Chariot	Elephant	Horse	Foot
Patti	..	1	10	1,000	100,000
Senāmukha	..	3	30	3,000	300,000
Gulma	..	9	90	9,000	900,000
Gaṇa	..	27	270	27,000	2,700,000
Vāhinī	..	81	810	81,000	8,100,000
Pṛtanā	..	243	2,430	243,000	24,300,000
Camū	..	729	7,290	729,000	72,900,000
Anīkinī	..	2,187	21,870	2,187,000	218,700,000
Akṣauhiṇī	..	21,870	218,700	21,870,000	2,187,000,000

[1] Cf. the Khalimpur Plate of Dharmapāladeva (Ep. Ind. IV, 253) ; the Belava Inscription of Bhojavarmadeva (Ibid. XII, 40) ; the Tarpandighi Grant of Lakṣmaṇasena (Ibid. XII, 9) ; the Rāmpāl Copper-plate Inscription of Śrīcandradeva (Ibid. XII, 139 ff.) In the Nāsik cave inscription No. 15. Rehhila is mentioned *as gaṇapaka.* (Bomb. Gaz. XVI, 579).

[2] See Ep. Ind. XII, 43 f.n.

[3] Nīti-p. VII. 6-11, 27-30.

It is hardly necessary to add that this exorbitant calculation could not possibly have been based upon actual military usage. Even if the whole manhood of India—including children and old men—could be marshalled into one grand army, it would fall immeasurably short of a complete *akṣauhiṇī* force, as given above.

3. Discipline, Drill and Exercises

We have scanty information about rules connected with the maintenance of discipline in the army. In the Arthaśāstra (Bk. II. ch. 33) there is a statement that the commander-in-chief should pay special heed to the maintenance of discipline in his army "not merely in camping and marching, but in the thick of battle." In the Śāntiparva (97, 20-22) there is cited a rule that a deserter from the ranks might be killed, and might even be burnt to death. The Nītiprakāśikā (VII, 60-63) advocates summary punishment to soldiers, guilty of disobedience or treachery. "A king should in time of war," says the author, "put to death those men who oppose his orders, the soldiers who run away and do not keep their weapons, avaricious generals who fight treacherously, men who do not face the enemy, who fight against each other, who deceitfully tell the enemy the designs of the king, who give way to the enemy and enjoy the king's misfortune." The Śukranīti (ch. IV. sec. vii. 11. 763-778) lays down that military regulations should be communicated to the soldiers once every eighth day, that the troops "should always forsake violence, rivalry, procrastination over state affairs, indifference to the injuries of the king, conversation as well as friendship with the enemies," that they must never enter a village without a royal 'permit,' and that there should be no credit-transactions between them and the village-folk. It is further enjoined that soldiers themselves were to be held responsible for the tidiness and careful handling of arms and uniforms. "They should keep the arms, weapons and uniforms quite bright (and ready for use)." A subsequent verse (11. 777-778) perhaps implies that those who disobeyed military regulations were punished with death.

The importance of drill and exercises for the army seems to have been realised from very early times. A pre-Kauṭilyan political thinker maintained the view that a small army of trained troops was better than a large army of "effete persons." Kauṭilya argues that it is possible to infuse spirit and enthusiasm even in the timid "by means of discipline and training."[1] Elsewhere (Bk. V. ch. 3)

[1] Kauṭ. tr. p. 864.

he says: "Footmen, horses, chariots and elephants shall be given necessary training in the art of war at sunrise on all days but those of conjunction (of planets); on these occasions of training, the king shall ever be present and witness the exercise." Kāmandaka in his Nītisāra puts in a vigorous plea for the daily exercise of troops. "By constant practice," he says, "one becomes an adept in fighting from chariots, horses, elephants and boats, and a past-master in archery; by constant and regular practice (*nitya-kriyā*) an intelligent man can perform the difficult feats."[1] Elsewhere he enjoins that even when the army is in a camp, the daily drill should not be discontinued. On the contrary, "every day the drill and exercises of soldiers should be performed with various appliances and on grounds cleared of shrubs, stones, trunks, earthen mounds and water."[2] Śukra also lays the utmost emphasis on the drill and training of troops. "The untrained, inefficient and raw recruits," he says, "are all like bales of cotton. The wise should appoint them to other tasks besides warfare."[3]

The methods followed in the training of troops must have differed from age to age, and perhaps also from region to region. Elsewhere we have sought to give an idea of the elaborate scheme of training devised for elephants and horses. In the Arthaśāstra (Bk. X. ch. 6), Kauṭilya says: "The *nāyaka* or the brigadier will, by means of trumpet sounds, flags and ensigns (*tūryaghoṣa-patākābhiḥ*), signalise to the constituents of his army as to when they are to form into divisions (*aṅga-vibhāge*), when to unite into a compact body (*saṁghāte*), when to halt (*sthāne*), when to turn back from the combat and when to make onslaughts." It is only logical to conclude that troops were trained in times of peace in the technique of movements according to signs and sounds. In the Nītiprakāśikā (VI, 58) it is stated that "the king should instruct his troops in those thirty-two movements of war which are acknowledged by polity." What these thirty-two movements were we do not know. The Śiva-Dhanurveda, however, provides us with a long list of technical movements and poses, in which the archers were trained. But it will be too tedious to repeat them here.[4] The Dhanurveda-saṁhitā of Vaśiṣṭha says that besides the

[1] Kām. XVI, 50. Comp. also Nītiv. pp. 121-3, where we have: *varamalpamapi sāravadbalaṁ, na bhūyasī muṇḍa-maṇḍalī.*

[2] Ibid. XVII, 16, 18-19.

[3] Śukranīti, ch. IV., sec. vii, 11. 32-33.

[4] Comp. e.g., Vaś. pp. 19-21 (Bengal ed.); Śār. No. 1789-1796. See also Ag. P. 249, 10-18.

different poses of archery, the foot-soldiers "should be trained in moving backward (*paścādgamanam*), standing still (*sthirīkaraṇam*), lying (*śayanam*), running apace (*dhāvanam*), rushing headlong into the hostile army, and moving in different directions in accordance with signals."[1]

4. Pay and Emoluments, Rewards and Honours

Most ancient writers strongly emphasise the necessity of making regular payment to troops. In the Sabhāparva (5, 48-49), a sage asks a king: "Do you give to your troops the sanctioned rations and wages at the appointed time? Or do you cause resentment by withholding them? Do you know that the irritation caused by arrears of pay and irregularity in the distribution of rations goads the troops to mutiny?"[2] In the Śānti-parva (58-9), Bhīṣma emphasises the supreme importance of keeping the army contented and gratified, for discontent among troops is a source of grave danger to the state. In the Arthaśāstra (Bk. VIII. ch. 5). Kauṭilya considers the withholding of soldiers' pay as one of the primary causes that breed discontent and trouble in the army. According to the Agni Purāṇa (239, 31), again, regular payment to troops is a factor of great importance contributing to the growth of a strong army.[3]

From the above one may reasonably draw the conclusion that the army in ancient India usually received its wages and rations from the state. But of the rates of pay and rations, drawn by officers and privates, we hardly know anything. There is, however, a chapter in the Arthaśāstra (Bk. V. ch. 3), which dwells on the salaries to be given to different categories of officials of the state. From this we get the following details regarding the salaries and wages of commanders, corporals, troops and servants in the military establishment:

	Officer	Salary per annum[4]
1.	Commander-in-chief	48,000 *paṇas*
2.	Nāyaka (captain)	12,000 "

[1] Vaś. (Bengal ed.), p. 63.

[2] We have the same query in the Rām. Ayodhyā. 100, 32-3.

[3] Comp. Nītiv. p. 85: *kiṁ tena jaladena yaḥ kāle na varṣati. sa kiṁ svāmī ya āśriteṣu vyasane na prati-vidhate;* also Yuktikalpataru, p. 5, v. 29; also Mānas. p. 80, vv. 568-9.

[4] Dr. N. N. Law, however, believes that the salaries are monthly, not annual Ind. Hist. Quart., 1929, p. 788.

	Officer	Salary per annum
3.	Officers-in-charge of elephants, horses, chariots and infantry and heads of guilds (śreṇīmukhya)	8,000 *paṇas*
4.	Superintendents (*adhyakṣas*) of infantry, cavalry, chariots and elephants ..	4,000 „
5.	The physician of the army, chariot-driver (*rathika*), horse and elephant-trainer	2,000 „
6.	Superintendent of the armoury ..	1,000 „
7.	Trained soldiers or privates ..	500 „
8.	Trumpet-blowers (*tūryakara*) ..	500 „
9.	The elephant driver	500 to 1,000 *paṇas* according to efficiency
10.	Stationary (*saṁsthāḥ*) spies ..	1,000 *paṇas*
11.	Wandering (*sañcarāḥ*) spies ..	500 „
12.	Servants leading the spies	250 „ or in proportion to the work done.

It will be noted that the scale of pay was fairly high. Assuming, as scholars do, the value of the *paṇa* to be about an English shilling, we get 48,000 shillings or £2,400 as the annual salary of the commander-in-chief. The pay of an ordinary trained soldier, again, was 500 *paṇas*, which is roughly equivalent to £25. The liberality and lavishness with which the Mauryan army was paid has been noted before. When one considers that the prices of commodities in those days were incomparably lower than what they are now, one finds in the above account an Indian corroboration of what the Greek ambassador says. Incidentally, it may be noted that the scales of pay for both the civil and military officers of the state, as given in the Arthaśāstra, suggest its author's association with an extensive and prosperous empire.

There is another point which calls for attention. Kauṭilya allots a salary of 4,000 *paṇas* to the superintendents of infantry, cavalry, chariots and elephants; but he assigns only 1,000 *paṇas* as the salary of other departmental heads (*adhyakṣas*). It is logical to conclude, therefore, that in the age of Kauṭilya the state attached much greater importance to the army than to its civil departments.

It may be presumed that the practice of making cash payment to troops was continued in the Gupta and post-Gupta periods. Referring to the prince of Balharā, Sulaimān writes that he gave regular pay to his troops, "as is the practice among the Arabs."[1] Berūṇī writes that as a rule the Hindu kings in the 11th century A.D. encouraged prostitution. "The kings," he continues, "make them an attraction for the cities, a bait of pleasure for their subjects, for no other but financial reasons. By the revenues which they derive from the business both as fines and taxes, they want to recover the expenses which the treasury has to spend on the army."[2]

Besides salaries and wages in cash, officers and privates in the army were sometimes rewarded with exemptions from land-revenue, sometimes with assignments of land. In a previous chapter it has already been noted how Kauṭilya speaks of villages which were exempted from taxation in lieu of the military services which they rendered to the state. Elsewhere in the Arthaśāstra (Bk. II. ch. 1), while describing the methods and measures for colonisation of lands, the author says: "Superintendents, accountants, gopas, sthānikas, veterinary surgeons, physicians, horse-trainers, and messengers shall be endowed with lands, which they shall have no right to alienate by sale or mortgage." In another context (Bk. V. ch. 3), however, he remarks that a king, who wants to maintain some uniformity of standard throughout his kingdom, must on no account endow his officers and servants with villages.

Whether Kauṭilya approved the system of paying officers with endowments of land is not quite clear. Probably he did not. But whether he liked it or not, the system came to prevail.[3] As early as the 2nd century A.D. an inscription of Siri Pulumāyi shows military officers holding large fiefs of land.[4] Describing the political practices of the 7th century A.D., the Chinese pilgrim, Hiuen Tsiang, says that "the king reserved one-fourth of the crown-lands to be bestowed on great public servants,"[5] and that "ministers of state and common officials all have their portion of land, and are maintained by the cities assigned to them."[6]

Further, epigraphic evidence proves that in the post-Harṣan epoch land-grants were frequently made by kings to their successful

[1] Elliot. I, 3. [2] Sachau. II, 157.

[3] The Śāntiparva (87, 6-8) and the Manusaṁhitā (VII, 119) have recommended it as a maxim at statecraft.

[4] Ep. Ind. XIV, No. 9. [5] Beal. I, 87.

[6] Watters. I, 177.

generals. For instance, an inscription of the Eastern Cāḷukya king, Amma I (c. 918-925 A.D.) describes how his general Mahākāla "more than once annihilated the enemy's army," and how the gratified king rewarded his general with the grant of the village of Drujjuru in the Pennāṭavaḍiviṣaya.[1] Another inscription describes the same king awarding the village of Goṇṭuru, together with twelve other hamlets, to a general named Bhaṇḍanāditya (*alias* Kuntāditya), who had a glorious record of service to the state.[2] In still another epigraphic record, originally found at Ātakūr and now preserved in the Mysore Government Museum, it is stated that in recognition of the valour displayed in battle by Manaleva, Betuga II gave him the circle of villages known as the Ātakūr twelve and also a village named Kādiyūr or Kāḍiyūr in the Beḷvola district. This grant is described in the record as a *bāḷgachchu* or "sword-washing grant," meaning, no doubt, that it was accompanied by the ceremony of laving Māṇalera's sword.[3] Similarly the Carkhari Plate of the Cāndella king, Vīravikramadeva, (dated 1254 A.D.), mentions the grant of a village in the Dāhīviṣaya to one Rāüta Abhi in recognition of a special deed of valour performed by him in the battle of Sondhi.[4] Sometimes also these land-grants were made in favour of vassal chiefs in recognition of their military services. Thus in the Pithapuram Inscription of Pṛthivīśvara (śaka 1108), it is stated that prince Kudiyavarman II of Velanāṇḍu, a vassal of the Eastern Cālukyas, rendered considerable military aid to his over-lord, Vimalāditya-deva. "Then, pleased by (his) assistance, king Vimalāditya bestowed on prince Kudyiavarman (II) the Gudravāra-dvaya," that is, the pair of districts called Gudravāra. For similar military aid given by Vedura II, a subordinate chief, against an unnamed Pāṇḍya monarch, king Vīra-Coḍa conferred on him the Sindhuyugāntara-deśa, that is, the country probably between the Kṛṣṇā and the Godāvarī.[5]

The above instances, however, show that land-grants were usually made in favour of officers who had distinguished records of service to their credit. But land-grants to officers in normal circumstances, perhaps in lieu of cash wages, were not unknown. The Icchāwar Plates, already referred to, state that the Cāndella king, Paramardideva, granted the village of Nandinī in the

[1] Ep. Ind. V, 134. [2] South Ind. Inscr. I, 42-43.
[3] Ep. Ind. VI, 52.
[4] Ibid. XX, 132. Instances like these may be easily multiplied. Comp. e.g., ibid. I, 345 ff. "Blood-fiefs" are often mentioned in the Ep. Carn.
[5] Ep. Ind. IV, 36 ff.

Nandāvana viṣaya to his general (*senāpati*), Madanapālaśarman. A Rock Inscription of the time of Bhojavarman (end of the 13th century) says that one Maheśvara was appointed by the Cāndella Kīrtivarman as the *viśiṣa* of Kālañjara, and endowed with the grant (of the village) of Pipalāhikā.[1] Similarly another officer named Vāśe or Vāśeka, on being appointed as the guardian of the fortress of Ajayagaḍh, received the village of Varbhari.[2]

Besides pay, either in the shape of salaries or land assignments, officers and troops were occasionally given special allowances on the eve of an expedition.[3] Moreover, soldiers who displayed special pluck and courage in the course of a battle were sometimes rewarded with an increase in their pay and rations, sometimes with special monetary allotments, and, in the case of officers, by promotion in rank and honour.[4] A recommendation to this effect in the Mahābhārata has already been quoted. In the Arthaśāstra (Bk. X. ch. 3), we come across a graded list of monetary rewards to be given to troops for acts of special merit. "A hundred thousand (*paṇas*)," says Kauṭilya, "for slaying the king (enemy); fifty-thousand for slaying the commander-in-chief and the heir-apparent; ten thousand for slaying the chief of the brave; five thousand for destroying an elephant or a chariot; a thousand for killing a horse, a hundred (*paṇas*) for slaying the chief of the infantry; twenty for bringing a head; and twice the pay in addition to whatever is seized." There are similar recommendations in the Nītisāra of Kāmandaka (XX, 18-21), the Agni Purāṇa (242, 34-35), and the Nīti-prakāśikā (VI, 88-99). The last-named work adds that this system of monetary rewards to troops in excess of their regular pay would inspire them to special feats of valour.

Further, it seems to have been considered a prime duty of the state to support the wife and dependents of soldiers dying young while on duty. The Vāśiṣṭha-Saṁhitā (XIX, 20) prescribes the rule that "the wives (of slain soldiers) should be provided for."[5] Kauṭilya (Bk. V. ch. 3) says the same thing, though in more

[1] Ep. Ind. I, 336. [2] Ibid. I, 337.

[3] Cf. Sabhāparva 5, 57; Śiśupālavadha XIX, 57. The Rājat. often speaks of "marching allowances" claimed by the Kasmirian soldiery on the eve of an expedition (VII. 1457; VIII, 808, etc.)

[4] Nīti-p. VI, 92; comp. also Mānas. pp. 133-4, vv. 1163-1167. The testimony of both the Dharmaśāstra and nīti literature further proves that troops were sometimes given a share of the booty. Cf. Manu VII, 96-98; Gautama X, 20-23; Nīti-p. VI, 106-8.

[5] Comp. also Sabhāparva 5, 54; Śāntiparva 86, 24.

general terms. "The sons and wives of those who die while on duty shall get subsistence and wages. Infants, aged persons, or diseased persons related to the deceased servants shall also be shown favour. On occasions of funerals, sickness, or child-birth, the king shall give presentations to his servants concerned therein." In the Nīti-vākyāmṛta (ch. 30) it is stated that "the king incurs a debt if he does not maintain the relations of an officer, who has died in the service of the state."[1] The Garra Plates of the Cāndella Trailokyavarman, dated 1261 v.s.=1205-6 A.D., show that occasionally land-grants were made for the maintenance of the dependents of slain soldiers. They record the grant of two villages by king Trailokyavarman for the maintenance of a person whose father had been killed in a battle with the Turks. It is expressly stated in the plates that the grant was made "by way of maintenance for the heirs of one who suffered death on the field of battle."[2]

It may be added that officers and commanders who had won laurels on the battle-field were sometimes rewarded with titles and other marks of distinction. One such mark of distinction was the right of going in public with a special band playing, called *pañca-mahāśabda* (because it was produced by the five primary musical instruments). Occasionally also high-sounding titles were conferred on a victorious general. The Nilgud Inscription of Taila II (dated śaka 904) provides us with an example of this kind. It says that king Tailapadeva, being immensely pleased with the achievements of his general, Śobhana, conferred on the latter a string of titles, such as *Neramodegaṇḍa*, the wrestler of mountain strong-holds, the crest-jewel of feudatories, the camp's rampart, etc.[3] In the Yādava kingdom of Deva-giri a special form of conferring distinction on a soldier or general was to permit him to accept betel leaf at the royal hands.[4]

[1] Com. also Nīti-p. VI, 106-8.
[2] Ep. Ind. XVI, 272 ff.
[3] Ep. Ind. IV, 208.
[4] Rice, *Mysore and Coorg*, p. 171; Saletore, *Social and Political Life in the Vijayanagar Empire*, I, 448.

CHAPTER X

ARMY ON THE MARCH

1. Time for marching

Most of the ancient writers are agreed on one important principle of military strategy, viz., that no foreign expedition should be undertaken when there were internal troubles within the state, or apprehension of an attack from the rear. It has always proved a profitable policy in warfare to embarrass an enemy either by inciting other powers to attack it from the rear or by fomenting internal troubles within its territory. Hence the importance of the rear being kept safe (*viśuddha-pṛṣṭha*) has been most zealously advocated. "Of the two things," says Kauṭilya, "slight annoyance in the rear and considerable profit in the front, slight annoyance in the rear is more serious; for traitors, enemies and wild tribes augment on all sides the slight annoyance which one may have in the rear."[1] Elsewhere he remarks that even when there was no such threat of an immediate attack from the rear, the king launching upon a foreign expedition should leave behind "one-third or one-fourth of his army to protect his base of operations against his rear-enemy and wild tribes in his vicinity."[2] Arguing in the same strain, Kāmandaka adds that "one should never sacrifice that which is within grasp for that which is yet unseen."[3]

There is another point on which most ancient writers seem agreed. It is in the emphasis they have laid on certain seasons of the year as peculiarly well-suited for military operations. The seasons thus preferred were autumn and spring.[4] The reasons for this preference are thus explained in the Śāntiparva (100, 11) : "It is the time of the harvest and of plentiful water-supply. These seasons, moreover, are neither very hot, nor very cold." According

[1] Kaut. Bk. IX, ch. 3.

[2] Ibid. Bk. IX, ch. I; also tr. p. 357: "One whose base is undefended is easy to be subdued, but not one who has marched out with a part of the army after having made arrangments to defend the rear."

[3] Kām. XVI, 5, 14-16; Cf. also Manu VII, 184.

[4] Comp. Manu. VII, 182-3; Viṣṇu III, 40-41; Yājñ. I, 348; Śāntiparva 100, 10, etc.

to the Udyogaparva (83, 7), the famous march of the Pāṇḍava army to the field of Kurukṣetra took place in the month of *Kaumuda* (October-November). And here again we have an enumeration of the special virtues of this season for military operation : "This is the month when you get abundance of food and fuel (*yavasendhanaḥ*), when all plants and herbs are vigorous and fresh, and all trees full of fruits. This is the time, again, when flies are scarce, roads free from mud, and climate extremely pleasant, because it is neither very hot nor very cold."[1] In the Raghuvaṁśa, Kālidāsa makes Aja start on his *vijaya-yātrā* in autumn. In the same season, according to Vākpati, Yaśovarman commenced his *dig-vijaya* campaign.

In spite of this general preference, however, military operations do not seem to have been restricted to these two seasons. It was a recognised maxim of state-craft that when the enemy was beset with troubles and difficulties, military expeditions might be undertaken at any time of the year.[2] According to Kauṭilya, the time for a military expedition should depend primarily on the nature of one's objective and the composition of one's forces. If it be the object of the invader "to destroy the enemy's rainy crops and autumnal handfuls (*muṣṭi*)," he should march during the month of *Mārgaśīrṣa* (November-December). If his object is to destroy the enemy's autumnal crops and vernal handfuls he must march in *Caitra* (March-April). Similarly, under special circumstances, and for the achievement of special objects, expeditions might be undertaken during other seasons of the year. But it is not merely the nature of the objective that should decide the timing of the expedition. The character of one's forces should also be taken into consideration. If, for instance, the invader's army consisted largely of elephants, he should preferably march in the rainy season; for "elephants with profuse sweat in hot weather are attacked by leprosy." Moreover, when there is scarcity of water, they often lose their agility and "become obstinate."[3] For similar reasons, the

[1] Udyogaparva 142, 16-17.

[2] Kauṭ. Bk. IX, ch. I: "Older teachers say that one should invariably march against the enemy in troubles." Kauṭ. however strikes a note of dissent. "When one's own resources are sufficient," he argues, "one should march, since the troubles of an enemy cannot be properly recognised; or whenever one finds it possible to harass or destroy an enemy by marching against him, then one may undertake a march." Cf. also Śāntiparva 100, 12; Manu. VII, 183; Viṣṇu. iii, 40-41: Kām. (XV, 1-2) says: *paraṁ durantavyasanopapannaṁ yāyānnarendro vijayābhikāṁkṣī.*

[3] Kauṭ. tr. p. 398; cf. also Kām. XVI, 7.

invader should march against a barren or desert country only during the rains.[1] On the other hand, an army in which war-cars and horses preponderated should be made to march in other than the rainy season.[2]

2. Consultation with astrologers

When an expedition was decided upon, astrologers were consulted, especially in the later centuries, to ascertain the most lucky moment for the formal departure of the army. With his intensely practical outlook, Kauṭilya was opposed to this reliance on the guidance of stars. "Wealth," he says, "will pass away from that childish man who enquires most after the stars." But his advice fell on deaf ears. The few accounts of ancient marches that have come down to us, whether legendary or historical, prove that rulers frequently consulted astrologers before starting on an expedition. We find references to this fact even in the Mahābhārata. "That king," says Bhīṣma in the Śāntiparva (100, 26), "who sets out under a proper constellation and an auspicious lunation, always succeeds in winning victory." Bāṇa informs us that king Harṣa consulted "a troop of astronomers numbering hundreds" on the eve of his *dig-vijaya* campaign. The astrologers "fixed an hour of marching suitable for the subjugation of all the quarters."[3] It is mentioned in the Chach-nāma that when Rai Chach prepared a grand army for an expedition "to the boundary of Hindusthan which adjoined the kingdom of the Turk," he consulted a number of astrologers. "The astrologers fixed an auspicious time, at which he departed."[4] Chach followed the same procedure on the eve of an expedition against Armābel.[5] To the last the *naimittakas* or astrologers formed an important feature of Hindu court life.[6] It is noteworthy that in contrast with Kauṭilya, later writers on nīti and arthaśāstra have devoted long chapters of their works to a discussion of omina and portenta.[7] These prove beyond doubt the tremendous hold of these ideas on the public

[1] Kauṭ. Gan.'s ed. III, 49-50: *deśamalpavarṣapaṅkaṁ varṣati maru-prāyaṁ caturaṅgabalo yāyāt.* Cf. also Kām. XVI, 7.

[2] Śāntiparva 100, 24.

[3] *Harṣacarita,* tr. by Cowell and Thomas, p. 197.

[4] Elliot. I, 140.

[5] Ibid. I, 151; cf. also I, 145.

[6] Ep. Ind. XIV, No. 15.

[7] See Kām. XVII, 23 ff.; Yukti-kalpataru, pp. 177 ff.; Ag. P. 232, 1 ff.; 233, 1-10, etc; Mānas. pp. 97 ff. Knowledge of prognostics was consideded as an important qualification of the *senāpati.* Kām. XIX, 37-8.

mind in the last centuries of our period. The same fact is illustrated by a curious story, recorded by the Muslim historian, Minhāj, regarding the birth of Lakṣmaṇasena. The writer says that Lakṣmaṇasena's father died when he was still in his mother's womb. "When the birth of Lakhmaniah drew near, the astrologers represented that if the child should be born at that hour, it would never attain to sovereignty; but if it should be born two hours later, it would reign 80 years. Whereupon the queen-regent kept herself suspended with her head downwards and legs bound together. When after two hours she was taken down, she gave birth to Lakhmaniah and immediately after died." The same writer narrates how an unfavourable prediction of astrologers demoralised the whole body of officials and chiefs in Bengal on the eve of the invasion of the country by Muḥammad bin Bakhtiyār. This blind faith in the occult must have occasionally hampered rational military operations.[1] It also proved an obstacle to the Hindus' success in war, as it must have often prevented them from taking the most obvious advantages of the enemy.

3. Observance of Religious Rites

Apart from this consultation with astrologers, the king was also expected to perform certain propitiatory rites and ceremonies on the eve of an expedition. It is stated in the Udyogaparva (197, 1 ff.) that the Pāṇḍavas performed a fire-service before they advanced to the field of battle.[2] "The day before the battle," says Kauṭilya, "the king should fast and lie down on his chariot with weapons. He should also make oblations into the fire, pronouncing the *mantras* of the Atharva-veda, and cause prayers to be offered for the good of the victors as well as of those who attain to heaven by dying in the battle-field. He should also submit his person to the Brāhmaṇas."[3] Likewise, Kāmandaka (XIX, 2) maintains that the king should worship "the gods and the twice-born Brāhmaṇas" on the eve of an expedition.

[1] Kalhaṇa (VII. 760-9) records an instance of this kind. A Kasmirian general, who was proceeding with a battalion of mounted men, "was delayed by evil omens."

[2] Udyogaparva (125, 2) indicates that the ceremony was performed by the royal priest. In the Sabhāparva (23, 3 ff.) we notice similar propitiatory rites being performed by a "renowned" priest before Jarāsandha goes out for battle. Cf. also Āśvalāyana Gṛhya Sūtra iii, 12, 1 ff.

[3] Kauṭ. tr. p. 426.

The devoutness with which king Harṣa of Kanauj embarked on his *dig-vijaya* campaign is thus described by Bāṇa: "The king had bathed in golden and silver vessels . . . ., had with devotion offered worship to the adorable Nīlalohita; fed the up-flaming fire . . . . , bestowed upon Brāhmans sesamum vessels of precious stones, silver and gold in thousands, myriads also of cows having hoofs and horn tips adorned with creepers of gold-work; sat upon a throne with a coverlet of tiger-skin; duly anointed first his bow and then his body down to the feet with sandal bright as his own fame; put on two seemly robes of bark silk marked with pairs of flamingos; formed about his head a chaplet of white flowers . . . ; and wound upon his forearm together with the seal-bracelet an amulet to prosper his going. After being sprinkled on the head with a spray of lustral water scattered by the hand of the highly honoured and delighted Purohit, he had sent away valuable equipages, and divided among the kings ornaments anointing the heaven with a copious light of jewels, had loosed the prisoners, and bestowed suitable gifts of favour upon distressed pilgrims and nobles . . . Finally upon all good omens pressing forward officiously, like devoted servants, in the van, amid a clamorous cry of "Victory" from the delighted people, he issued forth from his house . . ."[1]

It may be added that the custom of performing religious rites prior to an expedition was continued in the later Hindu kingdom of Vijayanagara. Nuniz speaks of the "offerings" and "sacrifices to idols" performed by Kṛṣṇa Deva Rāya before "he left the city of Bisnaga with all his troops."[2]

4. Order of March

We can glean a few details regarding the order of march from the manuals of Kauṭilya and Kāmandaka. According to the former, for instance, the march was to be conducted as follows. In the fore-front and a little ahead of the main army was posted

[1] Harṣacarita, tr. by Cowell and Thomas, pp. 197-8.

[2] Sewell, *Forgotten Empire*, p. 320. The Ag. P. (236, 1-21) prescribes that a king should undertake a series of religious ceremonies for a whole week prior to his departure on a campaign. For similar references to religious ceremonies on the eve of battle, comp. Mānas. p. 132, vv. 1151-1155. Moreover, a ceremony called *nīrājana* was usually performed by kings and generals in the month of Āśvin (a month described as eminently suitable for campaigning). It was a semi-military, semi-religious ceremony, in which the royal priest, ministers and all the component parts of the army, together with the arms and implements of war, were consecrated by means of sacred *mantras*. Cf. Yukti-kalpataru, pp. 178 ff.; Ag. P. 258, 1 ff.

the director of labour (*praśāstā*) with his retinue of artificers and workmen, preparing the path for those coming behind. The commander (*nāyaka*) was to proceed in the van of the army. The king with his harem was to be stationed in the centre (*madhye kalatraṁ svāmī ca*). On his two sides were to be posted his body-guards and horsemen. The elephants were to proceed in the rear, and the baggage and provisions on all sides.[1]

The description of the order of march in the Kāmandakīya is substantially the same, but there are a few minor differences. "The nāyaka", says Kāmandaka, "should proceed in front accompanied by the picked men of the host. The king should be stationed in the centre along with the harem, the treasure-chests as well as the weaker troops (*phalgu ca yad balam*). The flanks of the army should be occupied by the horsemen, while the car-warriors should be placed beside them on both sides. The elephantry should march beside the carmen, and beyond the elephantry should be placed troops recruited from forest tribes. The commander-in-chief should proceed in the rear of the army, encouraging the weak and worn-out troops."[2]

Most ancient writers seem agreed that in the event of any apprehension of danger, the army should be formed into a perfect battle-order even while on the march. "When there is a threat of attack in front, it should form itself into a crocodile array, and then proceed. If, on the other hand, the threat is in the rear, the army should march in a wagon-like array. When threatened on either side, it should proceed in a diamond-like array. If, again, the danger be apprehended from all sides, it ought to form itself into a *sarvatobhadra* array. While going along a narrow pass through which only one man can pass at a time, it should proceed in a needle-like array." This is from Kauṭilya (Bk. X, ch. 2), but we have the same injunctions in Manu (VII. 187-8), in the Kāmandakīya (XIX, 48-9), in the Agni Purāṇa (242, 4-8), and the Śukranīti (ch. IV. sec. vii, vv. 265-6).

5. Description of an army on the march

We have quite a good description of an army on the march in the Udyogaparva (ch. 151). The Pāṇḍava army is marching

[1] Bk. X. ch. 2.

[2] Kām. XIX.; cf. also Ag. P. 242, 4-6, where the above passage is reproduced verbatim. Ancient writers also stress the need of special precautions under certain abnormal circumstances. Cf. Kauṭ. tr. p. 423; Kām. XIX, 50-52; Ag. P. 242, 9 ff.

ahead to the field of Kurukṣetra. Composed of the four traditional arms ('limbs'), it moves on as an irregular body amidst the blare of conch-shells, the beating of drums and frequent war-cries. In the van of the army march Bhīmasena and several other knights, all in suits of armour. In the second line are the Prabhadrakas and the Pāñcālas. The king is in the centre, surrounded by carts and wagons filled with stores and provisions, tents, treasure-chests, arms and machines. Behind the king, proceed the main army, headed by the knights. The movement of the army causes such a tremendous din that, as the poet says, it seemed like "the roars of the deep when the tide is highest on the day of the new moon."

The Harṣacarita of Bāṇa provides us with a more realistic description of the manner in which Harṣa commenced his march. "At the close of the third watch," says Bāṇa, "when all creatures slept and all was still, the marching drum was beaten with a boom deep as the gaping roar of the sky elephants. Then, after a moment's pause, eight sharp strokes were distinctly given anew upon the drum, making up the number of the leagues in the day's march.

"Straightway the drums rattled, the *nāndīs* rang out joyously, the trumpets brayed, the *kāhalas* hummed, the horns blared; the noise of the camp gradually increased. Officers occupied themselves in arousing the courtiers. The heavens were confounded by a confused noise of drumsticks added to a rapid tapping of mallets. Commanders mustered crowds of barrack superintendents. Thousands of torches lighted by the people made inroads upon the darkness of night with their glare. Loving pairs were roused from sleep by the tramp of the women of the watch. Shrill words of command from the marshals dispelled the slumbers of blinking riders. Awakened elephant herds vacated their sleeping stalls. There was a shaking of manes from troops of horses risen from sleep. The noisy camp resounded with mattocks uprooting ground fastenings."

"Leathern bags, bursting with fullness, were extended upon the dusty backs of elephants . . . . . Servants of house-builders rolled up awnings and cloth screens belonging to tents and marquees. Leathern sacks were filled to roundness with bundles of pegs. Store-room stewards collected stores of platters. Many elephant attendants were pressed to convey the stores. The houses of the neighbourhood were blocked with clusters of cups and vessels, which were lifted upon numerous elephants, while the riders kept the animals steady. Wicked elephants were loaded with a cargo of utensils hurriedly tossed upon them by travel-practised domestics. Amid the laughter of the crowd helpless corpulent bawds lagged as they were with difficulty dragged along with hands and legs sprawling sideways . . . . . Camels, as sacks were set on their backs, bellowed at the outrage. The carriages of the high-born nobles' wives were thronged with roguish emissaries sent by princes of rank . . . . ."

"Stablemen dragged along half-eaten shoots to be eaten at the morning manoeuvres. Loud grew the uproar of foragers shouting to one another. Much crashing of stables resounded as the young rearing horses swerved in the confusion of starting. Women, hastening at the call of riders whose elephants were in readiness, presented unguents for the animals' heads. The low people of the neighbourhood, running up as the elephants and horses started, looted heaps of abandoned grain. Donkeys ridden by throngs of boys accompanied the march. Crowds of carts with creaking wheels occupied the trampled roads. Oxen were laden with utensils momentarily put upon them. Stout steers, driven on in advance, lagged out of greed for fodder lying near them. In front were carried the kitchen appliances of the great feudatories. First ran banner-bearers. Hundreds of friends were spectators of the men's exits from the interior of their somewhat contracted huts. Elephant keepers, assaulted with clods by people starting from hovels which had been crushed by the animals' feet, called the by-standers to witness the assaults. Wretched families fled from grass cabins ruined by collision. Despairing merchants saw the oxen bearing their wealth flee before the onset of the tumult. A troop of seraglio elephants advanced where the press of people gave way before the glare of their runners' torches. Horsemen shouted to dogs tied behind them. Old people sang the praises of tall Taṅgaṇa horses which by the steady motion of their quick footfalls provided a comfortable seat . . . . . The whole world was swallowed up in dust."

"At the hour of marching the front of the king's residence became full of chieftains arriving from every side, mounted on female elephants, with riders holding up bows striped with gold leaf, swords grasped by confidential servants occupying the inner seats, chowries waved by betal bearers, sheafs of javelins in cases under the charge of those who sat at the back, and saddles curving with scimitars and bristling with golden arrows . . . . ."

"When the adorable sun arose, the signal conch rang out repeatedly announcing the moment of the king's arraying the army."

After a brief interval he came forth, riding upon a female elephant, beautifully caparisoned, and surmounted by a white umbrella. The company of feudatory kings, who were awaiting his arrival, greeted him, and bowed "with bodies dutifully bent down." The emperor, in his turn, "distributed among them tokens of his favour, such as quarter glances, side glances, full glances, raised eyebrows, half-smiles, jests, plays upon words, inquiries after their health, return greetings, careless movements of the brow, and instructions, according to their several deserts." He then reviewed the army and the march began.

"Meanwhile a multitudinous babble was going on as follows. 'March on, my son.' 'Good sir, why do you lag? Here is a galloping horse.' 'Friend, you hobble like a lame man, while the vanguard here is coming furiously upon us.' 'Why are you hurrying the camel? Do you see, you pitiless brute, the child lying there?' 'Ramila, darling, take care not to get lost in the dust.' 'Don't you see the barley-meal sack leaks? What's the hurry, Go-ahead?' 'Ox, you are leaving the track and running among the horses.' 'You female elephant, you want to go among the males.' 'Porridge man, your jar is broken.' 'Laggard, you can suck the sugar-cane on the way.' 'The road in front is all ups and downs; old fellow, see you don't break the sugar kettle.' 'The load of grain is too heavy, Gaṇḍaka; the bullock cannot carry it.' 'Quick, slave, with a knife cut a mouthful of fodder from this bean field; who can tell the fate of this crop when we are gone?' 'The wagon is stuck fast; harness a strong pulling steer to the yoke.' 'Mad man, you are crushing women: are your eyes burst?' 'This way, boy! in the thick of the dense elephant squad there is no getting out'."

"Here groups of elephant men, bachelors, knaves, donkey boys, camp followers, thieves, serving men, rogues and grooms sated with an easily acquired meal of plentiful readily pounded remnants of grain, expressed their approval of the camp in bold boisterous jubilation. There poor unattended nobles, overwhelmed with the toil and worry of conveying their provisions upon fainting oxen provided by wretched village house-holders and obtained with difficulty, themselves grasped their domestic appurtenances, grumbling as follows:—'Only let this one expedition be gone and done with.' 'Let it go to the bottom of hell.' 'An end to this world of thirst'."

"Here, with cries of 'the labour is ours, but when paytime comes some other rascals will appear,' village servants, set to scare on the feeble oxen tripping at every step, were indiscriminately badgering the whole body of nobles. There the whole countryside had come in eager haste from both directions out of curiosity to see the king, and fools of grant-holders, issuing from the villages on the route and headed by aged elders with uplifted water-pots, pressed furiously near in crowds with presents of curds, molasses, candied sugar, and flowers in baskets, demanding the protection of the crops: flying before their terror of irate and savage chamberlains, they yet in spite of distance, tripping and falling, kept their eyes fixed upon the king, bringing to light imaginary wrongs of former governors, lauding hundreds of past officials, reporting ancient misdeeds of knaves."

Amidst such manifold scenes and incidents, the first day's march ended. A distance of sixteen miles was covered, and the army halted in an encampment previously fitted up for the purpose.[1]

Lesser in details, but equally interesting, descriptions of the army on the march are to be found in the Tamil historical poem, Kalinguttu Paraṇi,[2] Māgha's Śiśupālavadha (XII), Somadeva's Kathā-sarit-sāgara,[3] and a number of epigraphic records. It is needless to reproduce them here, for they are more or less of the the same pattern. They reveal, however, certain common characteristics. For instance, they show that the army, at least while it moved through a friendly zone, moved as a disorderly mass, the only precaution observed being perhaps to keep king in the centre. Secondly, they prove that an army on the march was accompanied by a host of women—"the cavalcade of the royal seraglio." This included not only the king's harem, and the wives and mistresses of the great nobles and feudatory chiefs, but also a great retinue of courtesans. Reference has already been made to the fact that as early as the fourth century B.C. Megasthenes noticed the employment of courtesans for purposes of espionage in the camp. Curtius says that when an Indian king was bound on a distant expedition, "he is accompanied by a long train of courtesans carried in golden palanquins, and this troop holds a separate place in the procession from the queen's retinue, and is as sumptuously appointed." Twelve centuries later, Māgha noticed the same ugly phenomenon in the Indian military system. "As soon as the army reached the encampment," he says in his Śiśupālavadha (V, 27), "the prostitutes pitched their tents, spread their beds, made themselves more attractive by putting on new robes, and like old residents, with offerings

[1] Harṣacarita, tr. by Cowell and Thomas, pp. 199-211.
[2] Ind. Ant. XIX, 329 ff. [3] Tawney. II, 89.

of water and betel leaf, began to receive strangers."[1] The third common characteristic which most ancient writers seem to emphasise is that an army on the march wore the spectacle of a gorgeous procession, with banners unfurled, standards displayed and music playing. Describing the march of an army, the author of the Kaliṅgattu Paraṇi (X, 33-4) says: "The conch-shells sounded, the big drums thundered, and the reeds and pipes squeaked till the ears of the elephants, which guarded the eight points, were deafened. Rows of umbrellas and banners were unfurled, crowded so that the day-light was hidden and darkness ensued." Similarly, the Anamkoṇḍa Inscription of the Kākatīya king, Rudradeva, refers to the march of a Kākatīya army as follows: "The earth was pounded by the hoofs of his excellent horses, prancing and tall; the sky was pervaded by the number of his excellent umbrellas which possessed (white) radiance of the moonlight; the regions were filled by the masses of his *cauris* which were as beautiful as a number of full moons." Similar descriptions occur almost everywhere. The two phenomena, which no writer has omitted to mention, are the terrific noise and 'clouds of dust' produced by a marching host.[2]

6. Transport, Crossing of Rivers, etc.

From the fourth century B.C. onwards, the usual means of transport consisted of elephants, camels, pack-ponies, bullocks and bullock-carts.[3] In the early Mauryan period, transport and commissariat arrangements were in charge of a special committee in the War Office. Strabo says that the committee worked in co-operation with the "superintendent of the bullock trains," which were used for transporting engines of war, food for the soldiers, provender for the cattle, and other military requisites. They supply servants, "who beat the drum, and others who carry gongs; grooms

[1] Duarte Barbosa notes that the later Vijayanagara army was similarly accompanied by "numerous unmarried women." See Vol., I, p. 225.

[2] Cf. Ind. Ant. XI, 18; Ep. Ind. I, 132, 264 etc.; II, 165, 191; Gauḍalekhamālā. II, 78; Somadeva's Kathā-sarit-sāgara, tr. by Tawney, I, 182; II, 89.

[3] For later references to these, comp. Harṣacarita, op. cit; Śiśupālavadha V, 5, 65 which speak of camels with jingling bells carrying wagons and provisions for troops (also ib. XII, 18). Ibid. V, 62 mentions bulls used for the same purpose. In the Nīti-p. (VI. 50), it is stated that the king must have an adundant supply of bulls, mules and far-going camels for carrying loads and burdens. Śukra says: "The elephant, the camel, the bull, the horse, are excellent beasts of burden in the descending order. Carriages are the best of all conveyances except in the rainy season." (ch. IV. sec. vii, 11. 852-3).

also for the horses, and mechanists and other assistants. To the sound of the gongs they send out foragers to bring in grass, and, by a system of rewards and punishments, ensure the work being done with despatch and promptness."[1] Kauṭilya enjoins that in the absence of the normal mode of transport, the troops themselves were to be entrusted with the task of carrying provisions and stores.[2]

In such circumstances, forced labour was also sometimes employed. According to Kauṭilya, one of the important functions of commandeered labour (*viṣṭiḥ*) was to carry the machines, weapons, armours, instruments and provisions.[3] The Junāgaḍh Rock Inscription of Mahākṣatrapa Rudradāman contains an early allusion to such employment of "forced labour."[4] But nowhere perhaps was this used with such ruthlessness as in the northwestern state of Kasmir, where the nature of the country as well as the absence of proper roads rendered it necessary to employ load-carriers in preference to other means of transport. We learn from the Rājataraṅgiṇī (V, 172-4) that towards the close of the ninth century king Śaṅkaravarman not only gave to this corvée a systematic organisation, but frequently used it as a means of fiscal extortion. Villagers, who did not turn up to carry their allotted loads, were fined by the value of the latter at enhanced rates, and the same fine was levied the following year a second time from the village as a whole. Sir Aurel Stein says that in consequence of this system of forced labour and their concurrent abuses, "expeditions outside the valley have at all times been dreaded by the agriculturists, on account of the hardships implied by the increased requisitions for carriage."[5]

Regarding methods employed in crossing rivers and streams, the Arthaśāstra has the following account: "Waters may be crossed by means of elephants, planks spread over pillars erected, bridges, boats, timber and mass of bamboos, as well as by means of dry sour gourds, big baskets covered with skins, rafts, *gaṇḍikā*

[1] McCrindle, *Ancient India*, pp. 54-55.

[2] Kauṭ. Bk. X. ch. 2. [3] Ibid. Bk. X. ch. 4.

[4] The inscription, however, says that Rudradāman abstained from the employment of 'forced labour.' Ind. Ant. VII. 261.

[5] Stein, Chronicles etc. I, 209, f.n. It may be noted here that a somewhat similar system of forced labour was employed by the Moghul emperors. Describing the oppression of the Moghul army, Manucci says that "on the villagers' heads they load their baggage, and by dint of blows force them to carry it." Manucci, ed. by Irvine, II, 452.

and *veṇikā*. When the crossing of a river is obstructed by the enemy, the invader may cross it elsewhere, together with his elephants and horses, and entangle the enemy in an ambuscade (*sattra*)."[1] In spite of this theoretical multiplicity, the most usual way of crossing rivers appears to have been by means of boats. Such was especially the case from the Gupta period onwards. Both the Raghuvaṁśa (IV, 31) and the Śiśupālavadha (XII, 71) contain references to armies being transported across rivers by means of boats. Some post-Gupta epigraphic records, already referred to, demonstrate the same fact.[2]

[1] Kauṭ. Bk. X, ch. 2.

[2] See ch. VII.

CHAPTER XI

THE CAMP

I

The usual terms for camp in Sanskrit are *śivira, skandhāvāra, kaṭaka,* etc.[1] In the Śilparatna, a work of unknown date, a distinction has been made in the meaning of the first two terms. "In a foreign country or in one's own," it says, "the military camp of a man desirous of conquests, and having the four-fold army, is called *śivira.* That camp, again, in the vicinity of which two or more kings are fighting with each other, is called *skandhāvāra.*"[2] In actual practice, however, this subtle literary distinction appears to have been usually ignored.

Ancient military opinion attached great importance to the selection of a suitable site for entrenching the camp. In the Arthaśāstra (Bk. X, ch. 1), Kauṭilya says that the site for the camp should be selected and measured by experts in *vāstu-vidyā,* the commander (*nāyaka*), the chief artificer (*vārdhaki*) and the astrologer. In the Śāntiparva (100, 16-17), Bhīṣma recommends a region near a forest as the best site for camping. Most recorded instances, however, show that the neighbourhood of a river was generally preferred. Thus the Pāṇḍu camp in the Mahābhārata was laid close to the river Hiranvatī.[3] In the Harṣacarita it is stated that the imperial camp, where Bāṇa met the emperor, was pitched near Manitāra along the Ajiravatī river.[4] The author of Chachnāma says that when Chach "arrived at the banks of the Sini, he pitched his camp there."[5] There are numerous epigraphic records

[1] There were other terms also in use, e.g., *upakārika,* occuring in the Barrackpur copper-plate of Vijayasena (N. G. Mujumdar, *Inscriptions of Bengal,* III, 57 ff.). In the Raghuvaṁśa (XVI, 55) we have *upakārya* more or less in the same sense.

[2] I. H. Q. III, 832. There is also a definition of *skandhāvāra* in Kām. XVII, 38-39.

[3] Udyogaparva 60, 2.

[4] Harṣacarita, tr. by Cowel and Thomas, p. 56.

[5] Elliot. I, 152, 153.

which refer to the 'camp' or 'victorious camp' of later kings and emperors. Most of them, it would appear, were laid out on the banks of rivers.[1] This preference for river-banks may have been due to two causes—first, the desire to secure an adequate supply of fresh water for the army, and second, the need of filling the moat round the camp from the stream.

The Udyogaparva of the Mahābhārata contains quite an early account of the manner in which a royal camp was pitched.[2] On their arrival at the field of Kurukṣetra, the first thing that the Pāṇḍus did was to drive off the outlying posts (*śainikāḥ gulmāḥ*) of the enemy. Then "on a part of the field that was level, cool and abounding with grass and fuel," the commander with his generals marked out the camp limits (*śiviraṁ māpayāmāsa*). In doing this, however, they "avoided cemeteries, temples and compounds consecrated to the deities, asylums of sages, shrines and other sacred spots." Then with the help of "skilled mechanics in receipt of regular wages," innumerable tents were erected for the troops, generals and allied kings. These tents were not only stocked with "food, fuel and drink," but also with arms and weapons of all kinds. To protect the camp against surprise attacks, a moat was dug about it (*khānayāmāsa parikhāṁ*) and patrols with proper instructions were posted.

The Kuru camp was laid out more or less in the same manner. Spreading over an area of five *yojanas*, it also contained countless tents and pavilions stored with provisions and arms. As in the opposing camp, so also here troops were relayed for outpost and patrol duty. But besides fighting men, both the camps included a large and motley host of non-combatants such as bards, panegyrists, priests, vendors, traders, prostitutes and women of rank.

II

In the Arthaśāstra of Kauṭilya (Bk. X, ch. I) we get a clear enunciation of the principles of encampment as understood or practised in the Mauryan and post-Mauryan epoch. The camp, says Kauṭilya, might be of any shape—circular, rectangular or square, as the occasion or available space required (*bhūmivaśena vā*). It was to consist of four gates, six roads and nine divisions. It was also to be fortified with earthen ramparts (*vapra*), ditches

[1] Comp. Ep. Ind. II, 193, v. 39; ibid. II, 194, 299, 360; V. 204-5; X, 103; XI, 126 ff., etc.

[2] Udyogaparva 152, 1 ff.; 195, 12 ff.

(*khāta*) and watch-towers (*āṭṭālaka*)—especially so when there was the possibility of prolonged stay or apprehension of danger from the enemy. The quarters of the king were to be fixed in one of the divisions of the camp, to the north of the centre. It was to be 100 *dhanus* in length and 50 in breadth. Immediately to the west of it was to be fixed the royal harem. The guards of the harem (*antarvaṁśika-sainyaṁ*) were to have their quarters near at hand.

In front of the royal pavilion there was to be an audience tent for the king (*purastād upasthānam*). On its right were to be the treasury and other administrative offices; and on its left the stables for horses and elephants mounted by the king.

Surrounding the royal pavilion there should be four enclosures, each distant from the other by a hundred *dhanus* (500 cubits). The first of these was to be set up by means of carts (*śakaṭa*), the second by thorny shrubs (*methīpratati*), the third by wooden posts or columns, and the fourth perhaps by an earthen wall (*sāla*). In the forefront of the first enclosure the prime minister and the royal priest should have their quarters. To their right were to be the store-house and the kitchen, and to their left the store of raw products and the armoury. In the second enclosure were to be located the quarters of the commander-in-chief, of *maula* and *bhṛta* troops, and horses and chariots. The third enclosure was to be occupied by elephants, gild levies and artificers; and the fourth by commandered labour, allied troops and forest tribes. Merchants and courtesans were to live beside the main road of the camp (*anumahāpatham*).

Outside these enclosures were to be posted huntsmen and keepers of dogs, and spies and sentinels with trumpets and fire. To prevent the enemy from springing a surprise upon the camp, the ground round about was to be barricaded by means of secret pits, mounds and thorns. The sentinels employed to guard the camp were to be divided into eighteen groups, changing their watches in rotation. Life in the camp was to be under strict discipline, and "all disputes, drinking, social gatherings and gambling" were to be interdicted. Troops must be kept in a state of concentration and readiness for immediate action. A system of pass-port for entrance to, and exit from, the camp was also to be enforced.

III

The above summary represents a clear enunciation of Hindu ideas on encampment, as they had developed in India till the age of Kauṭilya. To what extent, and in what respects, these were altered or modified in the light of later experience, we do not know. The later works on nīti do not help us in the matter. Kāmandaka has a lengthy chapter on the subject,[1] but he has reproduced parrot-like the ideas of his master. On one principle, however, he lays the utmost emphasis. It is the paramount necessity of keeping the communications safe. The camp required reinforcements of men, cattle, ammunitions, provisions and stores of all kinds. Any interference with these by the enemy, he says, might mean the complete destruction of the camp.[2]

Ordinarily tents were pitched for the residence of troops and officers in the camp. We have already quoted Bāṇa's reference to "cloth screens belonging to tents and marquees." Referring to a camp, Māgha says that "the residences of chiefs were circular like the moon, made of white cloth, and kept in their position by means of ropes."[3] But occasionally a camp was also made up of wooden huts. The Rājataraṅgiṇī (VIII. 2509-10) provides us with an instance of this kind. To capture Śiraḥśilā, a royal camp was pitched in front of the castle. "By troops of wood-cutters and other workmen, Dhanya had rows of houses constructed resembling a town on the bank of the Madhumatī. He, strong and capable, cleared the thicket of trees of darkness, turned forest-land into habitations, and provided the camp with all supplies in abundance."

Commenting on the epic camp, Hopkins says that it was "a miniature town."[4] A Hindu camp appears to have retained this character throughout our period. Bāṇa's account of Harṣa's camp near Maṇitāra supports the above view;[5] and Māgha's account of a typical eighth-century camp further confirms it.[6] Provided with sutlers and traders of all sorts, with panegyrists, priests and prostitutes, a typical Hindu *skandhāvāra* was the prototype and fore-runner of a later-day Moghul imperial camp. Describing the imperial camp of Aurangzeb, Catrou remarks: "To sum it up, it may be said that Aurangzeb dragged in his train a travelling city as large and as peopled as his capital."[7]

1 Kām. XVII. 2 Ibid. XVII, 40.

3 Śiśupālavadha V. 52; V. 61; XII. 4 etc. Similarly, describing the camp of a Pāṇḍya king, the Mullaippāttu (41-46) says that the king's tent in the centre was "surrounded by tents of women-guards enclosed by partitions of cloths" and "the tents of body-guards." S. K. Aiyangar, *Some Contributions of South India to Indian Culture*, pp. 330-31.

4 J. A. O. S. XIII, 219.

5 Harṣacarita, tr. by Cowell and Thomas, pp. 46 ff.

6 Śiśupālavadha, V, 21 ff.

7 Irvine, *The Army of the Indian Moghuls*, p. 197.

CHAPTER XII

ARMY IN THE FIELD

1. Importance of Position

Ancient military opinion appears to have attached great importance to the position of an army in the theatre of war. A pre-Kauṭilyan teacher stresses the importance of position by means of the following homely analogy: "A dog seated in a convenient place may drag a crocodile, and a crocodile seated in a low ground can drag a dog."[1] In the Arthaśāstra (Bk. X. ch. 4), Kauṭilya says: "Favourable positions for infantry, cavalry, chariots and elephants are desirable both for war and camp. For men who are trained to fight in desert tracts, forests, valleys, or plains, and for those who are trained to fight from ditches or heights, during the day or night, and for elephants which are bred in countries with rivers, mountains, marshy lands, or lakes, as well as for horses, such battle-fields as they should find suitable are to be selected." It is thus evident that according to Kauṭilya the primary consideration which should weigh with a general in selecting a position must be the character and composition of his forces. It was universally recognised that the different arms required different grounds for the proper discharge of their functions.[2] A commander was expected to keep this fact persistently in view, and dispose troops in harmony with the ground on which they were to act. In another context, however, Kauṭilya says: "That part of the country in which his army finds a convenient place for its manœuvres and which proves unfavourable to his foe is the best; that part of the country which is of the reverse nature is the worst; and that which partakes of both the characteristics is a country of middling quality."[3] In other words, the amount of advantage which a position offered to the belligerent was to be the sole criterion of its merit or demerit. A general in command must have the military insight to recognise whether a particular position

[1] Quoted in Kauṭ. Bk. IX, ch. I; Kām. repeats it in XVI, 38.

[2] These have been described by most ancient writers. Cf. Kauṭ. Bk. X. ch. 4; Śāntiparva 100, 21-23; Ag. P. 242, 30; Kām. XX, 10 ff.

[3] Bk. IX, ch. 1.

would be advantageous for the evolution and manœuvre of his troops.[1]

2. Battle-orders

When two hostile armies faced each other, and conflict was imminent, it was the usual practice to draw them up in battle-orders.[2] The term for battle-order in Sanskrit is *vyūha;* and the ranging of an army in battle-array was one of the essential qualifications of the commander-in-chief. Battle-orders were many and various, and they have been dwelt upon at considerable length in all ancient texts on war.

The testimony of military writers reveals three stages of tactical evolution among the ancient Hindus. The first stage is probably represented by the code of Uśanas, according to whom an array should consist of three divisions, viz: wings (*pakṣau*), vanguard, (*urasyam,*) and rear-guard (*pratigraha*). The next stage is marked by the code of Bṛhaspati, who added flanks (*kakṣau*) to the above list.[3] In later works like the Kāmandakīya (XX, 30), the Agni Purāṇa (241, 41-2), and the Nīti-prakāśikā (VI, 11) a battle-order has been described as consisting of seven divisions (*saptāṅga*), viz. wings, flanks, vanguard, centre (*madhya*), rear-centre (*pṛṣṭha*), rear-guard and *koṭi.* (?)[4]

[1] Yet Kauṭilya would not give the *senāpati* absolute latitude in the choice of position. The army should not be arrayed, he says (Bk. X. ch. 3), facing the south or the sun, or against the wind. Nor must it take up a position, where long stay or whence speedy retreat would not be possible. Elsewhere (Bk. X. ch. 2) he says that it is a good thing to take a position in front of, but not distant from, "a mountainous or river fortress with all its resources." The evidence of the Greek and the early Muhammadan chronicles shows that this particular piece of advice was often followed in actual practice. Compare, for instance, the position occupied by the Kathians, the Malloi and the Oxydrakai when fighting with Alexander, as also that taken up by Dāhir when he fought with Muḥammad bin Kāsim. But such a position had its disadvantages. With a place of safety close at hand, an army was often tempted to flee to the fort at the first serious onslaught of the enemy. Comp. also Elliot. II, 20 for another instance of this nature.

[2] As stated before, an army was sometimes formed into a battle-order while marching through a dangerous zone. Vide supra. Cf. also Kām. XIX, 44 ff.

[3] Kauṭ. Bk. X. ch. 6. *Pakṣāvurasyaṁ pratigrahaity-Auśanaso vyūhavibhāgaḥ. Pakṣau kakṣāvurasyaṁ pratigraha iti Bārhaspatya.* Cf. also Kām. XX, 31.

[4] In the Mānas. (p. 135, vv. 1178-1181) we have a still more grandiloquent list of divisions in a battle-order. These are *mukham, uras, praurasyam, pratigraha, kakṣau, prakakṣau, pakṣau, prapakṣau* and *pṛṣṭham.*

Descriptions of battle-orders occur in the Mahābhārata, the Arthaśāstra of Kauṭilya, and later manuals on nīti and Dhanur-veda. For instance, we are told in the Mahābhārata, that on the first day of the war, the Pāṇḍus arrayed their troops in a "needle-shaped" (*sūcī*) order, and on the day following in the form of a 'heron' (*krauñca* or *krauñcāruṇa*). On the third day Bhīṣma led off with a 'rhomboid' (*garuḍa*) array, while the Pāṇḍus drew up an order in the shape of a crescent.[1] On the fifth day we have the 'hawk' (*śyena*) array on the Pāṇḍu side, and the 'crocodile' (*makara*) on that of the Kurus.[2] On the seventh day Bhīṣma, 'skilled in battle-orders' drew up a 'circular' (*maṇḍala*) array,[3] while the Pāṇḍu king formed the 'thunderbolt' (*vajra*).[4] The day following Bhīṣma drew up an array 'like the sea'; and to meet it the Pāṇḍu commander was ordered by the king to array his hosts in the '*śṛṅgāṭaka*' order.[5] On the next day, Bhīṣma disposed his troops in the '*sarvatobhadra*' array;[6] the Pāṇḍus too formed a strong counter-array, but it is not given any name.[7] The most ponderous of all arrays, however, came on the fourteenth day. Droṇa formed an array, half of which was in the shape of a 'wagon' (*śakaṭa*), and the other half in that of a 'lotus' (*padma*). The 'wagon' extended over twelve *gavyūtis* in length and covered the front, while the 'lotus' forming the rear was five *gavyūtis* deep. And within the 'lotus' was formed another solid array called the 'needle' (*sūcī*).[8] In other words, the 'lotus' at the back of the 'wagon' served as an enclosure for the 'needle.' We have thus three different arrays made and perfected into one composite master-array.[9] On all other days we have either no names for the arrays formed,[10] or mere repetitions of the orders previously devised on one side or the other.[11]

When we come to study the details of these epic battle-orders, we find ourselves on more shaky ground. The poet here seems to give free scope to his fancy; and the metaphors used in the names

1 Udyogaparva 19, 34-35; Bhīṣmaparva 50, 40; 51, 1 ff.
2 Bhīṣmaparva 69, 7-12; 69, 2 ff.
3 Ibid. 81, 12.
4 Ibid. 81, 23.
5 Ibid. 87, 5; *sāgarapratimaṁ ghoram*; also ib. 87, 17.
6 Ibid. 99, 1.
7 Ibid. 99, 14.; *mahā-vyūhaṁ prativyūhyasudurjayam.*
8 Droṇaparva 85, 23; *sūcī padmasya garbhastho guḍho vyūhaḥ kṛtaḥ punaḥ.*
9 J. A. O. S. XIII, 213 ff.
10 Karṇaparva 46, 11 ff.; 46, 28 ff.; Śalyaparva 8, 24 ff.
11 Karṇaparva 11, 14 ff.; 11, 28 ff.

of the 'orders' are usually kept up in the narration of the details. Let us, for instance, take the case of the 'rhomboid' (garuḍa) array formed by Bhīṣma on the third day of battle. The commander, we are told, was on the 'beak' (*tuṇḍe*), two chiefs on the head (*śīrṣam*), two more made the 'eyes' (*cakṣuṣī*), others were on the 'neck' (*grīvā*) and still others in the rear (*pṛṣṭha*), tail (*puccha*), right wing (*dakṣiṇaṁ pakṣam*) and left flank (*vāmaṁ pārśvam*).[1] Similarly the 'hawk' array formed by the Pāṇḍus on the fifth day had the following parts: face (*mukha*), eyes, head, neck, wing and rear.[2] In the same way, the sixth day's crocodile' array had its head, eyes, mouth, neck, back, feet and tail.[3] Similar details are repeated in connection with the other orders.[4]

We get, however, a more rational discussion about battle-orders in the Arthaśāstra of Kauṭilya and post-Kauṭilyan texts on war. Broadly speaking, battle-orders are divided under four main heads, viz. *daṇḍa* ('staff'), *bhoga* ('snake'), *maḍala* ('circle'), and *asaṁhata* ('detached order').[5] Each of these, again, is subdivided into several varieties. Thus the *daṇḍa* comprised seventeen, the *bhoga* five, the *maṇḍala* two, and the *asaṁhata* six varieties of arrays. But apart from these, there were various other arrays known.

Uśanas and Bṛhaspati defined a *daṇḍa* ('staff') as an array in which the troops stationed in the different divisions were arranged in curved lines or columns. According to Kauṭilya, however, it meant a kind of battle-order in which the wings, flanks and vanguard of the army were maintained in equal strength. The seventeen varieties of this order were as follows:

"A *daṇḍavyūha* is called *pradara* ('breaking the enemy's army') when its flanks are made to project in front. It is, again, known as *dṛḍhaka* ('firm') when its wings are stretched back. It is called *asahya* ('irresistible') when its wings are stretched forward towards the enemy. When after the formation of the wings, the front is made to bulge out, it is called *śyena* ('hawk'). These four varieties are called *cāpa* ('bow'), *cāpakukṣi* ('the centre of the bow'), *pratiṣṭha* ('hold') and *supratiṣṭha* ('a stronghold') respectively when they are arranged in the reverse order. That variety of the *daṇḍavyūha* in which the wings are arranged in the shape of a bow

[1] Bhīṣmaparva 51, 1 ff. [2] Ibid. 69, 7-12. [3] Ibid. 75, 4-12.

[4] Ibid. 87, 18-19; 99, 1 ff.; Droṇaparva 19, 7 ff.; Karṇaparva, 11, 13 ff.; 14, 10-28, etc.

[5] Kauṭ. Bk. X. ch. 6; Kām. XX, 41; Ag. P. 242, 49; Nīti-p. VI, 8.

is called *sañjaya* ('victory'). The same with a projected front is called *vijaya*. The array which has its wings drawn up in the shape of a flat ear is called *sthūlakarṇa;* the array in which the wings are made twice as flat as those of a *vijaya* is known as *viśāla-vijaya* ('great victory'); that in which the flanks and the vanguard are stretched towards the wings is called *camūmukha;* and the same is called *jhaṣāhya* when it is arayed in the reverse form. That variety of *daṇḍa* in which the troops are made to stand one behind another, is called *sūcīmukha* ('needle-faced') array. When the array consists of two such lines, it is called *valaya*; and when of four lines, it is called *durjaya* ('invincible')."[1]

According to Uśanas and Bṛhaspati, the *bhoga* meant a battle-order in which the troops in the different divisions were arrayed in one continuous chain. Kauṭilya says, however, that the chief distinctive feature of this battle-order was the fact that its wings, flanks and front were of unequal depth. The five varieties of this order were: *sarpasārī* (which has a serpentine movemnt), *gomūtrika* (course of a cow's urine), *śakaṭa* (wagon), *makara* (crocodile) and *pāripatantaka*. Some of these have been defined. Thus the 'wagon' is explained as "that variety of *bhoga* in which the front is divided into two parts, and the wings are arranged in the form of staffs." The reverse of this is described as the 'crocodile' array. The *pāripatantaka*, again, is said to have been a variety of the 'wagon,' having in its columns a large number of elephants, horses and chariots.[2]

The *maṇḍala* (circular array) has been defined as a battle-order in which the wings, flanks and front stood in close proximity to one another, without having any intermediate space between them.[3] Its two varieties were known as *sarvatobhadra* and *durjaya* When the battle-order was so arranged as to face in all directions, it was called *sarvatobhadra*. When, again, though having the flanks as usual, its front was split up into two halves and the wings into four, it was termed *durjaya*.[4]

The *asaṁhata* has been explained as an array in which the wings, flanks and front were stationed apart from each other. The

[1] Cf. also Kām. XX. 43 ff.; Ag. P. 242, 51-52; Nīti-p. VI. 4-5. Kām. XX, 44 has *sthūṇākarna* instead of *sthūlakarṇa*.

[2] These five varieties of *bhoga* are also noticed in Kām. XX, 48-9; Ag. P. 242, 56; Nīti-p. VI, 6.

[3] *Pakṣa-kakṣorasyānām ekībhāve maṇḍalaḥ,*

[4] Kauṭ. Bk. X. ch. 6; Kām. XX, 50; Ag. P. 242, 57-8; Nīti-p. VI, 8.

six varieties of this order were known as the 'thunderbolt' (*vajra*), 'alligator' (*godhā*), 'park' (*udyānaka*), 'crow-footed' (*kākapadī*), 'crescent' (*ardha-candrikā*), and *karkaṭa-śṛṅgī*.[1]

Besides the above, battle-orders might be formed in various other ways. In the Arthaśāstra (Bk. X. ch. 6), Kauṭilya writes: "The array in which the chariots form the front, the elephants the wings, and horses the rear, is called *ariṣṭa*; that in which infantry, cavalry, chariots and elephants stand one behind the other is called *acala*; that in which elephants, horses, chariots and infantry stand in order one behind the other is known as *apratihata*."[2] When, again, the wings were occupied by elephants, the flanks by horses, and the front by war-cars, it was called a *cakra* (wheel) array. When the front was occupied by elephants, the flanks by chariots and the wings by horses, it was known as a *madhya-bhedī* array. There was also what has been described as an *antarbhedī* array. In this the flanks were occupied by elephants, the wings by chariots and the front by cavalry.[3]

It is needless to expand the list further. From the foregoing enumeration it is clear that the disposition of troops on the battle-field might in fact take any form or shape.[4] The nature of the battle-order to be adopted by a general on any particular occasion was determined by various considerations. In the first place, the composition of the forces at his disposal was a factor to reckon with.[5] A second determining factor was the character of the theatre of operations. Kauṭilya says: "The even, uneven and complex nature of the ground in the front or on the sides or in the rear should be examined. On an even site the *daṇḍa* and the *maṇḍala* array should be formed; on an uneven ground *bhoga* and *asaṁhata* arrays should be made; and on a site of a complex nature, the battle-order should be of the *viṣama* type."[6] We have a re-iteration of the same view in the later Śukranīti, where the

[1] Kām. XX, 51 has *uddhāna* instead of *udyānaka*. Compare also Ag. P. 242, 59 and Nīti-p. VI, 7-8, where the nomenclature is slightly different.

[2] Cf. also Kām. XX, 36.

[3] Kauṭ. Bk. X. ch. 5; Kām. XX, 37-8; Ag. P. 242, 45-6.

[4] The Nīti-p. VI, 10, says that the *vyūhas* are to be counted in thousands.

[5] In Bk. X. ch. 5 of the Arthaśāstra, Kauṭilya speaks of "pure" (*śuddha*) and "mixed" (*miśra*) arrays. When an array was formed by only one arm, e.g. the infantry or the cavalry, or the chariots or the elephants, it was called *śuddha*. But when it was formed by a combination of various arms, it was of the "mixed" type.

[6] Kauṭ. tr. p. 427. Here the translation has been slightly altered to make the meaning clear.

author maintains that "the ruler should devise one, two or more of these *vyūhas* or a mixture of them according to the number of troops and the character of roads and battle-fields."[1] The third factor which decided the nature of the array was the strength and character of the enemy's battle-order. "One should," says Kauṭilya, "assail the *pradara* by means of the *cāpa, pratiṣṭha* by means of the *supratiṣṭha, sañjaya* by means of the *vijaya, sthūlakarṇa* by means of the *viśāla-vijaya,* and *pāripatantaka* by means of the *sarvatobhadra.* One may assail all kinds of arrays by means of the *durjaya.*"[2] In several texts, again, it is enjoined that a large force, fighting against a small one, should be arrayed in extended lines, but a small force, in order to compete with a large one, should charge in one long narrow column, concentrating all its strength at one point.[3]

Besides the formation of battle-orders, ancient writers provide us with a few other details regarding the disposition of the army on the field of battle. It is stated, for instance, in the Arthaśāstra (Bk. X. ch. 5) that foot-soldiers should be so arrayed that the space between any two men might be equivalent to one *śama* (fourteen finger-breadths); horses should be arrayed with three *śamas* (two and one-third feet) as the intervening space; while chariots and elephants should be stationed five *śamas* (three and eight-ninth feet) apart. In more extended arrays, however, the intervening space between any two individuals should be doubled or trebled. When the army consisted of a large contingent of archers, the rules appear to have been slightly different. Thus the space intervening between any two bowmen was to be equivalent to a *dhanus* (five cubits), that between horses fifteen cubits, and that between war-cars and war-elephants twenty-five cubits. This increase in space was probably necessitated by the fact that archers required more room for the effective use of their weapons. With regard to the different divisions of an array, Kauṭilya holds that in

[1] Śukranīti, ch. IV, sec. vii, 11. 566-7.

[2] Kauṭ. Bk. X. ch. 6.

[3] Cf. Manu VII, 191; Ag. P. 236, 27. The Mahābhārata affords an illustration of this maxim. Yudhiṣṭhira, finding himself in possession of a much smaller force than the Kurus, suggested to his brother the adoption of the *sūcīmukha* or the solid oblong array. Arjuna recommended the *vajra* or the 'thunderbolt' array for the same reason. It is not difficult to guess what was meant by either, especially as the purpose of the Pāṇḍus was offensive rather than defensive. A narrow front or a close column was to be formed with a view to breaking the enemy's line. Cf. Bhīṣmaparva 19, 4; 43, 102.

ordinary circumstances they should be ranged twenty-five cubits apart from each other. The Agni Purāṇa (236, 35) maintains that care should be taken in every case to provide ample space for the free movement of the different divisions, and that neither *en masse* nor individually should the troops be inconveniently crowded.

Qualitatively, troops were considered as falling under four classes: viz. *sāram,* (best), *anusāram* (second best), *tṛtīyasāram* (third in rank), and *phalgu* (weak troops). Kauṭilya lays it down that in drawing up an array the general should place the weaker troops (*phalgu*) in the fore-front of each division. Then should come the *tṛtīyasāram,* and then the best. The second best (*anusāram*) is to be placed in the rear line. The reason offered for this arrangement is typically illustrative of the intensely practical nature of Kauṭilyan military precepts. If the weakest troops be placed in the front line, he argues, the first shock of the enemy's charge would fall upon them, and not a single troop of the better type would perish. When the enemy is thus grappled in an encounter with the riff-raff of the army (*phalgu-bala*), the general should manoeuvre his best troops, swoop down upon the enemy and annihilate him.[1] Elsewhere, however, the author recommends that the best troops should be placed in the van, and the weaker troops in the rear.[2] This was also the advice of later writers like Kāmandaka (XX, 34). and Someśvara (Mānas. vv. 189-191).[3] The Agni Purāṇa emphatically (236, 41-42) maintains that weak troops should never be placed in the van, for when attacked they would easily give in and thus create confusion in the rest of the army. On the other hand, if brave troops be placed in the front line, their example would serve as an inspiration to the weaker troops in the rear.

3. Conduct of Battles

Though much ingenuity was expended on the formation of battle-arrays, it does not seem that they had any decisive influence on the conduct of battles. The epics give one the impression that after the first plunge into the fight, no order whatever was maintained. "As soon as the armies meet," says Hopkins, "we read that there was complete disorder. This is caused in three ways. The mass is helpless and imbecile, left to itself; the knight

[1] Kauṭ. Bk. X. ch. 5.

[2] Ibid.

[3] Comp. also Śāntiparva 100, 44-46.

is reckless and foolhardy. Instead of remaining to attack the division allotted to him at the outset of the day, he rushes about wherever he pleases, and the slightest incident sends him shooting transversely across the field, discomforting his friends almost as much as his foes. The knightly proficiency in 'manœuvres,' either of weapon-skill or of chariot-skill, leads directly to this individual excellence and weakness of the mass. It is a combat of duels and push. Each knight flings himself in front of another, and the two then 'circle,' or wheel about each other, in the method admired by the Greek observer, until one is confused or weakened; for the charioteers do the twisting (except incidentally), while the knights have to keep the balance and shoot. As the cars constantly tip over, the shooting must have been as described rather wild. Meanwhile the regiments led by the knights into the field either stand stock-still and look on at the spectacle, or they fling themselves against each other, two unheeded masses, and cutting and chopping each other in a promiscuous manner, lend their weight against the foe. More than weight we can scarcely call it. No individual common man is important. While this by-play goes on, one knight is slain or flees. Then all his soldiers run away, since they fight not for a cause but for a leader."[1]

Nothing could have been a better description of the manner in which battles were conducted in the so-called epic period. But it is doubtful whether the description is applicable to ancient Indian warfare in general. We have indeed a few accounts of battles in post-epic literature and inscriptions, but as they were written mostly by priests and literary men, without military experience, they appear to follow a conventional standard.[2] It will, therefore, be risky to make any deduction from these accounts. On the other hand, we have in the Arthaśāstra and other military texts, a clear enunciation of some fundamental principles of tactics, which perhaps prove that commanders of armies followed some definite plan in conducting a campaign. For instance, it is laid down that when an army is drawn up in battle-order, the general must not move it *en masse* against the foe but should rather assail the latter with one or two divisions, and when the enemy is thrown into confusion, should follow up the first onset with the remaining divisions.[3] A second principle enunciated is that a commander

[1] J. A. O. S. XIII, 223.

[2] Comp. e.g., Raghuvaṁśa, Śiśupālavadha and Kaliṅgattu Paraṇi; also South Indian Inscr. vol. I, pp. 153-4; vol. III, p. 37 etc.

[3] *vyūhaṁ tu sthāpayitvā pakṣakakṣorasyānāmekena dvābhyāṁ vā praharet śeṣaiḥ pratigṛhṇiyāt.* Kauṭ. Bk. X, ch. 5.

must begin a battle by striking that portion of the hostile army which is occupied by weak and treacherous troops.[1] Thirdly, it is emphasised that he should make a rear-attack on the enemy, when a frontal attack is considered disadvantageous, and a frontal attack under contrary circumstances. Similarly when an attack on one wing or flank is deemed unwise, the other wing or flank may be assailed. Having struck the front of the hostile army, the commander should follow it up by an attack from the rear. He may also strike at the enemy's rear, and then when it has wheeled round, must attack it from the front.[2] Finally, it is laid down that a commander must not press hard a weak but desperate foe, secure in a strong position; for "when a broken army, reckless of life, resumes its attack, its fury becomes irresistible."[3]

It may be presumed that these and other similar principles of tactics, which we find embodied in ancient military manuals,[4] were not merely reproduced from foreign copy-books, but learnt from the school of hard experience, and that once learnt they were not easily forgotten. But we have no sufficient data to appraise the extent to which they were a controlling factor in military operations. There is reason to believe, however, that some of the characteristics of epic warfare persisted till almost the close of our period. It is probable, for instance, that to the last a battle was often a 'combat of duels and push'; it is certain that there was always an element of single combat, in the sense that when the king, who usually commanded in person, fell or fled, his army also fled. Thus, as we have already seen, the fight for Sind in 712 A.D. was decided by the fall of Dāhir, the king of the country; while an important victory gained by Sultan Maḥmūd in 1008 A.D. was due to the flight of the elephant on which his opponent was mounted.[5] To kill, or put to flight, the opposing king was thus the primary object in each battle.[6]

4. Some Usages of the Battle-field

Before closing this chapter, it is necessary to refer to a few interesting usages of the battle-field. One such usage was the

[1] *Yataḥ vā duṣyaphalgubalaṁ tataḥ abhihanyāt.* Bk. X. ch. 3.

[2] *Purastādabhihatya pracalaṁ vimukhaṁ vā pṛṣṭhato hastyaśvenā-bhihanyāt. Pṛṣṭhataḥ abhihatya pracalaṁ vimukhaṁ vā purastād sārabalenābhihanyāt.* Kauṭ. Bk. X. ch. 3. This particular piece of tactics was employed by Alexander in the battle of the Hydaspes.

[3] Kauṭ. Bk. X. ch. 3.

[4] Besides Kauṭ., comp. also Kām. XX, 55 ff.

[5] Vide supra.

[6] This is plainly recognized in the Mānas. p. 138, vv. 1215-19.

delivery of harangues by kings, generals and priests to rouse the troops to heroism and stir them to action. The Mahābhārata records a few instances of this practice. In the Bhīṣmaparva (17, 6 ff.), for instance, we notice Bhīṣma making a short, encouraging speech to the chiefs, reminding them of their duty as warriors. In the Karṇaparva (93, 54 ff.), the Kuru king is seen haranguing his disheartened troops in order to inspire them to a supreme effort. He refers to the smallness of the enemy's force, points out that even by flight they could not escape destruction by the Pāṇḍus, and finally extols the virtues of death on the battle-field. "There is no greater sin for a Kṣatriya," he says, "than flight from battle. There is no surer path to heaven than death in battle." The Śānti-parva (100, 32 ff.) lays it down as an injunction that the king or the commander-in-chief should address words of encouragement to the army before the commencement of a battle. It also contains the specimen of such a speech, from which we may quote the following: "Let us swear to conquer and never desert one another. Let those who are overcome with fear stay behind. Let those also stay behind who would cause their chiefs to be slain by themselves neglecting to act heroically in battle. Let only such men come who would never turn back from battle or cause their comrades to be slain . . . The consequences of fleeing away from battle are loss of wealth, infamy and reproach . . . Those that flee from battle are wretches among men. They simply swell the number of human beings on earth, but for true manhood, they are neither here nor hereafter . . . When enemies coming to battle tarnish the fame of a person, the misery which he feels is more poignant than the pangs of death. Know that victory is the root of religious merit and of every kind of happiness . . . Resolved upon acquiring heaven, we should fight, regardless of life or death; and with this determination to conquer or die, attain a blessed end in heaven."

This necessity of addressing encouraging words to the troops on the eve of a conflict is also emphasised in the Arthaśāstra of Kauṭilya and post-Kauṭilyan works on nīti. "A virtuous king," says Kauṭilya, "should call his army together, and, specifying the place and time of battle, address them thus: 'I am a paid servant like yourselves; this country is to be enjoyed (by me) together with you; you have to strike the enemy specified by me." The minister and priest of the king should also similarly harangue the army. They should say: "It is declared in the Vedas that the goal which is reached by sacrificers, after performing the final ablutions, in sacrifices in which the priests have been duly paid for, is the very goal which brave men are destined to attain." It is further enjoined that bards and astrologers in the king's entourage should point out to the troops the impregnable nature of their array, belittle the strength of the enemy, and assert that, owing to their association with the gods and their knowledge of the auguries, they were convinced that the king was sure to win the day. Sooth-sayers (*sūtāḥ*) and courtbards (*māgadhāḥ*) should humour the troops by extolling "their caste, corporation, family, past deeds and character," and the followers of the priest should loudly proclaim that sacrifices were being performed for the complete annihilation of the foe.[1]

Passages like the above also occur in later texts,[2] but it is needless to dilate upon them any further. It is already clear, we presume, that like the ancient Greeks and Romans, the Hindus frequently harangued their troops, and appealed, through the imagination, affections and conscience to their love of honour and glory, to enthusiasm, to patriotism, to revenge, and to pride of race and birth. Like the Greeks and Romans also, they appear to have made solemn and constant use of superstition, associated with religious ceremonies, and resorted to prodigies and preternatural omens to animate their troops and induce them to attempt deeds of valour.[3]

(b) War Music

Another interesting usage of the battle-field was military music. "Make them march to music," said Marshall Saxe, who considered music as a detail of great military importance. "There is the whole secret, and it is the military step of the Romans. Everyone has seen people dance the whole night, cutting capers at the same time. But take a man, and make him dance without music for quarter of an hour, and see how he stands it; that proves that music has a secret power over us, and enables us to undergo great exertion."

[1] Kauṭ. Bk. X. ch. 3.

[2] E.g. comp. Manu VII, 194; Ag. P. 236, 51-55.

[3] Referring to the Paurava army, Curtius Rufus says that "an image of Herakles was borne in front of the infantry, and this acted as the strongest of all incentives to make soldiers fight well. To desert the bearers of this image was reckoned a disgraceful military offence, and they had even ordained death as penalty for those who failed to bring it back from the battle-field, for the dread which the Indians had conceived for the god when he was their enemy had been toned down to a feeling of religious awe and veneration." This fact, however, is not mentioned by Arrian. Moreover, so far as we know, the practice is nowhere referred to in ancient Sanskrit literature.

The history of military music in India goes back to the early Vedic period. The Ṛgveda (VI, 47, 29-31), contains the following beautiful hymn in praise of the war drum (*dundubhi*) :

"Send forth thy voice loud through earth and heaven, and let the world in all its breadth regard thee, O Drum, accordant with Gods and Indra, drive thou afar, yea, very afar, our foemen. Thunder out strength and fill us full of vigour; yea, thunder forth and drive away all dangers. Drive hence, O war-drum, drive away misfortune; thou art the Fist of Indra; show thy firmness. Drive hither those, and these again bring hither; the war-drum speaks aloud as battle's signal."

Similar beautiful verses in praise of the battle-drum occur also in the Atharva-veda (V, 20-21), wherein it is described as "shrill-crying," "loud-noised," thundering "like a lion," "exciting the weapons of the warriors," and "overpowering hostile plotters."

Music filled an important rôle in epic military affairs. No expression is perhaps more frequent in the battle-scenes of the Mahābhārata than the following: "Then there arose a tumultuous uproar, caused by the blare of trumpets, thundering of drums, the blowing of conch-shells, etc., besides shouts and cries." Music was played when the army marched; it heralded the beginning of the battle; it announced the fall of a chief or knight; it was employed for signalling orders across the field. The Śānti-parva (100, 46) recommends that "to encourage crowds (in battle) let such noises as these be made, *kṣveḍāḥ kilakilā* and *krakaca,* with horns and drums." The instruments used in producing battle music were many and varied, collectively called *vāditrāṇi.* Chief among these were the drum, tambourine, trumpet, conch-shell, horn (especially cow's horn) and lyre.[1]

[1] Cf. Udyogaparva, 151, 52; Bhīṣmaparva 51, 23 ff.; ibid. 44, 4 ff. Droṇaparva, 38, 31; Karṇaparva 11, 36-37, etc. See also J. A. O. S., XIII, 318 ff. The Jātakas also make frequent references to military music. The Soṇananda Jātaka (Cowell's tr. V, 170), for instance, contains the following:

"Who marches here with tabour, conch, and beat of sounding drums
Music to cheer the heart of kings? Who here in triumph comes?"

In the Mūga-pakkha Jātaka (Cowell's tr. VI, 14), a king orders as follows:
"The horses to the chariots yoke,—bind girths on elephants and come;
Sound conch and tabour far and wide, and wake the loud-mouthed kettle-drums.

Let the hoarse tom-tom fill the air, let rattling drums raise echoes sweet,—
Bid all this city follow me,—I go my son once more to greet."

Curtius Rufus says that king Porus had a number of drummers in his army, and he posted them with the infantry and archers behind the elephants.[1] In one of his Rock Edicts (No. VI), Aśoka speaks of *bherīghoṣa* (the sound of the war-drums) as a symbol of martial policy. In the Arthaśāstra (Bk. V. ch. 3), Kauṭilya mentions *tūrya-karas* (trumpet-blowers) and assigns them double the wages of ordinary musicians (*kuśīla*). Elsewhere (Bk. X. ch. 6), the sound of the trumpet (*tūrya-ghoṣa*) is mentioned as one of the means to signalise *nāyaka's* orders to his troops.

References to military music in the Harṣacarita have been quoted in a previous chapter. Hiuen Tsiang says that Emperor Harṣa was always accompanied in his marches by several hundred persons with golden drums called "music-pace-drums," beating one stroke at each step.[2] Similar references to battle music occur also in the Raghuvaṁśa (VII, 38), and the Śiśupālavadha (XVIII, 3, 54; XIX, 26, etc). A Cālukya grant of king Kīrtivarma II, dated 758 A.D., refers to *ḍhakkā* drum, a 'lotus-mouthed' triumpet and a drum called the "roar of the sea."[3] The Kurram Plates of the Pallava king, Parameśvaravarman I, speaks of the "thunder-like sound" of kettle-drums and conch-shells, inspiring terror in the battle-field.[4] Similarly *paṭaha* and *ḍhakkā* drums are mentioned as instruments of war music in the Kadba Plates of Prabhūtavarṣa,[5] and kettle drums, "loud jharjharas," "shrill ḍamarus" and tabors in the Nagpur Stone Inscription of the rulers of Mālava, dated 1104-5 A.D.[6] The Mānasollāsa enjoins that at the commencement of a battle, "the very skies should be rent" (*sphoṭayan diśaḥ*) by the beating of drums, the blowing of conch-shells and *kāhalās*, and the blare of trumpets.[7]

From the Rājataraṅgiṇī (VIII, 2568), we learn that in Kasmir kettle-drums were beaten between the night watches in a fort or camp,[8] and that a surprise attack was often announced by the blare of trumpets and drums. For instance, when Sujji (VIII, 1879) made a night attack on the retreating Kasmirian troops, he

[1] McCrindle, *India and its Invasion by Alexander*, p. 208.
[2] Beal, *Life*, p. 173.
[3] Ind. Ant. VIII, 28.
[4] Ep. Ind. XVII, 343.
[5] Ep. Ind. IV, 348.
[6] Ibid. II, 192. For further epigraphic references to war music, see Ep. Ind. I, 235; IV, 95; VI, 103; IX, 181, 206; Ind. Ant. XII, 13, etc.
[7] Mānas. p. 137, v. 1209.
[8] *Tūrya-karas* beating the night watches is also referred to in Kauṭ. Bk. I, ch. 19.

"announced to the opponents his surprise attack" by drum-beats. Elsewhere (VIII, 2942), we read: "Then at night-fall, there arose from the middle of the village a great noise of drums, and the shouting of troops which announced an attack." In both cases the immediate result was the complete demoralization of the enemy. In another context (VIII, 1080-1081), Kalhaṇa mentions that a war-lord, Pṛthvīhara, "on hearing the noisy music which arose from his shouting army, counted from curiosity the musical instruments. Apart from the numerous kettle-drums and other (big instruments), he could, in his curiosity, count twelve hundred small drums such as are carried by *śvāpakas*."

It is clear from the above review that the instruments of war music were many and various. But the chief of them appear to have been the drum, the tambourine, conch-shells, trumpet and horn. An early Muhammadan historian refers to the "crow-faced" Hindus trumpeting "their white shells on the backs of the elephants."[1]

(c) Ambulance

Another useful custom was the provision of medical aid to wounded officers and troops. The Mahābhārata refers to surgeons and physicians marching with the Pāṇḍava army to the field of

[1] Elliot. II, 215. The drum itself was of many varieties, called *dundubhi, bherī, paṭaha, puṣkara, ānaka* or *mahānaka, peśī, jharjhara, ḍamaru, ḍiṇḍima, ḍhakkā, pratiḍhakkā, kāhalā, koṇikā, āḷambara* or *aḍambara*, etc. The fact that two or more of them are often mentioned together probably shows that they were not merely different names of one and the same instrument. Thus *bherī* and *dundubhi* are mentioned together in Bhīṣmaparva, 99, 11: (*bherī-mṛdaṅga-śaṅkhānāṁ dundubhināñca nisvanaiḥ*), *bherī* and *peśī* in ibid. 43, 8, (*tato bheryaśca peśyaśca krakacā goviṣāṇikāḥ*); *bherī* and *anīka* in Droṇaparva 86, 1-2, (*tāḍyamānāṣu bherīṣu . . . anīkānāñca nirhrāde*); *bherī and paṇava* in Bhīṣmaparva 99, 11 (*bherī-mṛdaṅga-paṇavān*); and *paṇava* and *ānaka* in Virāṭaparva 72, 27 (*paṇvānaka-gomukhāḥ*). Similarly the Kakkaṭa Jātaka (Cowell II, 237), speaks of *ānaka* and *āḷambara* as drums of two distinct varieties. In the same way, *paṭaha, kāhalā* and *koṇikā* are mentioned together in the Harṣacarita (ch. VII); *paṭaha, jharjhara* and *ḍamaru* in the Nagpur Stone Inscription (Ep. Ind. XI, 192); *paṭaha* and *ḍhakkā* in the Kadba Plates of Prabhūtavarṣa (Ep. Ind. IV, 348). Of the different kinds of drums, the *dundubhi* was of earlier origin, and was the instrument *par excellence* during the Vedic period; but at a later epoch it appears to have been superseded by the *bherī*. Aśoka's remark (Rock Edict. VI): *bherīghoṣa aho dhammaghoṣa* (*jātā*), tends to prove that the *bherī* had become the chief instrument of military music in the 3rd century B.C.

Kurukṣetra.[1] In the Śāntiparva (69, 59) Bhīṣma recommends that a king must maintain in a fort four kinds of physicians, among whom there must be some who have specialised in cases of poisoning and the extraction of arrow-heads. In the Arthaśāstra (Bk. X. ch. 3), Kauṭilya remarks: "Physicians with surgical instruments and appliances and healing ointments and bandages, and women with food and drink should stand behind, encouraging the fighting men."[2] The later Nītiprakāśikā (VI. 43, 50) enjoins that the king should have in his camp not merely a rich store of medicine, but also expert physicians equipped with surgical instruments (*sarvopakaraṇair-yuktān vaidyāṁśca suviśāradān*).

The chief importance of references like the above lies in the fact that they show that provision of medical aid to sick and wounded troops was regarded as an important duty of the state. But to what extent such aid was actually provided, how it was organized, how far it was effective are questions on which no light is thrown by our records. The Rājataraṅgiṇī (VIII. 740-41), however, preserves the memory of one Kasmirian king, who is said to have spent large sums of money in providing medical aid for his troops. About 1120 A.D. Srinagar, the capital of Kasmir, was besieged by ḍāmara rebels, headed by Bhikṣācara and Mallakoṣṭha. The siege was long and protracted, for the reigning monarch, Sussala, defended the city with great vigour. "Ever he was seen arranging that the wounded should have their hurts bandaged, the arrow-heads removed, and proper presents given. The sums which the king spent on the troops by giving marching allowances, gratuities and medicines were beyond calculation."[3]

1 Cf. Udyogaparva, 151. For surgeons attending on a wounded knight see Bhīṣmaparva 120, 55.

2 Elsewhere Kauṭilya speaks of veterinary surgeons employed by the state to look after the health of elephants and horses. Cf. Bk. II. ch. 30 and 32.

3 The Tamil poem, Nedu-nal-vādai, gives a beautiful description of the Pāṇḍya king, Neduj-Chelyan II, going out at midnight to see the wounded in his camp. See Kanakasabhai, *The Tamils 1800 Years Ago*, p. 85.

CHAPTER XIII

FORTIFICATION AND SIEGECRAFT

1. Pre-historic fortification

In dealing with the history of fortification in ancient India, we have two sets of facts to consider—archeological and literary. To some extent this has been done in previous chapters also, but archeological evidence acquires a relatively special importance in any study of architecture, not less so of military architecture.

Both these streams of evidence, however, carry the history of fortification in India to a very remote antiquity. It is not yet quite clear whether the newly discovered city of Mohenjo-dāro was protected either by wallings or by fortifications. Sir John Marshall believes that the city walls would naturally be buried beneath the deep alluvium of the surrounding plains, where no excavations have yet been carried on.[1] But whatever be the fact about Mohenjo-dāro, remains of fortifications belonging to the same chalcolithic age have been revealed by Mr. N. G. Majumdar after his examination of two more sites in the Indus valley. Both these sites, known respectively as Ali Murad and Kohtras Buthi, lie in the narrow corridor between the Indus and the Beluchistan border. Partial excavations carried out at the former place have led to the discovery of a long rampart wall of irregularly dressed stone blocks, each about 2′ in length, 1′ in height, and 1′ or a little more in thickness.[2] The latter place is a hill commanding the camel track from Arabjo Thana to Taung. The hill rises to a maximum height of 95 feet on the north, gradually sloping down to only 10 feet above the surrounding plain on the south. On the east, west and north, it is quite steep, rugged and difficult of approach. As one ascends the hill from the south, "there is first of all, above the incline, a low rampart wall, and next a second wall much more substantial than the first, both built of stone boulders laid

[1] Sir John Marshall, *Mohenjo-dāro and the Indus Civilisation*, Vol. I, p. 9; also p. 282, f.n.

[2] Memoirs of the Arch. Survey of India, No. 48, pp. 89-90.

without any mortar." Mr. Majumdar considers the second wall, which must have been originally of huge proportions, as an example of cyclopean masonry. Besides these walls, there are also traces of four ruined bastions and an entrance on the south-east.

"There is no doubt from the objects recovered," says Mr. Majumdar, "that the site is one of the chalcolithic period. But the remains cannot be those of an ordinary settlement. The cyclopean wall, with which the area is girt and protected, suggests its being the site of a fortress. The difficulty of access from three sides no doubt contributed to its safety. Standing on the top of the hill one could have a clear view for miles around, the importance of which from a strategic point of view would be immense. To the west of the Buthi is a flanking chain of the Khirthar on the way to Taung, in which at places gaps have been filled up by constructing massive stone walls."[1]

It is clear, therefore, that some of the fundamental principles of fortification were known and practised in India as early as the chalcolithic age, and that towns and settlements were sometimes protected by stone walls, both for strategic reasons and for the protection of the life and property of the inhabitants from marauding bands in the neighbourhood.

The oldest literary record of India, viz. the Ṛgveda also testifies to the pre-historic origin of the art of fortification. There are numerous passages throughout the work which point to the conclusion that the pre-Aryan inhabitants of India (called *Dāsas* or *Dasyus*) were excellent builders in their days, and had numerous forts and strong-holds in their possession. Thus Sambhara is said to have had ninety (Ṛv. i, 130, 7), ninety-nine (ib. ii. 19, 6) or a hundred (ib. ii. 14, 6) forts. Sambhara is called a Dāsa (ib. vi. 26, 5). He was the formidable foe of the Aryan chief, Divodāsa Atithigva. Besides, the Ṛgveda sometimes refers to the non-Aryans as being in possession of "iron castles." In ii. 20, 8, for instance, we have: "When they placed the thunder-bolt in his (Indra's) hand, he slew the Dasyus and overthrew their iron castles." Perhaps the epithet iron is used to connote excessive strength.

It is probable also that the Vedic Aryans, when they slowly and steadily pushed their way into India, found themselves, under the stress of the concentric attack of the surrounding non-Aryan

[1] Ibid. pp. 132-33.

population, compelled to fortify their positions. The resources of fortification, which they captured from the non-Aryans, probably stood them in good stead, and they utilised them to the best of their ability. Where the captured non-Aryan *enceinte* was susceptible of repair, it was probably repaired; and occasionally also new strong-holds must have been created to protect life and property in view of the general insecurity of the time. We have no definite knowledge as to the character of these strong-holds. They are sometimes spoken of as made of stone (*aśmamayī*, iv, 30, 20), sometimes of sun-dried brick (*āma*, lit. raw, 'unbaked,' ii, 35, 6); but more often they were probably built of "hardened earth with palisades and a ditch."[1] Occasionally, it may be, these forts were of considerable size, for we find one described as "broad" (*pṛthvī*) and "wide" (*urvī*).[2]

In the post-Vedic period, as the country became more thickly settled, the tendency to surround towns and cities with defensive works for protection against enemies appears to have become more marked. In the Jātakas, for instance, we read of cities being fortified with walls and ramparts, with buttresses, watch-towers and massive gates. The city of Vesālī or Vaiśālī is said to have been encompassed by a triple wall, with gates and watch-towers;[3] the city of Mithilā had "its walls, gates and battlements;"[4] and so also had the city of Potali.[5] In the Mahā-Ummagga Jātaka, we read the following: "He caused a great rampart to be built for the city. Along the rampart were watch-towers at the gates, and between the watch-towers he dug three moats—a water-moat, a mud-moat and a dry-moat . . . . . This was done as a defence against future danger."[6]

[1] Vedic Index. I, 539.

[2] Ṛv. i. 189, 2. For a detailed account of Vedic references to fortifications see Muir, Original Sanskrit *Texts*, II, 378-383.

[3] Cowell, *The Jātaka*, I, 316.

[4] Ibid. VI, 30.

[5] Ibid. III, 2.

[6] Rhys Davids, *Buddhist India*, p. 63. The Taṇḍulanāli Jātaka states that the walls of Benares (Bārāṇasī) were twelve leagues round by themselves. The Mahājanaka Jātaka (No. 539) refers to Campā, the capital of Aṅga, with its gate, watch-tower and walls. In the epics we find more elaborate descriptions of fortified cities. Cf., for instance, the description of Indraprastha in the Ādiparva, 207, 30 ff., of Ayodhyā in Rām. Ayodhyā. 5, 10 ff., and of Laṅkā again in Rām. Laṅkā. 3, 4, 11-17. Hopkins maintains that these descriptions belong to the latest amplification of the original Mahābhārata (and Rāmāyaṇa) and that "the accounts of full fortifications must be regarded as foreign to the first form of the poem." (J. A. O. S. XIII, 175). He further holds that though walled cities were known in early

Remains of an old fortress belonging to the 6th or 7th century B.C. have been unearthed at Rājgir. Local traditions affirm that it is the same as the town of Girivraja, referred to in the Mahābhārata as the capital of Jarāsandha. According to Buddhist annals, king Śreṇika or Bimbisāra left the old city and commenced the construction of a new town at the foot of the hills, about two-thirds of a mile north of the old town. It is, therefore, legitimate to infer that Girivraja (or old Rājagṛha) belonged to the pre-Bimbisāra or pre-Buddha epoch of Indian history.

The town stood on an admirably selected site—an uneven valley with hills on all sides. The hills themselves constituted the walls of the outer town, and the natural defences which they afforded were further strengthened by artificial fortifications. Explorations carried out on the spot have revealed that there were two lines of walls round the city; an outer and an inner line, the length of the latter being four and one-fourth miles. The outer line goes up and down hill from Vaibhāragiri over Sona-giri, thence to Udayagiri and along the southern range of hills to Giriyak, and then back at intervals over Saila-giri, Chaṭhāgiri, Ratnagiri and Vipulagiri.

The Archeological Report of 1909-10 gives the following account of the construction of these walls: "The faces of the walls are built of massive undressed stones between 3 and 5 feet in length, carefully fitted and bonded together, while the core between them is composed of smaller blocks carefully cut and laid with chips or fragments of stone, packing the interstices between them. No mortar or cement is visible anywhere in the stone-work."[1]

The walls are standing to their greatest height on the west of the Bangaṅgā Pass, where their elevation is between 11 and 12 feet. "On the west of Sonagiri, and on the Vaibhāragiri, Vipulagiri and Ratnagiri, the walls are much ruined and seldom rise higher than 7 or 8 feet. From the fact that whenever the height of between 11 and 12 feet is reached, the walls are invariably finished off with a course of stone work, and that there are no fallen blocks of stone

times, "strong stone walls and battlemented towers belong to the late Mbh-Rāmāyaṇa period." (Ibid. XIII, 174 f.n.). This is possible. But the premise on which the whole argument is obviously based, viz. that there are no "purely Hindu remains antique enough to prove that stone-walled cities were known before Alexander" can no longer be upheld in the face of recent archeological discoveries.

[1] Report of the Arch. Surv. of India, 1909-10, pp. 88-89.

lying near, we may assume that this was the original height of the massive masonry described above. Above this substructure, there was no doubt a superstructure composed either of smaller stone work or of bricks baked or unbaked, or possibly of wood and stone or brick combined."[1] The thickness of the fortifications varies on the different hills from 14′ to 17′ 6″.

A further point of importance is that bastions (towers) are found attached to the outside of the walls, wherever special strength was required. Altogether sixteen such structures have been discovered, but it is possible that originally there were more. "They are solid rectangular buildings, constructed after the same fashion as the wall and built on to it at irregular intervals. In plan, they measure 47′ to 60′ long by 34′ to 40′ broad, the long side always coinciding with the face of the wall on to which they abut. They rise to the same height as the wall and, like it, were, no doubt, provided with superstructures which have now disappeared."[2]

Another noticeable feature about the outer walls is the stairs or rather ramps, built in the thickness of the wall along its inner face, in order to give access to the top. Nine such ramps have so far been discovered. They measure approximately 5′ 6″ wide and 15′ long.

These defences were further supplemented by separate watch-towers erected at various prominent points on the hills. Two of these exist on the Vaibhāra hill, four on the Vipula hill, and one on the easternmost peak of the Ratnagiri.[3]

We have described the fortifications of old Rājagṛha at considerable length mainly for two reasons. In the first place, they show that stone fortification had perhaps a continuous history in India from the chalcolithic period onwards, and consequently the accounts of fortified cities which we find in the Jātakas and the epics need not be considered as mythical or as late. Secondly, they illustrate that in making strongholds, the strategical strength of the site was taken into consideration and advantage taken of the natural features of the ground.

II Forts and strong-holds in the 4th century B.C.

The classical chronicles make it evident that when Alexander invaded India in the 4th century B.C., forts and strong-holds held

[1] Ibid.
[2] Ibid. pp. 89-90.
[3] Ibid. pp. 89-90.

by Hindu chiefs were scattered thickly over the country. The captial of almost every state, however small, appears to have been fortified with defensive works of varying solidity. Where the ground offered natural barriers, full advantage of these was taken. Such, for instance, were Massaga or Mazaga, Bazira, Aornos etc. With regard to Massaga, Curtius supplies us with an elaborate description of the defences with which both nature and man had provided the city. "An army of 38,000 infantry," he says, "defended the city which was strongly fortified both by nature and art. For on the east, an impetuous mountain-stream with steep banks on both sides barred approach to the city, while to the south and west nature, as if designing to form a rampart, had piled up gigantic rocks, at the base of which lay sloughs and yawning chasms hollowed in the course of ages to vast depths, while a ditch of mighty labour drawn from their extremity continued the line of defence. The city was besides surrounded with a wall of 35 stadia in circumference which had a basis of stonework supporting a superstructure of unburnt, sundried bricks. The brickwork was bound into a solid fabric by means of stones so interposed that the more brittle material rested upon the harder, while moist clay had been used for mortar. Lest, however, the structure should all at once sink, strong beams had been laid upon these, supporting wooden floors which covered the walls and afforded a passage along them."[1] Concerning Bazira, Arrian tells us that it "stood on a very lofty eminence and was strongly fortified in every quarter."[2] Aornos, again, was a place of extra-ordinary strategic strength, but does not appear to have had any artificial fortifications. Arrian says that the 'rock' had a circuit of about 200 stadia, and at its lowest elevation a height of eleven stadia. "It was ascended by a single path cut by the hand of man, yet difficult. On the summit of the rock there was, it is said, plenty of pure water which gushed out from a copious spring. There was timber besides, and as much good arable land as required for its cultivation the labour of a

[1] McCrindle, *India and its Invasion by Alexander*, pp. 194-5. In connection with the above description, Messrs. Heitland and Raven make the following pertinent observation: "How the arrangement was to prevent the upper part of walls from settling down is a mystery as the text stands; and we can only suppose that (*a*) Curtius has not understood his authorities, or (*b*) he has left out some important steps in the description, or (*c*) that the text is mutilated so as to conceal his real meaning." *Alexander in India*, p. 107.

[2] McCrindle, *India and its Invasion by Alexander*, p. 69. Sir Aurel Stein has identified the place with the ancient fortress of Bir-kot in the Swat. See Memoirs of the Archeological Survey of India, Vol. 42, pp. 23 ff.

19

thousand men."[1] Diodorus describes the rock as a natural stronghold, 100 stadia in circumference, 16 stadia in height, and with a level surface forming a complete circle. The Indus washed its foot on the south; elsewhere it was surrounded by deep ravines and inaccessible cliffs.[2] Sir Aurel Stein, who has successfully located Aornos on the rock-girt site adjoining Mount Una, observes: "The precipitous nature of that slope would lend itself to easy and effective defence, in particular by rolling down large stones, a formidable method of defence the actual use of which Curtius here specially mentions."[3]

But towns which were not so favoured by nature were not left at the mercy of every invading or marauding band from outside. Nearly all of them were surrounded with defensive works, the size and character of which depended upon the situation, probable exposure to attack, and the wealth of the inhabitants. For instance, Arrian tells us that the city of the Aspasioi was encompassed by a double line of walls. The outer wall "was but rudely constructed," but the inner wall was remarkably strong.[4] With regard to Sangala, the capital of the Cathaeans, the same writer says that it was "strongly fortified," and that its walls were of brick.[5] Similarly most of the towns in the territory of the Malloi and the Oxydrakoi were well fortified. Arrian speaks of the capital of the Malloi as "the strongest of all the cities that lay near." The city was defended by walls, and within them there was a citadel with gates, towers and parapet.[6] About another of their towns, identified by Cunningham with Kot-Kamalia, a small but ancient town situated on an isolated mound on the northern bank of the Ravi,[7] we are informed that it was not only defended by a wall, but had within it a citadel, "seated on a commanding height and difficult of access."[8] The classical authors mention a third Malloi city, identified by Cunningham with Tulamba, which was defended by brick walls and enormous mounds of earthen ramparts.[9]

[1] Ibid. p. 71. [2] Ibid. p. 271.

[3] Stein, *On Alexander's Track to the Indus*, p. 154. Cf. also Memoirs of the Archeological Survey of India, Vol. 42 for a full discussion of the grounds of identification.

[4] McCrindle, *India and its invasion by Alexander*, p. 62.

[5] Ibid. p. 119. Curtius (ib. p. 217) adds that it was also defended by a morass.

[6] Ibid. pp. 145-6, 288.

[7] Cunningham, *Ancient Geography*, pp. 208-10.

[8] McCrindle, op. cit., pp. 140-141.

[9] Ibid. p. 142.

Other fortified cities in the Punjab and Sind, referred to by classical writers, were the capital of the Brahmanas,[1] Sindimana, the capital of Sambos,[2] the city in which Proticanus, king of Praesti, shut himself up,[3] and the capital of Sophytes.[4] Far to the east, in the tongue of land formed by the junction of the Son and the Ganges, was the city of Palibothra, Palimbothra or Pāṭaliputra, the capital of Magadha. In the time of Megasthenes, it was considered to be by far "the largest city in India"—a long, narrow parallelogram in shape, measuring about nine and one-fifth miles in length and one and a half miles in breadth. It was not defended by any brick wall, but by a massive wooden palisade, pierced by sixty-four gates and crowned by five hundred and seventy towers. The palisade had loop-holes for the archers to shoot through, and outside there was a ditch, 30 cubits deep and 400 cubits (6 plethra) broad. The ditch was filled from the waters of the Son.[5]

It is important to take note of two salient facts in the above account. First, though cities were surrounded with various defensive works, there was no uniformity in their character. As before stated, the character of defensive works depended on various factors, such as the situation of the city, probable exposure to attack and the wealth of the inhabitants. In this connection it is worth recalling a statement recorded by Arrian regarding Indian cities of this age. He says that those Indian towns "which are down beside the river or the sea are made of wood; for towns built of brick would never hold out for any length of time with the rains on the one hand, and, on the other, the rivers which rise above their banks and spread a sheet of water over the plains. But the towns which are built on elevated places out of reach of these are made of brick and lime."[6] This will explain why the defensive works round Pāṭaliputra, the capital of a far-flung and prosperous empire, were built of timber and not of brick, as certain cities in

[1] Ibid. p. 143. It had a citadel within it, to which the beseiged took refuge when the outer walls were found to give way.

[2] Ibid. p. 159. Curtius (ib. p. 254), who refers to this place without giving the name, describes it as the "strongest of all the cities which belonged to this people." Alexander took it "by making a passage into it underground"—a device which many centuries later was repeated by Aurangzeb in capturing Surat.

[3] Ibid. pp. 253-4. There was a citadel within this city also. It was strengthened by towers.

[4] Its walls and towers are referred to by Curtius (ib. p. 219).

[5] Megasthenes, Frag. 25; Strabo, XV, c. 702.

[6] Megasthenes, Frag. 26; Arr. Ind. 10.

the northwest appear to have been. Secondly, it is important to note that the age witnessed a significant development in the history of military architecture in India. Most of the towns mentioned above were defended by means of surrounding walls, but in some cases, as a measure of additional protection, strongly-fortified citadels were added within the walls. It will appear from a careful perusal of the texts that the citadel was built in one corner of the town—usually in the part which was most secure and well-defended—and that a continuation of the town wall formed its outer side. The citadel served as the ultimate refuge of the besieged, when the outer defences of the town were captured or destroyed by the assailing force. It was the last resort to which the garrison retired in desperate extremity.

III Kauṭilya's Conception of Fortification

Nowhere perhaps are the ancient Hindu ideas on fortification better delineated than in the Arthaśāstra of Kauṭilya. In common with his predecessors in the field of political speculation, Kauṭilya considered the fort as one of the seven constituent elements of the state. Doubtless it was not the most important, but it was more important than the treasury, the friend and the army itself.[1] "For it is in the fort that the treasury and the army are safely kept, and it is from the fort that secret war (intrigue), control over one's partisans, the upkeep of the army, the reception of allies and the driving out of enemies are successfully practised. In the absence of forts, the treasury is to the enemy, for it seems that for those who own forts, there is no destruction."[2] Elsewhere he says that "the haven of the king and of his army is a strong fort."[3]

[1] Kauṭ. Bk. VI, ch. I. [2] Ibid. tr. p. 379.

[3] Ibid. p. 302. These ideas were shared by all later writers. In the Manusaṁhitā (VII. 73-74), for instance, it is stated that "foes cannot injure a king who has taken refuge in his fort." "One bowman, placed on a rampart, is a match in battle for one hundred (foes), one hundred for ten thousand; hence it is prescribed (in the śāstras that a king shall possess) a fortress." Similarly in the Yuktikalpataru (p. 17), king Bhoja emphatically asserts that the ordinary military strength of a king is, in fact, no strength. His real strength lies in the fort, for a king with a meagre force becomes powerful on account of the invincibility of his stronghold. Somadeva (Nītiv. p. 80) emphasises the importance of fortifications by introducing a homely analogy. "A king without a fort," he says, "has no refuge, just like a bird let loose from a ship in the midst of the ocean." Another writer (cf. Śārṅgadhara-Paddhati, ed. by Peterson, p. 220) compares the king without a fort to the snake without poison, or an elephant without rut.

With these preliminary remarks about the importance of fortifications, Kauṭilya next goes on to classify forts on the basis of their location. In his view, forts might be classified under four principal heads, viz. *pārvata* (hill fort), *audaka* (water-fort), *dhānvana* (desert fort), and *vanadurga* (forest fort). He defines a hill fort as one which is either perched on a rocky precipice (*prāstaraṁ*) or built in a valley in the midst of an encircling range of hills (*guhā*). A water fort, he says, may be situated on an island in the midst of a river (*antardvīpaṁ*), or on a plain surrounded by low ground or morass in which water is stagnated (*nimnāvaruddhaṁ sthalam*). Similarly a forest fort is either encompassed by many bogs and fens, interspersed with trees and bushes (*khañjanodakaṁ*), or is girt by thickly-set tall trees with undergrowth (*stambagahaṁ*). Finally, a desert fort is one which is located either in the centre of a wild tract devoid of water or even of thickets (*nirudaka-stambaṁ*), or in a region sterilised by desert salt (*iriṇa*).[1]

Of these different varieties, Kauṭilya gives his preference to hill-forts and considers them as the most unassailable. In Bk. VII, ch. 12, for instance, he says: "Of forts such as a fort on the plain, in the centre of a river and on a mountain, that which is mentioned later is of more advantage than the one previously mentioned."[2] In an earlier chapter (ch. 10) of the same Bk., he explains the reasons which led him to this view. "Of two fortified kings," he says, "one who has his forts on a plain is more easily reduced than the other owning a fort in the centre of a river, for a fort in a plain can be easily assailed, destroyed or captured along with the enemy in it, whereas a fort surrounded by a river requires twice as much

[1] Kauṭ. Bk. II, ch. 3. Classification of forts was a stock-in-trade with all writers on nīti, though they do not appear to follow one uniform principle. The Viṣṇu-saṁhitā (III, 6) mentions five classes: *"Dhānva-nṛ-maru-vṛkṣa-giri-durgāṇ."* The Śāntiparva (86, 5) adopts a six-fold division: *Dhanva-durgaṁ mahī-durgaṁ giri-durgaṁ tathaiva ca. Manuṣyadurgaṁ mṛd-durgaṁ vana-durgañca tāni ṣaṭ.* Manu (VII. 70), while adhering to this six-fold classification, substitutes for the earth-fort (*mṛd-durgam*) variety of the Śāntiparva the water-fort (*audaka*) variety of Kauṭilya. This form of classification is also seen in the Ag. P. 222, 4-5 and the Mat. P. 216, 6-7. For similar lists of forts comp. Rām. Laṅkā. 3, 20-22; Mānasāra X, 90-91, etc. Bhoja in his Yuktikalpataru classifies forts under two heads, viz. *akṛtrima* (natural) and *kṛtrima* (artificial); the same has been done in Somadeva's Nitiv. (pp. 79-80). In the Mānas. p. 78, vv. 541-549, again, forts have been classified under nine heads in accordance with the nature or method of defence.

[2] Kauṭ. tr. p. 354.

effort to capture, and supplies the enemy with water and other necessaries of life." Again: "Of two kings, one owning a fort surrounded by a river, and another having mountainous fortifications, seizing the former's land is better, for a fort in the centre of a river can be assailed by a bridge formed of elephants made to stand in a row in the river, or by wooden bridges, or by means of boats; and the river will not always be deep and can be emptied of its water, whereas a fort on a mountain is of a self-defensive nature, and not easy to besiege or to ascend; and where if one portion of the army defending it is routed out, the other portions can escape unhurt, and such a fort is of immense service, as it affords facilities to throw down heaps of stone and trees over the enemy."[1]

With this estimate of the relative value of forts, Kauṭilya asks the ruler to create defensive works "on all the four quarters of the boundaries of the kingdom," "on grounds naturally best fitted for the purpose."[2] But apart from these, the king must have in the centre of his kingdom, "in a locality naturally best fitted for the purpose, such as the bank or the confluence of rivers, a deep pool of perennial water, or of a lake or tank,"—a fortified capital. This might be of any shape, circular, rectangular or square, in consonance with the requirements of the ground.[3] It has to be surrounded by three successive ditches, the first 84 feet (14 *daṇḍas*), the second 72 feet (12 *daṇḍas*) and the third 60 feet (10 *daṇḍas*) wide, "with depth less by one-quarter or one-half of their width." The sides of the ditches were to be built of stones or bricks (*pāṣāṇopahitāḥ pāṣāṇeṣṭaka-baddha-pārśvāḥ*), and they were to be filled with perennial flowing water drawn from some neighbouring river. Crocodiles and lotus plants were to be nurtured in the ditches so that no enemy could swim across them with impunity.

At a distance of 24 feet from the inner-most ditch, a rampart (*vapra*) 36 feet high and twice as broad, is to be erected "by heaping mud upwards and by making it square at the bottom, oval at the centre, pressed by the trampling of elephants and bulls."

[1] Ibid. pp. 349-50. In this view of the relative importance of forts, other writers follow in the footsteps of Kauṭilya. Comp. Manu (VII. 71); the Ag. P. 222. 5 has *sarvottamaṁ śailadurgamabhedyaṁ cānyabhedanaṁ;* the same view is expressed in the Mat. P. 217, 7; *sarveṣāmeva durgāṇāṁ giridurgaṁ praśasyate.*

[2] Kauṭ. tr. p. 54.

[3] *Vṛttaṁ dīrghaṁ caturasraṁ vā vāstukavaśena.*

Gaps in the rampart must be filled up with fresh earth. The intervening space between the rampart and the ditch is to be strewn with throny bushes, sharp instruments and entanglements of various kinds.

Above the rampart are to be erected walls or parapets (*prākāra*), built of brick. They might be of any number, with a space of 12 to 24 cubits between them; and they should be twice as high as they are broad. The parapets are to be interspersed at regular intervals with towers or bastions (*aṭṭālaka*), square throughout and provided with movable staircases.

"In the intermediate space measuring 30 *daṇḍas* between two towers, there shall be formed a broad street in two compartments covered with a roof and two and a half times as long as it is broad." This street appears to have been intended for patrol of the sentinels, protected overhead by the roofs. The bifurcation of the street is for facilitating the double movements, forward and backward, of the guards on duty. "Between the tower and the broad street shall be constructed an *Indrakośa,* which is made up by covering pieces of perforated wooden planks affording seats for three archers." The entrance gate to the fort should be "one-sixth as broad as the width of the street," and above the gateway should be constructed a turret, its face resembling a large lizzard. Besides the main gate, there must also be special secret passages for flight or exit in an unassailable part of the rampart.

In addition to the above, the author gives other details regarding the construction of roads and buildings within the fort. He also speaks of the construction of canals (*kulya*) to hold weapons. "In these canals, there shall be collected stones, spades (*kuddāla*), axes (*kuṭhāri*), varieties of staffs, cudgels (*musṛṇṭhi*), hammers (*mudgara*), clubs, discus, machines (*yantra*), and such weapons as can destroy a hundred persons at once (*śataghnī*), together with spears, tridents, bamboo-sticks with pointed edges made of iron, camel-necks, explosives (*agni-saṁyogas*) and whatever else can be devised and formed from available materials."[1] In the chapter on the Superintendent of Armoury (Bk. II, ch. 18), he gives a list of various immovable machines (*sthira-yantra*), which from the commentator's explanation appear to have been specially stored in forts to repulse assaults upon them. He further recommends that articles of food, fodder and fuel should be "stored (in the fort) in such quantities as can be enjoyed for years together

Kauṭ. tr. p. 57.

without feeling any want." "Of such collection," he adds, "old things shall be replaced by new ones when received."[1]

IV Forts and Strong-holds from the Gupta Period Onwards

The foregoing account will serve as an illustration of the typical ideas on fortification as they had developed in India till the time of Kauṭilya. To what extent, and in what respects, these ideas were altered or modified in the light of later experience, we have no means of knowing. During the next thousand years or more , there were no great inventions or mechanical developments to make any sudden changes in the art of war or any of its branches. One is, therefore, justified in inferring that such changes as did occur in the art of fortification were evolutionary rather than revolutionary. The evidence of the Chinese pilgrims and of the early Muslim chroniclers points to the conclusion that the character of the permanent defences constructed around cities remained in general unchanged during this period, although there was perhaps a gradual increase in the size of the walls and in the dimensions of the ditches, in order to combat the growing efficiency of siege machinery. It is probable also that there were improvements in the height and strength of the towers, and of other arrangements for protecting the ditches along the weaker portions of the wall—that is, the curtains between the towers.

But the chief note in the history of military architecture of this period was the increased tendency to construct hill forts. This was in consonance with the teachings of Kauṭilya and other military writers. The typical site preferred for a hill fortress was a precipitous cliff sloping to a river on one, two or even three sides and with steep slopes falling away on the other side. At the highest point was built a fort serving as a citadel.[2] Some of these were like eagles' nests on lofty cliffs, places of last refuge rather than strategical positions. But others were of real strategical strength,

[1] Ibid. p. 60. Most ancient writers emphasise the importance of adequately provisioning a fort. Comp., for instance, Manu VII, 75; Śāntiparva 69, 45-60. According to Somadeva (Nītiv. p. 80) abundance of food, fuel and water constitutes one of the essential factors of the strength of a fort. In the absence of these, he says, a fort is no better than a prison-house. Comp. also Mat. P. 217, 29-33, where a long list of weapons and other materials, which are to be stored in a fort, is given; also Mānas., p. 79.

[2] Cf. A. S. R. V, 102 ff.; ibid. 1905-6, p. 12; Stein, *Chronicles of Kasmir*, II, 229-30; also the author's note on viii, 2528.

commanding the countryside or the approaches to a state. Muhammadan historians acknowledge that Sultan Maḥmūd could not accomplish his design of conquering Kashmir owing to the impregnable nature of the fortresses of Rājagiri and Lahūr, described by Berūnī as "the two strongest places I have ever seen."[1] It is also a matter of common knowledge that the eight forts of Bundelkhand, along with the natural ruggedness of the country, long enabled the rulers of this territory—first the Cāndellas and later the Bundelas—to maintain their independence against powerful foreign invaders.

Of the numerous hill fortresses established in Northern India during the last five or six centuries of our period, the most celebrated at the time of the Muhammadan invasions were Kāliñjar (Kālañjar), Gwalior,[2] Ajayagaṛh [3] and Maniyāgaṛh in Central India; Chitorgaṛh, Ranthombhor and Maṇḍor[4] in Rajputana; Bhīrā (Bhatia) and Kangra (Nagarkot, Bhimnagar, etc.) in the Punjab; and Loharokoṭṭa, Bānaśālā and Śirahśilā in Kashmir. It is noteworthy that the early Muhammadan historians have referred to some of these forts in terms of enthusiastic admiration. In connection with the fortress of Kāliñjar, for instance, Hasan Nizami says that it was "celebrated throughout the world for being as strong as the wall of Alexander."[5] The same writer describes the fort of Gwalior as "the pearl of the necklace of the castles of Hind, the summit of which the nimble-footed wind from below cannot reach, and on the bastion of which the rapid clouds have never cast their

[1] Sachau. I, 208; Elliot. II, 455, 466.

[2] In epigraphic records the fort is called Gopa-giri, Gopādri, Gopācala-durga and Gopādridurga, of which the present name is merely a corruption.

[3] In contemporary inscriptions it is called Jaya-pura-durga.

[4] The old name of the city was Maḍḍodara, according to one inscription (Ep. Ind. IX, 280, 1, 13), and Maṇḍavaya-pura-durga according to another (J. R. A. S., 1894, p. 5, 1. 6). The date of the castle's foundation may probably be placed in the sixth century A.D. Its remains are thus described in the Archeologic Survey Report, 1909-10, pp. 93-04: "Its walls, though badly damaged and partly buried beneath their own debris, still rise to a considerable height on the north and west sides. On the east, and to some extent on the south also, they were built at the edge of a precipitous scarp, their width averaging some 24 or 25 feet, and were further strengthened and protected by bastions on the outside, of which several are still preserved on the north and west sides. Along the curtain of the walls these bastions are either square or rectangular in plan; but the one at the northwest angle is circular, and it is probable that those at the other three corners were of the same form."

[5] Elliot. II, 231.

shade."[1] 'Utbi refers to the fort of Bhatia as follows: "The walls of which the wings of an eagle could not surmount, and which was surrounded as by the ocean with a ditch of exceeding depth and breadth."[2] Regarding the fort of Ranthombhor, again, Minhajus Sirāj says that it "is celebrated in all parts of Hindustan for its great strength and security. It is related in Hindu histories that it had been invaded by more than seventy kings, and no one had been able to take it."[3]

But beyond vague generalisations and hyperboles, the Muhammadan historians give us no useful details as to the manner in which these hill forts were originally constructed. Nor can we know these details from other sources. This is chiefly because some of these forts have now disappeared, others are lying in rolling heaps of brick debris, while the few which are still standing have been so completely transformed during the Middle Ages as to retain little of their original character. Unfortunately, moreover, the military architecture of this period has received comparatively little attention from archeologists, and the data at present available are not sufficient to enable us to discriminate with confidence between successive periods of building, or to determine which parts are attributable to the Hindu founders and which to the Muhammadan dynasties that followed them.[4]

Owing to this two-fold difficulty, we can only guess the outline of these structures as they originally stood. They were usually constructed by running massive stone walls round the summit or top contour of the hills. The walls, built of large blocks of stone, laid without cement, usually rose from the very edge of the hill, being a continuation of the scarp of the rock. Occasionally, too, walls of masonry appear to have been erected to guard against access at places where the difficulties of the ascent in its natural state might possibly be overcome. The walls were further strengthened by bastions or towers constructed at irregular intervals.[5] But whatever their original character, these hill forts were looked

[1] Ibid. II, 227. [2] Ibid. II, 28-29. [3] Ibid. II, 324-5.

[4] A reference to the history of the forts of Kangra (A. S. R. 1905-6, p. 12 et. seq.), Deogir and Kāliñjar will bear out the truth of the above statement.

[5] See Rajputana Gazetteer, vol. II-A, 1908, p. 101; District Gazetteers of the United Provinces, Vol. XXI, pp. 165-6, 234-5; Eastern States (Bundelkhand) Gazetteer, Vol. VI-A, 1907, 264-5 etc. Stein says that castles in and about Kashmir were built of rough, unhewn stones set in a frame-work of wooden beams, and were therefore liable to rapid decay if once neglected. "This fact is sufficiently illustrated by the wholly ruinous condition of many

upon as the best that the engineering skill of the age could produce. In contemporary estimation they were well-nigh impregnable. This need not cause any surprise. A hill with steep sides might be easily made unapproachable by such cumbrous structures as towers and rats, while the height of the hill, added to the height of the walls, would be too much for besiegers' missiles. If the sides of the hill were precipitous and rocky, mining became impossible and the site was perfect for defence.

Despite this general preference for hill forts, the old practice of creating defensive works around cities in the plains was continued. The account of Hiuen Tsiang, the Chachnāma and other early Muhammadan chronicles go to show that towns, even of a small size, were often enclosed by walls.[1] The most celebrated of these walled towns in northern India at the time of Muhammadan invasion were Delhi, Kanauj, Ajmir, Multan, Jālor (Jālewar), Asnī, Thangar, Kol, Meerut (Mīrāt) etc. The Muhammadan historians have referred to the fortifications of these cities in general terms. Thus Delhi is described as "among the chief (mother) cities of Hind," consisting of "a fortress which in height and breadth had not its equal nor second throughout the length and breadth of the seven climes."[2] Kanauj is said to have had seven detached forts.[3] The fort of Ajmir, "one of the most celebrated in Hind," is spoken of as enclosed with four walls.[4] Regarding Multan, Idrisi says that it was a large city commanded by a citadel, which had four gates and was surrounded by a moat.[5] Kīzwinī speaks of the city as "large, fortified and impregnable."[6]

of the forts which the Sikhs erected on the routes to Kashmir in the early part of this (nineteenth) century." This fact also coupled with the destructive action of the heavy monsoon rains and the equally heavy snowfall to which the southern slopes of the Pir Pantsāl are exposed, accounts for the more or less complete disappearance of the once famous fort of Lohara or Loharakoṭṭa (Stein, *Chronicles of Kashmir,* II, 300).

[1] The Chinese pilgrim says: "The towns and villages have inner gates; the walls are wide and high . . . . The earth being soft and muddy the walls of the towns are mostly built of brick or tiles." Beal, *Life,* I, 73-74. According to the Chachnāma (Elliot. I) the kingdom of Dāhir in Sindh had a large number of well-fortified cities, such as Nīrūn (p. 163), Debal, Lohāna, Lakha, Askalanda (p. 203), Sikka (pp. 142, 203-4), Multan (pp. 142, 204), Shākalha Budapur, Siwistan, Brahmanabad, Rāwar (p. 154), Sisam (p. 159), Bahitlūr (p. 162), Bahrur, Dhalila (p. 174) and Alor (p. 192). The ruins of some of these fortified cities have been described by Lieut.-Col. B. R. Branfill in Ind. Ant. 1882, p. 7 *et seq.*

[2] Elliot. II. 216.
[3] Ibid. II, 46, 458.
[4] Ibid. II, 226.
[5] Ibid. I, 82.
[6] Ibid. I, 96.

Jālor (Jālewar) is described as a strong fort with gates and bastions,[1] and Thangar as a "fortress which assembled a hill of iron."[2]

It must not be supposed for a moment that these walled towns were confined to the north alone. They spread like a net-work over the entire country. Some of them in Kathiawad and Gujerat have been described by Mr. Altekar.[3] Mr. V. Kanakasabhai has likewise described the fortifications of certain ancient towns of the Tamil land, such as Uṛaiyūr, Madurā, Vañchi or Karūr, Kanappār and Takadūr.[4] We are told, for instance, that Madurā was a fortified city. "There were four gates to the fort, surmounted by high towers, and outside the massive walls which were built of rough-hewn stone was a deep moat, and surrounding the moat was a thick jungle of thorny trees. The roads leading to the gates were wide enough to permit several elephants to pass abreast, and on the walls on both sides of the entrance there were all kinds of weapons and missiles concealed, ready to be discharged on an enemy."[5] Likewise, Vañchi was also "strongly fortified, and on the battlements were mounted various engines to throw missiles on those who attacked the fort. Over the gates in the walls were towers plastered with white mortar and adorned with flags. Surrounding the walls was a broad moat in which man-eating alligators of large size abounded."[6] Contemporary epigraphic records also throw light on the defences of a few cities. For instance Kāñcī or Kāñcīpura, the Pallava capital, is thus described in one inscription: "Whose high walls were insurmountable, and hard to be broken, which was surrounded by a huge moat that was unfathomable and hard to be crossed, and which resembled the girdle of the southern region."[7] The Gadral plates of Vikramāditya I refer to the city in almost similar terms.[8] Again, the town of Viḷanam is referred to as follows in the Madras Museum plates of the early Pāṇḍya king, Neḍuñjaḍaiyan (Jaṭilavarman): "Which has the three waters of the sea for its ditch, whose strong and high walls which rub against the inner part of the receding sky, rise so high that the sun has to retire in his course, which is (as strong as) the fort in the beautiful (island of) Ilaṅgai (Laṅkā)."[9]

It is perhaps clear from the above—and this is also the testimony of archeology—that to the last days of our period, the wall

[1] Ibid. II, 238. [2] Ibid. II, 226.
[3] Altekar, *Ancient Towns and Cities of Gujerat and Kathiawad.*
[4] Kanakasabhai, *The Tamils 1800 years ago*, pp. 12-13, 15-16, 24, 86, 100 etc.
[5] Op. cit. [6] Op. cit. [7] Ind. Ant. VI, 77.
[8] Ep. Ind, X, 105. [9] Ind. Ant. XXII, 73-4.

with towers remained the leading idea of fortification. The towers provided flanking fire along the front; they also afforded refuges for the garrison in case of a successful escalade, and from them the platform could be easily enfiladed. Usually, too, but not invariably, the wall was reinforced by a ditch, which had three advantages; it increased the height of the obstacle, made the bringing up of the engines of attack more difficult, and supplied material for the filling of the wall.[1]

V. Siegecraft

The military science of ancient India seems to have been more skilful in defence than in attack. The fortresses of the age could usually withstand the most powerful siege weapons known to the people. Of the tools of siegecraft but little is known. It is probable that the use of scaling ladders and battering rams was known, though there is no clear evidence to prove this.[2] Further, elephants were occasionally employed to batter in the gates of a fort. As stated before, ancient military writers considered this as one of the most important functions of war-elephants. Both Sanskrit and Tamil literature contain allusions to this mode of siegecraft. In the Mahābhārata, for instance, elephants have been described as

[1] As an additional protection strongholds were sometimes surrounded by a thick plantation of thorny trees and shrubs. We are told that the Coḷa capital Uṟaiyūr on the southern bank of the Kaveri "was strongly fortified with a wall and ditch, and a jungle of thorny trees surrounding the ditch." (Kanakasabhai, *The Tamils 1800 years ago*, p. 24; also p. 12, for another instance). In one inscription on the south wall, first tier, of the central shrine at Tañjavur, it is stated that Rājendracoḷa conquered the fort of Vanavāsī, which was "protected by walls of continuous forests" (S. I. I. Vol. III, pt. I, p. 94). Similarly in the Rājat. (VIII. 2260), Kalhaṇa refers to a *giridurga*, "surrounded by a dense forest." 'Utbi says that the advance guard, which Sultan Maḥmūd despatched to attack Kulchand's fort, had to penetrate "through the forest like the comb through a head of hair." (Elliot. II, 43). The same writer has noted the following in connection with the fort Āsī: "Around this fort there was an impenetrable and dense jungle, full of snakes which no enchanters could tame, and so dark that even the rays of the full moon could not be discerned in it. There were broad and deep ditches all around." (Ibid. II, 47).

[2] There is one passage in the Arthaśāstra (Bk. XIII, ch, 4) which may conceal an allusion to battering-rams. The passage runs thus: *"Dāraṁ ca guḍena nimnaṁ vā pāṁsumālayācchādayet. Bahulārakṣaṁ yantrair ghātayet."* *Parigha*, as defined in the Nīti-p. (II, 20; V, 45), probably meant a battering-ram. It is described as "of a round shape, as big as a palmyra-tree, and of good wood. Experts know that a whole troop is required to make it move and strike." Oppert, *Weapons*. p. 22. In earlier usage, however, *parigha* appears to have meant a kind of mace.

pura-bhettārah (town-breakers).[1] The Tamil poetess Avvaiyar speaks of 'brigades of war elephants,' 'with their tusks blunted by battering thy enemy's forts.'[2]

Another device occasionally employed was mining. In Bk. XIII, ch. 4 of the Arthaśāstra, while describing the various devices by which an enemy fort could be captured, Kauṭilya remarks that a besieging king "may assail the rampart and parapets by making use of underground tunnels and iron rods."[3] But it does not seem that mining ever came into general vogue. It is probable that as most of the Indian fortresses were built on high ground or upon a foundation of solid rock, mining was considerd entirely useless as a tool of siege-craft. But the word *suruṅgā* with its military implication continued to be known, and ultimately passed over into Hindi vocabulary. The ordinary Hindi word for a mine is *suraṅg* and *suraṅg urānā* is to spring a mine.[4]

The use of fire, too, for the reduction of a fortified place was not unknown. On this Kauṭilya supplies us with the following account: "Having captured the birds, such as vulture, crow, naptṛ, bhāsa, parrot, maina, and pigeon, which have their nests in the fort walls, and having tied to their tails inflammable powder (*agniyoga*), he may let them fly to the forts. If the camp is situated at a distance from the fort and is provided with an elevated post for archers and their flags, then the enemy's fort may be set on fire. Spies, living as watchmen of the fort, may tie inflammable powder to the tails of mungooses, monkeys, cats and dogs and let them go over the thatched roofs of the houses. A splinter of fire kept in the body of a dried fish may be caused to be carried off by a monkey, or a crow, or any other bird (to the thatched roofs of the houses)."[5] The author further describes the ingredients of

[1] Sabhāparva. 61, 17.

[2] Kanakasabhai, *The Tamils 1800 years ago*, p. 108. The Saṁgāmāvacara Jātaka (Cowell, II, 64-5) thus describes the part played by a state elephant in the capture of Benares: "Winding up his trunks about the shafts of the pillars, he tore them like so many toad-stools; he beat against the gateway, broke down the bars, and forcing his way through, entered the city and won it for his king." Ktesias mentions Indian war-elephants trained to demolish the walls of the enemy. "This they effect," he explains, "by rushing against them at the king's signal, and throwing them down by the overwhelming force with which they press their breasts against them." McCrindle, *Ancient India as described by Ktesias*, p. 35.

[3] *Suraṅgābala-kuṭikābhyāṁ vapra-prākārau hārayet.*

[4] Irvine, *The Army of the Indian Moghuls*, p. 274.

[5] Kauṭ., tr. p. 468.

which various inflammable compounds might be prepared and utilised for setting fire to an enemy fort. But he concludes with the following salutary advice: "When a fort can be captured by other means, no attempt should be made to set fire to it; for fire cannot be trusted; it not only offends gods, but also destroys the people, grains, cattle, gold, raw materials and the like. Also the acquisition of a fort, with its property all destroyed, is a source of further loss."[1] His advice, however, did not always restrain belligerents from resorting to this infamous method. Both literature and inscriptions record instances of towns and fortified places being burnt down by ruthless conquerors. Thus in an inscription of the 29th year of Rājarāja the Great, (dated 1047 A.D.), it is recorded that the Coḷa monarch set fire to Koḷḷippāk, (42 miles from Secunderabad in the Nizam's dominions), one of the capitals of Jayasiṁha.[2] The Pithapuram pillar inscription of Mallapadeva (śaka 1124) states that Guṇaga-Vijayāditya of the Eastern Cālukya dynasty burnt down a place called Cakrakūṭa (probably the same as Cakrakoṭṭa, which appears to have been situated in the dominions of the king of Dhārā, the capital of Mālava).[3] Kalhaṇa (VII. 766-772) records how Vijayamalla, a brother to king Utkarṣa, invested a fortified place and burnt "the houses with his troops, who had fixed fire-brands at the points of their darts." Elsewhere (VIII, 971-1004) the same author describes with harrowing details how during the reign of Sussala, the Ḍāmaras set fire to the famous temple of Cakradhara, in which many people of the neighbourhood "with their women, children, animals, rich stores and property sought an asylum."

But the most usual method employed to get over the resistance of a fortress was by strict investment and starving out. The besiegers tried to cut off the besieged from communication with the outside world, and thus to prevent them from receiving reinforcements or supplies and to make them dependent upon such stores as they may have been able to lay in beforehand, or might be able to produce within the town. In the Mahā-Ummagga Jātaka there is a very realistic description of how king Culani-Brahmadatta besieged the capital of the king of Videha and sought to capture the city by cutting off its water supply.[4] A strict and

[1] Ibid. p. 469.

[2] Ind. Ant. XLVIII, 119.

[3] Ep. Ind. V, 226 *et. seq.* For similar instances, compare Ind. Ant. XII, 221; Ep. Ind. IV, 38, n. 3 etc.

[4] See also Asātarūpa Jātaka (Cowell, *The Jātaka,* II, 243).

protracted blockade often led to the starvation of the garrison, and starvation in its turn to surrender. In the Chachnāma it is related that Rai Chach conquered the fort of Pābiya by following this method. "The chief of the place (Pābiya) gave battle, but after great fighting and bloodshed, the king of Pābiya fled and entered the fort. Rai Chach was victorious, and encamped in the field of battle for a time. When the store of provisions was exhausted, and grass and wood and fuel were all consumed, the enemy being in distress left the fort at the time when the world had covered itself with the blanket of darkness, and the king of the stars concealed himself in the gloom of the night."[1] The Rājataraṅginī also provides us with several instances of this sort. When king Harṣa (1089-1101 A.D.), for instance, laid siege to the fort of Pṛthvīgiri, he sought to starve out the garrison. "When he had stopped there for more than a month, the defenders of the fort became distressed owing to their food and other supplies being exhausted. How large were not the tribute and supplies which king Saṁgrāmapāla offered in order to save that garrison?" Harṣa was obstinate and rejected those offers. Thereupon the besieged chieftain bribed an officer of the hostile army, who instigated the soldiers to claim a marching allowance and thus fall into disorder, and at the same time spread a false and alarming report of an attack from the Turuṣkas. Harṣa was thus compelled to raise the siege and march off.[2] On another occasion an attempt to take the fort of Dugdhaghāta by starvation was frustrated by a sudden fall of snow.[3] But the investment of the castle of Śiraḥśilā by Dhanya was more successful. At the outset Dhanya took up his position on the bank of the Mudhumatī, near Śardi. And "though the troops thus stoutly kept their ground for three or four months, yet they were unable to seize those who were in the castle, because no such acts of hostility, as the cutting off of food supplies by means of an investment were undertaken, which might have reduced those arrogant (opponents) to straits." But Dhanya soon perceived this loophole and, moving his troops closer to the castle, occupied its main approach. Here he fortified his position, and constructing a line of block-houses round the castle-ridge from the south, effectually cut off the besieged rebels from the scanty supplies they were previously able to collect from the neighbouring hamlets. "Then unceasing encounters ensued at

[1] Elliot. I, 141.
[2] Rājat. VIII. 1158-59.
[3] Ibid. VII. 1181-1191.

every moment in which both sides lost countless men . . . . Those in the castle were few, while those in the (besieging) camp were many. Hence the former, though they killed many, were easily made to suffer. After the castle had been harassed with two or three assaults, it appeared with the closed folds of its gates as if shutting its eyes from fear. Those in the castle lost their confidence when they saw that Dhanya and other (ministers) were trying to win over the guards, create internal dissension and otherwise take advantage of a weak point. At night they did not sleep but shouted to each other to keep themselves awake. In the daytime, again, when they slept, they made the castle appear silent and deserted. Even the sound of the kettle-drums (beaten) by the several corps between the night-watchs, made them tremble at night, as the thunder (makes tremble) the sparrows in the hollows of the trees. The royal troops kept them in excitement day and night by all possible means and blocked (their access to) the water by boats which were moving about. Cut off from the river, they put up somehow with the pain of thirst, but they became disheartened when their foodsupply became exhausted owing to their inability to get outside."[1] Thus cut off from supplies, and deprived of water, the Ḍāmara lord of the castle agreed through messengers "to sell the king's enemies."[2]

As the investment of a fortress did not in general consist of anything beyond a blockade, sieges were often long and protracted. It is stated in the Chachnāma that the siege of Akhan Lohāna by Rai Chach "lasted for the period of one year."[3] After the first battle of Tarain in 1191 A.D. the Rajputs under Pṛthvīrāj laid siege to the fort of Sarhind; but it took them thirteen months to compel the garrison to capitulate.[4]

The methods of repelling a siege or assualt must have varied from age to age, and to some extent, from locality to locality. The Śāntiparva enjoins that on the occasion of a siege all thatch-covered houses within the fort should be plastered with mud as a protection against fire.[5] According to Kauṭilya, all possible impediments were to be placed before the enemy to prevent a close investment. Grass and firewood round the fortress were to be set on fire and destroyed as far as a *yojana* (five and five-fortyfourth miles); all water channels or pools were also to be either destroyed or vitiated; and a system of secret wells, hidden pits and barbed iron cords

[1] Ibid. VIII. 2509-2566.
[2] Ibid. VIII. 2598.
[3] Elliot. I, 147.
[4] Ibid. II. 296.
[5] Śāntiparva, 69, 47.

should be devised all around the fort.[1] From his chapter on *Āyudhāgārādhyakṣa* (Bk. II, ch. 18) it appears that heavy, immovable machines, worked by mechanical power, were placed over the gates and walls, kept in readiness for projecting large shafts at the foe or dumping rocks upon them. But the evidence of the early Muhammadan chroniclers proves that either these machines were crude and ineffective or that in general and except for the arrows, stones and other missiles thrown from the walls against the attackers, the defenders trusted rather to the size and strength of their walls and tried little in the way of an active defence.

As against mining, the best device which the besieged could employ was to countermine, and then attack the diggers below ground, drive them back, and fill up the hole they had excavated. The term for the countermine was *prati-suruṅgā*. We have the following account in the Arthaśāstra as to how and when it was to be constructed. "When the enemy attempts to dig an underground tunnel for the capture of the fort, the besieged should dig a ditch inside the walls so deep as to make water come out of the earth. If the digging of a ditch is considered impracticable, a number of wells may be constructed along the walls. In suspicious places along the parapet, empty pots or bronze vessels may be placed in order to find out the direction in which a tunnel is being dug by the enemy. When the direction of the tunnel is discovered, a counter-tunnel should be constructed; or having made a hollow passage to the tunnel, it may be filled with poisonous smoke or water."[2]

When the fort was on an eminence and stones were available in plenty, these latter were stored and rolled down the slopes upon the besiegers. As already mentioned, one of the reasons which Kauṭilya adduces in favour of hill-forts was the enormous advantage of this method of defence. We find an early instance of this kind in the defence of Aornos against Alexander. Curtius says: "As the barbarians rolled down massive stones upon them while they climbed, such as were struck fell headlong from their insecure and slippery positions."[3] The chronicle of Kalhaṇa shows that in Kashmir, where fortresses were almost invariably constructed on hills, this was a favourite mode of defence. In connection with the siege of Dugdhaghāta (VII, 1181), for instance, we are told

[1] *Tṛṇa-kāṣṭham ā yojanād dāhayet. Udakāni ca dūṣayet : avāsrāvayecca. Kūtakūpāvapātakaṇṭakinīśca bahirujjayet.* Kauṭ. Bk. XII, ch. 5.

[2] Kauṭ. Bk. XII, ch. 5.

[3] McCrindle, *India and its invasion by Alexander*, p. 199.

that the defenders (Darad soldiers) "threw down big boulders and other missiles" on their assailants. A more detailed account of the use and effect of this mode of defence is given in connection with the siege of Bānaśālā. "The royal troops were throwing stones from catapults, showers of arrows and various (other) missiles. And those in the castle defended themselves by rolling down stones. The royal army, though large, could not attack those in the castle, while stones were falling and arrows marked with Bhikṣu's name . . . Notwithstanding their great number they were so repulsed by the hail of stones from those (in the castle) that they became convinced of this (undertaking) not being achievable by sheer prowess. The heads which the stones carried off from the bodies of brave soldiers, appeared, with their streams of blood, like bee-hives, (thrown down by stone-hits) from the tops of trees with bees rising from them."[1]

Rājat. VIII, 1677-78, 1685-86. The use of stones continued as a favourite mode of defence for many centuries to come. Fryer saw "on the tops of the mountains, several fortresses of Seva Gi's, only defensible by Nature, needing no other artillery but stones, which they tumble down upon their foes, carrying as certain destruction as bullets where they alight." Fryer, *A New Account of East India and Persia*, p. 127.

CHAPTER XIV

NOTES ON ARMS AND ARMOUR

Like the history of fortification, the history of the development of arms and armour goes back to the remotest antiquity. Among the numerous objects of interest, which have been unearthed at Mohenjo-Dāro and Harappā, there have been discovered weapons of war and of the chase. It would seem that the chief weapons used by the people of the Indus valley were axes, spears, daggers, bows and arrows, maces, slings, and possibly—though not probably—catapults. But they do not appear to have known the use of defensive armours such as shields, helmets or greaves. At least, no trace of any of these has been discovered. The materials of which most of the weapons were made were either copper or bronze.[1]

In the succeeding ages numerous other weapons came into vogue. Some of these held the field for a time, and were superseded by other, more efficient prototypes. Some, again, in varying forms, outlasted the shocks of centuries and remained a permanent feature of the Indian military system. On the whole, it would seem that like many other things of life, arms and weapons underwent a gradual process of evolution. For instance, the sword which was not known to the people of Mohenjo-Dāro and Harappā, and, it would seem, rarely used by the Vedic Aryans, became one of the principal weapons of India in the post-Vedic period. The bow, which was a wooden staff bent into a curved shape in the Ṛgvedic period, was developed into a highly finished composite apparatus in later centuries. Moreover, with the advance of knowledge in science and metallurgy, powerful projectile machines worked by mechanical power appear to have been discovered and used in both offensive and defensive warfare. Such were the *yantras* and *mahā-yantras* mentioned in the epics, the Arthaśāstra and later literature.

[1] Sir John Marshall, *Mohenjo-Dāro and the Indus Civilisation*, I, 35-36; II, chs. 24 and 25.

Ancient writers have classified arms and weapons under certain heads. The Mahābhārata,[1] for instance, speaks of a four-fold classification of arms, but does not indicate the principle on which it is based. In the Arthaśāstra (Bk. II, ch. 18), Kauṭilya divides arms as engines of war, weapons with pointed ends like plough-shares, bows, swords, razor-bladed weapons, stones and armours. The Agni Purāṇa (249, 2), again, classifies weapons under five heads, viz., those thrown by machines (*yantra-mukta*), those thrown by the hand (*pāṇi-mukta*), those thrown and drawn back (*mukta-sandhārita*), those not thrown (*amukta*), and natural weapons such as the fist. Omitting the last, which is purely theoretical, the practical division is four-fold, and is probably the same as that referred to in the Mahābhārata. The Yukti-kalpataru of Bhoja divides weapons into two classes, viz., deceitful (*māyikaṁ*) and non-deceitful (*nirmāyaṁ*). The former is illustrated by combustibles (*dahanādikaṁ*) and the latter by weapons like the sword (*khaḍgādikaṁ*).[2] In the Nīti-prakāśikā (II, 11-13), again, arms are divided according to their nature into *mukta* (thrown), *amukta* (not thrown), *muktāmukta* (thrown or not thrown), and *mantra-mukta* (thrown by means of spells). These four classes of arms, the author adds, constituted the four feet of the Dhanur-veda.

For the purpose of the present study, we cannot accept the above classifications, each of which we realise on reflection is defective in one way or another. We may, therefore, more conveniently divide arms under two heads, viz., offensive and defensive. Offensive arms may, again, be subdivided into (*a*) missiles and (*b*) 'short' arms, those used at close quarters, corresponding to the European '*arme blanche*.'

I OFFENSIVE WEAPONS

1. Bow

The origin of the bow is lost in the mists of obscurity. The discovery of a number of copper and bronze arrow-heads at Mohenjo-Dāro and Harappā proves that the use of the weapon was known to the people of the Indus valley about the third or fourth millennium B.C. The evidence of comparative philology shows that the Indo--Aryans were acquainted with archery even

[1] Vanaparva 308, 11 has *astragrāmaṁ caturvidhaṁ.* Karṇaparva 7, 6 has *yasmin mahāstrāṇi samarpitāni citrāṇi śubhrāṇi caturvidhāni.* The same four-fold division is also referred to in the Śiśupālavadha XVIII, 11.

[2] Yukti-kalpataru, p. 140, vv. 30-31.

before they settled down in India. For, the names of the bow, bow-string and arrow are the same in Indo-Iranian and in part appear Indo-European.[1] The Ṛgveda is replete with references to the bow and arrow,[2] and Macdonell and Keith suggest that practically no other weapon played any substantial part in Vedic warfare.[3]

Starting from that dim past the bow had a continuous history in India till the beginning of the nineteenth century. It was only after the introduction of hand fire-arms, and the gradual extension of their use that it was ousted from its position as one of the leading military weapons of the country.[4] Throughout the ancient period, however, it was the weapon *par excellence* of the Hindus. It gave its name to military science (*dhanur-veda*),[5] and proficiency in its use was the measure of a man's reputation as a warrior.

The earliest bow must have been a very simple instrument made of bamboo, cane or wood. During the Vedic period, it was "composed of a stout staff bent into a curved shape (Av. iv. 6, 4)

[1] The arrow, Sanskrit *iṣu* = Avestan *iṣu* = Greek *iós*. Bow and bow-string are Indo-Iranian.

[2] E.g. Ṛv. ii, 24, 8; viii, 7, 4; 72, 4; ix. 99; x. 18, 9; 125, 6, etc.

[3] Vedic Index I, 388. The following prayer of Pāyu in the Ṛv. VI, 75, 2 ff. is an eloquent commentary on the esteem in which the weapon was held:

"With Bow let us win kine, with Bow the battle,
with Bow the victors in our hot encounters.
The Bow brings quiet and sorow to the foeman;
armed with Bow may we subdue all regions."

[4] It should be noted, however, that the use of the bow persisted throughout the eighteenth century, in spite of fire-arms having become extremely common by that time. In his *Reminiscences of the Great Mutiny* (p. 76), W. Forbes Mitchell says that he saw the bow being used by the rebels at the second relief of Lucknow in Nov., 1857.

[5] The use of the bow is referred to in countless ancient books and inscriptions. A collection of these references may easily form a separate volume. A few of these may be cited here at random. Cf., e.g., The Jātaka, Cowell's tr., No 68, 181, 465, 522, 539, etc. In the Saṁyutta Nikāya (P. T. S. II, 267-8), the Licchavis are described as "diligent (*appamatta*), zealous and active in archery." In the Sūtrālaṅkāra, Aśvaghoṣa includes archery in a list of subjects which a prince should carefully study. For references to the use of the bow in the epics, see J. A. O. S. XIII, 269 ff. In his XIIIth Rock Edict, Aśoka speaks of "*śarasake vijaye*," indicating thereby that victories in battles were achieved primarily through the instrumentality of bows and arrows. For a few other epigraphic references to the use of the bow in ancient warfare, see C. I. I. III, 12, 56, 207, etc.; Ep. Ind. I, 87, 132, 302, 312; II, 233; III, 57; IV, 314 ff.; VI, 34; XVII, 304 ff.; Ind. Ant. XI, 17; South Ind. Inscr. 1, 21 ff., 153; III, 63 etc. Kings are often referred to as distinguished archers. Comp., e.g., Ep. Ind. VIII, 61; Ind. Ant. XXII,

and of a bow-string made of a strip of cow-hide (Ṛv. vi. 67, 11; Av. i. 2, 3)."[1]

The Jātakas frequently refer to the ram's-horn bow, though it is likely that bamboo and wooden bows were also in use.[2] In the Arthaśāstra (Bk. II. ch. 18), Kauṭilya specifies palmyra (*tāla*), bamboo (*cāpa*), wood (*dāru*) and horn (*śṛṅga*) as the chief materials out of which bows in his age were made. Bows made of palmyra were known as *kārmuka*,[3] those of bamboo as *kodaṇḍa*, those of wood as *drūṇa*, while horn bows were called *dhanu*. Bow-strings were made of *mūrvā* (Sansaviera Roxburghiana) *arka* (Calotropis Gigantea), *śaṇa* (hemp), *gavedhu* (Coix Barbata), *veṇu* (bamboo bark) and *snāyu* (sinew).

The Śiva-Dhanur-veda mentions two kinds of bows, one made of bamboo (*vāṁśam*) and the other of horn (*śārṅgam*).[4] It lays down that bows of bamboo should consist of three, five, seven or nine knots. Those having four, six or eight knots should be discarded.[5] The bow-string, according to the same authority, should be made from silk-thread (*paṭṭa-sūtrāḥ*) twisted into a cord. It must be three-stranded, round, smooth and of the size of the little finger throughout. In the absence of silk-thread, Śiva recommends the sinews of deer and buffaloes as also cords prepared from the thongs of the fresh skin of goats for strings. He further adds that a good string could be made of the outer rind of bamboo with a silk-thread twisted round it. Fibres of *arka* (Calotropis Gigantea) might also be turned into a string of considerable strength.[6]

The Agni Purāṇa (245, 4 ff.) supplies us with the following account of the materials for the construction of the bow: "Bows are made of three things, viz. metal, horn and wood. The string of a bow is likewise made of three substances, viz., rattan (*vaṁśa*), hemp, (*bhaṅga*) and hide (*tvac*). The best bow is four cubits

78; ibid. V, 317; Ep. Ind. V, 187; also the 15th verse of the Pāṭa-Nārāyaṇa Stone Inscription of the Paramāra Pratāpasiṁha (of which, unfortunately, I have lost the reference).

[1] Vedic Index I, 388 ff.

[2] Cf. Khaṇḍahāla Jātaka (No. 68) and Sarabhaṅga Jātaka (No. 522).

[3] Hopkins derived *kārmuka* from *kṛmuka*, and thought that the latter was kind of wood of which bows were made. J. A. O. S. XIII, 269. This is obviously wrong, as the above statement in the Arthaśāstra proves.

[4] Vāśiṣṭha Dhanur-veda Saṁhitā, p. 11, v. 47; Śārṅgadhara Paddhati, No. 1760. It should be noted that the Bengal edition of Vaś. is only referred to. The relevant passage in the Bombay edition may be easily found.

[5] Vaś. p. 9, vv. 35-6; Śār. No. 1749-50.

[6] Vaś. pp. 12-13, vv. 50-56; Śār. No. 1761-1767.

long, the medium bow three and a half cubits, and the inferior bow only three cubits. The bow-stave is to be so prepared that it may not have any uneveness from its centre to the extremities. In order that it may be firmly held, a spare piece of wood should be fixed at the centre of the bow-stave. The ends of the bow should be made thin and tapering so as to resemble the eye-brows of a handsome woman. Metal and horn bows should be made either of iron or horn separately or of the two substances conjointly. The horn-bow should be well-shaped and decked with gold. Bows which are crooked or have cracks or holes in them are not good. The metal-bow is to be made of gold, silver, copper and black iron (steel). Horn-bows made out of the horns of buffaloes, *śarabha* and *rohiṣa* are praiseworthy. Bows are also made of sandal wood, rattan, sal wood *dhānvana* (a king of Hedyserum) and *kukubha* (Pentapterá arjuna). But the bow made of bamboo, which grows in autumn and which is cut and taken at that time, is the best of all."

It is quite probable that originally wooden and bamboo bows were alone used, and horn bows were later inventions. In search after materials to improve the casting power of the bow, man would naturally be struck by the elastic properties of the horns of animals. The combined testimony of the Jātakas, the epics and the Arthaśāstra of Kauṭilya proves that horn-bows had come into use in India before the beginning of the Christian era.[1] Probably the bow of pure horn was the link between the wooden bow and the composite bow of a later age. In making a bow of horn, whether of a pair of horns or of a single large horn, like that of a baffalo, split up to make the two limbs, the bow when made and unstrung would naturally take the shape of the horns when growing on the animal's head. It would at once be seen that the only way to get any spring from the bow would be to bend them the reverse way of the natural curve. Thus we have the reflex bow. This particular characteristic of the horn bows, viz. that they were drawn in the reverse direction to the curve which they assume when unstrung, will explain some of the otherwise inexplicable stories recorded in the epics.[2]

The passage quoted above from the Agni Purāṇa shows that the bow was sometimes made of iron; but the recoil of this, or,

[1] Vide supra. The bow of Viṣṇu in the Mahābhārata is called *śārṅga*. See J. A. O. S. XIII, 269.

[2] The stories emphasise the inability of renowned heroes to bend and string certain bows. Comp. e.g. the *svayamvara* episode of Draupadī.

indeed of any metal is so slow in comparison with that obtained from other materials, that a bow which would give the requisite swiftness of flight would be beyond the power of the strongest man to draw. Metal bows are, therefore, nowhere extolled and they do not seem to have ever come into general use in ancient India.

There are two passages in the Agni Purāṇa which suggest the existence of composite bows in the later centuries of our period. One of these runs to the effect that bows might be made of horn and iron conjointly. In the other we are told that the middle part of a bow should be joined with a spare piece of wood.[1] Now, the main constituents of the composite bow are three-fold—viz. horn, being a compressible substance for the belly; wood or metal to give stiffness to the centre; and sinew for the back, to give elasticity and 'cast.' The reticence of the Agni Purāṇa concerning this additional backing of sinews no doubt weakens, but by no means precludes, our inference. The double-curve bows portrayed in some Sānchi reliefs and on Gupta coins appear, in all probability, to have been of the composite form. The curve of these bows when fully drawn (illustrated, for instance, in the Lion-slayer and the Tiger-slayer types of Gupta coins) seems to be only practicable with those which are made of materials far more elastic and less liable to fracture than any wood.

It may be naturally asked as to why even after the development of horn and composite bows, the Agni Purāṇa so highly extols bows made of bamboo. The answer to this question is, no doubt, partially found in the elastic properties of bamboo. But the more important reason appears to have been that a highly finished horn or composite bow would always be an expensive weapon, whereas bamboo bows, though less effective, would be more easily come by.

Ancient writers throw some light on the length and size of bows. Hopkins points out that in the Mahābhārata the bow is "several times spoken of as *tālamātra* or palm-long, which, when compared with the numerical qualification employed in *saḍaratni*, may probably be interpreted as six cubits in length."[2] Elsewhere we have recorded a statement of Arrian that the bow carried by the infantry in the fourth century B.C. was of the same length as the bow-man.[3] Some of the bows represented at Sānchi appear to

[1] A separate piece of metal or wood fixed to the centre of the bow-stave is also referred to in the Śiśupālavadha XX, 12.

[2] J. A. O. S. XIII, 270. [3] See ch. III.

have been of this size, but others were shorter.[1] The Śiva-Dhanurveda contains the following rules regarding length and size of a bow: "A good bow is that which is a little less strong than its bearer. For that which is precious is not the bow, but the bow-man. If he is troubled by the bow, he cannot shoot with ease (lit. does not see his target). Hence the size of a good bow should be in proportion to the strength of its bearer. The bow which measures five and a half cubits is recognised to be the best. Of this length was the heavenly bow which Śaṅkara held in yore. Twenty-four *aṅgulas* make one cubit (*hasta*), and four cubits make one bow (*dhanu*). If the bow used by man be of this length, it should be considered auspicious . . . According to some authorities, however, the bow should measure nine *vitastis* (4½ cubits)."[2] A little further on the author says: "The weapon *par excellence* of Viṣṇu is his horn-bow. It was made by Viśvakarman and measures seven *vitastis* (3½ cubits). The horn-bow used by man for long many years is six and a half *vitastis* (3¼ cubits) in length."[3]

From the preceding quotations it is abundantly clear that the length of a Hindu bow usually varied from 3¼ cubits to 4½ cubits. It appears further that, generally speaking, horn bows were shorter than wooden or bamboo bows. Both the Śiva-Dhanurveda and the Agni Purāṇa recommend four cubits as the most appropriate length of bows. Thus, by a process of expansion in meaning, the word '*dhanus*' came to signify a measurement of four cubits (*hastas*).

Arrow and Quiver

The shaft of an arrow was usually made of *sara* reed (saccharum sara), sometimes also of wood and bamboo.[4] A butt (*puṅkha*) was often added to the shaft for the purpose of making a securer notch.[5]

[1] Cunningham, *Bhilsa Topes,* p. 216. The bows portrayed on Gupta coins seem to have been about 5½ feet in length.

[2] Vaś. pp. 8-9, vv. 30-34, 37; Śār. No. 1742-1745, 1748, 1750.

[3] Vaś. p. 11, vv. 44, 46; Śār. No. 1757, 1759.

[4] Besides the statement of Kauṭilya on the point (already quoted), comp. Droṇaparva 97, 7; Ag. P. 245, 12, etc. The Śiva-Dhanurveda contains a few rules regarding the preparation of the shaft. See Vaś. pp. 14-15, vv. 56-59; Śār. No. 1768-1770.

[5] The butt is often referred to as "gilded.' Comp. e.g., Virāṭa-parva 43, 15, where we have '*hema-puṅkhāḥ*'; Raghuvaṁśa III, 64 which mentions '*suvarṇa-puṅkha.*' Maisey's Pl. XXII shows that some of the arrows represented at Sāñchi are provided with butts.

An arrow was usually feathered for the purpose of stabilising its flight. The Śiva-Dhanurveda recommends the feathers of the following birds for arrows : heron (*kaṅka*),[1] goose (*haṁsa*), brown hawk (*śaśada*), osprey (*matsyāda-krauñca*), peacock, vulture and wild cock (*kukkuṭa*).[2] The Mahābhārata mentions all these and the feathers of flamingos besides.[3] The number of feathers preferred appears to have been usually four, and they were fastened by means of threads and sinews (*snāyu-tantubhiḥ*).[4] The feathers were generally trimmed six inches long, but those stuck up in arrows meant to be shot from a horn bow measured ten *aṅgulis*.[5]

The head of an arrow was usually tipped with horn, bone, wood or metal. Kauṭilya (Bk. II, ch. 18) mentions arrow-heads made of metal, bone or wood so "as to cut, rend or pierce." The Droṇaparva (188, 11 ff.) gives a list of forbidden weapons and mentions, *inter alia*, arrow-heads made of monkey-bone, cow-bone and elephant-bone. The Śiva-Dhanurveda says : "There are numerous kinds of arrow-heads, assuming different shapes in different regions, such as *ārāmukha* (head shaped like an awl) *kṣurapra* (head having a razor-like barb), *gopuccha* (head resembling a cow's tail), *ardha-candra* (crescent-shaped head), *sūcīmukha* (needle-shaped head), *bhalla* (broad-headed [?]), *vatsa-danta* (head shaped like a calf's tooth), *dvibhalla* (?), *karṇika* (ear-shaped head), and *kāka-tuṇḍa* (head shaped like a crow's beak)."[6]

Occasionally, it would seem, arrows had ignited matter wrapped round the point. In the Arthaśāstra (Bk. XIII, ch. 4), Kauṭilya gives three different recipes for the preparation of fire-arrows. In

1. Vaś. reads *kāka* (crow).
2. Vaś. reads *kurara* (female osprey).
3. Virāṭa-parva 42, 10 mentions *śuka-patra*. Vulture's feathers (*gārdhra-patra*) are mentioned in Droṇaparva 119, 42; 125, 28 etc. Feathers of *kaṅkas* and peacocks are mentioned in Karṇaparva 24, 21; Droṇaparva 125, 29. Raghuvaṁśa III, 56 has *mayurpatriṇā śareṇa*.
4. Vaś. p. 16, v. 62; Śār. No. 1772, 1773; also Ag. P. 245, 12 where we have '*snāyu-śliṣṭāḥ supatrakāḥ*.'
5. Vaś. p. 15, v. 61; Śār. No. 1772-3.
6. Vaś. p. 16, vv. 64-5; Śār. N. 1777-8. Most of these names occur also in the epics. For a detailed analysis, see J. A. O. S. XIII, 275 ff. Some of these are also mentioned in later Sanskrit works such as the Raghuvaṁśa (III, 59; IV, 63, 77; XI, 29), Mat. P. (149, 77), etc. The classical authors say that the arrow by which Alexander was wounded within the stronghold of the Sudracae (Kṣudrakas) was tipped with a barbed head. Cf. McCrindle, *India and its invasion by Alexander*, p. 241. Plutarch (ibid. p. 312) adds: "This arrow-head is said to have measured three fingers' breadths in width and four in length."

a well-known passage (VII, 90), Manu condemns the use of fiery arrows in civilised warfare, indirectly proving thereby that these were known. The later Mānasollāsa, on the other hand, recommends the use of arrows carrying burning matter, especially against elephants.[1] The Rājataraṅgiṇī (VII, 982-3) records an actual instance of the use of "burning arrows smeared over with vegetable oil, struck by which the enemies caught fire."

Arrows built entirely of iron were known as *nārāca.* We find mention of these in the Jātakas,[2] the Mahābhārata,[3] the Artha-śāstra (Bk. II, ch. 18), the Agni Purāṇa (245, 12) and a multitude of other works. The Śiva-Dhanurveda says that the *nārācas* were built entirely of iron, that five big feathers were attached to them, and that only the strongest archers could shoot with them.[4] There are reasons to think that these arrows were specially employed in fighting against elephants.[5]

Sometimes the shaft of an arrow bore the name of the archer inscribed upon it. The practice is referred to in the Droṇa-parva (169, 36), the Raghuvaṁśa (III, 35; VII, 38), the Pātāla-khaṇḍa (29, 88) and the Rājataraṅgiṇī (VIII, 1678).

The size and length of arrows seem to have varied considerably. In the Śatapatha Brāhmaṇa (VII, 5, 2, 10), the length of an arrow is stated to be five spans, about three feet.[6] In the Mahābhārata, the normal length is said to be equal to that of an axle of the war-car.[7] According to Strabo, Indian arrows in the Mauryan period were nearly three cubits long.[8] Cunningham maintains that the arrows represented in the Sānchi reliefs appear to be from three to five feet in length.[9] The Śiva-Dhanurveda describes the length of an arrow as two cubits or two cubits subtracted by a *muṣṭi* (fist), and its girth as equal to that of the little finger.[10] According to the Agni Purāṇa (249, 36), again, an arrow of the

[1] Mānas. v. 1213; comp. also vv. 1065 and 1067.

[2] Cowell, *The Jātaka,* No. 68 and 522.

[3] See J. A. O. S. XIII, 279.

[4] Vaś. p. 19, v. 73; Śār. No. 1787.

[5] Cf. Bhīṣma-parva 57, 13; Karṇa-parva 22, 5; Śiśupālavadha XVIII, 4. Kauṭilya mentions another variety of arrow, called *daṇḍāsana.* The commentator explains it as *ardha-nārāca.*

[6] Vedic Index I, 82.

[7] Droṇaparva 164, 18: "*rathākṣa-mātrairiṣubhiḥ.*"

[8] McCrindle, *Ancient India,* p. 73.

[9] Cunningham, *Bhilsa Topes,* p. 216.

[10] Vaś. p. 14, v. 59; Śār. No. 1770.

best class should measure twelve *muṣṭis* in length, while the Nītiprakāśikā (I, 17; IV, 28-9) maintains that it should be three cubits long and an *añjali* (the hollow of the two palms) in circumference. It may be inferred, therefore, that arrows usually varied from two to three cubits in length. Shorter arrows were probably meant for close and longer ones for distant combat.[1]

Direct references to the range of arrow shots are seldom available.[2] The Śiva-Dhanurveda, however, throws some light on the subject. While discussing the question of the distance at which the target for practice is to be located, the author says that "the target placed at a distance of 60 *dhanus* (240 cubits) is the best, that placed at a distance of 40 *dhanus* (160 cubits) is of medium quality, while one located only 20 *dhanus* (80 cubits) apart from the bowman is inferior."[3] It may be inferred from this that the distance which an arrow could traverse with force and efficacy was about 120 yards. Similarly, from another passage dealing with *nārāca*-shooting, it may be inferred that the range of the flight of an iron arrow was about 90 yards.[4]

The archer usually carried his arrows in one or two quivers slung over his shoulder.[5] Hopkins says that the quiver was fastened on the right of the back, and that it held from ten to twenty arrows.[6] The Sānchi reliefs seem to confirm this view.[7] The quiver was sometimes decorated with the figures of animals and birds.[8]

2. Yantras

Yantra is a generic term, often loosely used to denote "a contrivance of almost any kind." In the Mahābhārata, as Hopkins

[1] Droṇaparva 122, 53 ff. describes a class of arrows, "one span long" and specifically meant for fighting at close quarters.

[2] Droṇaparva 97, 9 seems to imply that arrows could be fired across as far as two miles (*krośam-atikrānte*). But this is hardly credible, and certainly an exaggeration.

[3] Vaś. p. 27, v. 6; Śār. No. 1819.

[4] Vaś. p. 27, v. 7; Śār. N. 1820. (The first line is left out in Vaś., probably owing to copyist's oversight).

[5] The normal practice was to carry one quiver only. But sometimes two were also carried. The dual use of the term *iṣudhi* and *tūṇa* in many passages of the Mahābhārata may be explained only on this assumption. Comp. e.g., Ādiparva, 225, 22, 32; Udyogaparva, 60, 12; Śalyaparva, 62, 9; Rām. Ayodhyākāṇḍa, 65, 17, etc.

[6] J. A. O. S. XIII, 274.

[7] Cunningham, *Bhilsa Topes*, p. 215.

[8] Comp., e.g., Virāṭaparva, 43, 15.

points out, it is used to denote a restrainer or protector, and serves as an armour or holder of a fastening, as the rope of the holder of a banner. It is part of the trappings of a war-car, the bands of the chariot: it is used to sail a boat with, and is even a drumstick.[1] In the Arthaśāstra it is found among the war accoutrements of elephants (Bk. II, ch. 32), and also among the surgical instruments used by physicians in the discharge of their professional duty (Bk. X, ch. 3).

But the *yantras* were also employed as military implements. In the Arthaśāstra (Bk. II, ch. 18), Kauṭilya speaks of two varieties of *yantras*, viz. *sthira* (immovable) and *cala* (movable), but both implements of war. In the epics and the Purāṇas, these along with *śataghnīs* are frequently mentioned as posted on the walls and gates of forts and fortified towns. In the Sabhāparva (5, 36), for instance, a sage asks a king: "Are your forts always filled with treasure, food, weapons, water, *yantras*, mechanics and archers?" In the Śānti-parva (69, 45), Bhīṣma enjoins that heavy *yantras* (*guruṇyeva yantrāṇi*) should be placed on the gates of fortresses (*dvāreṣu*). Moreover, the usual descriptions of towns in the epics inevitably leave the impression on the reader's mind that like the walls and moats, the *yantras* formed a part and parcel of the Hindu conception of fortification.[2] In the Agni Purāṇa (241, 28), it is stated that "that fort is said to be in distress in which the *yantras*, walls and moats are in a state of disrepair, and where the garrison is dwindling in number."

[1] J. A. O. S. XIII, 301. In the Laṅkā-kāṇḍa (22, 36) the term is used to denote an engine for carrying heavy stones:

Hastimātrān mahākāyāḥ pāṣāṇāṁśca mahā-balāḥ
Parvatāṁśca samutpāṭya yantraiḥ parivahanti ca.

Mr. Date (p. 92) refers to this verse in support of his theory that the *śataghnī* and *yantra*, between which he makes no distinction, were engines for throwing stones. That the *śataghnī* was an altogether different kind of weapon, and was never employed for throwing stones on the enemy, will be evident from the discussion under that heading.

[2] Cf. Rām. Ayodhyākāṇḍa, 5, 10: Vanaparva 15, 5; ibid. 283, 3-4, where we have a typical account of the defensive arrangements of a city:

Agādha-toyāḥ parikhā mīnanakra-samākulāḥ
Babhūvuḥ sapta durdharṣāḥ khādiraiḥ śaṅkubhiścitāḥ
Kapāṭa-yantra-durdharṣāḥ babhūvuḥ sahuḍopalāḥ
Āśī-viṣa-ghaṭā ghorāḥ sasarjara-sapāṁśavaḥ

Here the *kapāṭa-yantras* seem to be engines to guard the doors, and the following words indicate that they were designed to cast balls and stones. Cf. also *Abhilaṣitārtha-cintāmaṇi* (ed. by Dr. R. Shamasastry, Mysore, 1926), p. 96: *durge yantrāṇi kāryāṇi nānā-praharaṇāni ca.*

The question, therefore, naturally arises as to what were these *yantras* so often stated in the epic and post-epic literature as forming an essential part of a city's defence. We are inclined to believe that these were of the nature of catapults and ballistae used by the ancient Hebrews, Greeks and Romans in their warfare. Like them, these engines were enormous in size, and were used for propelling large arrows and stones. As already stated, Kauṭilya speaks of two varieties of *yantras*. Of these the "immovable" variety consisted of the following engines of war:

1. Sarvatobhadra.	4. Viśvāsaghāti.	7. Parjanyaka.
2. Jāmadagnya.	5. Saṁghāṭī.	8. Ardhabāhu.
3. Bahumukha.	6. Yānaka.	9. Ūrdhva-bāhu.

Kauṭilya himself does not say what exactly was the nature and purpose of these engines, save and beyond that they were enormous and heavy, and hence immovable. But the gap left by him has been filled in by his commentator. Thus *sarvatobhadra* is explained as "a cart with wheels and capable of rapid revolution." And then follows the remark: "This, when rotated, throws stones in all directions." *Jāmadagnya*, he says, was an engine to shoot large arrows (*mahāśara-yantra*); *bahumukha* "a tower situated on the top of a fort and provided with a leather cover," altogether so devised as to enable a number of archers to direct their arrows in all directions; and *viśvāsaghāti* "a cross-beam at the entrance of a city, and so placed as to be caused to fall down and kill enemies when approaching." The others have been similarly explained. Thus *saṅghāṭī* was a long pole to set fire to *aṭṭālaka* and other parts of a fort; *yānaka* a pole or rod mounted on a wheel so as to be thrown against enemies; *parjanyaka* a water-machine to put out fire, and so on and so forth.

It is obvious from the above that the *yantras* were of various kinds and were used for different purposes. But if the interpretation of the commentator can be relied upon, the first two in the above list were very similar to the ballista and the catapult as used in ancient and medieval Europe. And it is necessary to emphasise that we have no right to disbelieve the commentator, partly because his interpretation is not contradicted by any rival set of evidence, but more so because it is in general agreement with what we learn from other contemporary or semi-contemporary sources. In the same chapter in which Kauṭilya speaks of these engines, he also speaks of *yantra-goṣpaṇa-muṣṭi-pāṣāṇa*, i.e. stones thrown by *yantras*, *goṣpaṇa* (a kind of rod) and hand. If there were stones specifically meant to be thrown by *yantras*, there must have been engines also to propel stones on the enemy. This conclusion is upheld by epic evidence. In the Sundara-kāṇḍa (62, 24), there is a reference to *yantrotkṣiptā ivopalāḥ*, i.e. like stones thrown by machines. In the Laṅkā-kāṇḍa (3, 12 ff.) the poet, while describing the defences of Laṅkā, says: "There are big and strong *yantras* to throw stones and arrows, and these can repel a hostile army when it approaches the city." A few lines below we read: "At the gates of the city there are four broad bridges, provided with *yantras*. These prevent enemies from making an assault on the city and throw them into the surrounding ditches." Quotations like these may be multiplied, but it is abundantly clear that the *yantras* (not all, of course,) were large and heavy engines, generally used for discharging heavy bolts, stones and arrows.[1] We have no knowledge as to what supplied their motive power, or how they were constructed and worked. But it is on record that like their European counterparts, they produced terrific noise when in action.[2] They may, therefore, be looked upon as the artillery of the Hindu army, and as such they seem to have been regarded in ancient times. We have noted elsewhere that in the six-fold division of the Hindu army as contemplated in Manu (vii, 185) and Śānti-parva (103, 38), the *yantras* have been assigned one independent division.

3. The Sword

The sword appears to have come into use comparatively later than the bow. No sword or sword-blade has been discovered at Mohenjo-Dāro and Harappā.[3] And although it was known to the Vedic Aryans, it appears to have been seldom used in the battles of the period.[4] But as centuries elapsed, it came more and more into prominence. In the Śānti-parva (166, 3 ff.; 82 ff.) Bhīṣma, being asked as to which weapon in his opinion is the best for all kinds of fighting, replies that the sword is the foremost among

[1] This is further confirmed by the fact that in the Ag. P. (252, 18), the functions of the *yantra* and *kṣepaṇī* (sling or fustibal) are described as similar. Cf. also ibid. 249, 4, where like the sling and bow, the *yantra* is a propelling machine.

[2] Cf. Vanaparva 279, 36: *Visphārastasya dhanuṣo yantrasyeva tadā babhau*: also Aśvamedha-parva 77, 26.

[3] Sir John Marshall, *Mohenjo-Dāro and the Indus Civilization*, I, 35.

[4] See Vedic Index I, 47. The correspondence of the Latin *ensis* to Sanskrit *asi*, however, shows that the weapon must have been in use from very early times among Indo-European peoples.

arms (*agryaḥ praharaṇānāṁ*), but the bow is first (*ādyam*).[1] There are reasons to believe that in the later centuries of our period the sword came to rival the bow as a weapon of offence.

Early Arabic literature provides us with a curious illustration of the esteem with which Indian swords were looked upon in western Asia. A renowned Arab poet, Kaab bin Zuhair, composed a poem in praise of the Prophet, entitled Quasidah-i Burda, now known as Banat Suaad. One couplet of the poem was as follows: "Verily the Prophet is a light from which illumination is sought by all and a sharp sabre (*sarimun*) among the drawn swords of God." The Prophet, however, suggested an improvement, saying that *sarimun* should be replaced by *Al-muhannad* (the Indian sword).[2] Another early Arabic poet, Hellāl, describing the flight of the Hemyarites, says: "But they fled under its (i.e. the cloud's) small hail (of arrows) quickly, whilst hard Indian swords were penetrating them." And again: "He died and we inherited him; one old wide (cuirass) and a bright Indian (sword) with a long shoulder-belt."[3]

Certain regions of India appear to have enjoyed special reputation for excellent sword fabrication. In the Virāṭa-parva (42, 14), there is an eulogistic reference to swords manufactured in the country of the Niṣādhas (*naiṣadhya*). In the Sabhā-parva (51, 28) again, the Aparānta country is declared to be one of the best centres for the manufacture of swords and other steel weapons. The early Muslim chronicler, Ibn Haukal, says that in his days the territory known as Debal was "famous for the manufacture of swords."[4] The Agni Purāṇa (245, 21 ff.) provides us with the following account of the chief centres of sword manufacture: "Swords manufactured in Khaṭ or Khaṭṭara country are noted for their elegant appearance, those produced in Ṛṣika are well-known for their cutting capacity, those in Surpāraka for their strength, those in Aṅga for their sharpness, while swords manufactured in

[1] Śānti-parva 166, 66 contains a legend regarding the mystic and divine origin of the sword. Comp. Hopkins, *Epic Mythology*, 1915, p. 176.

[2] Muslim Hall Magazine, 1929.

[3] J. B. B. R. A. S. XIV, 240. Mr. B. K. Sarkar (*Hindu Achievements in Exact Science*, 1918, p. 45) says that the secret of manufacturing the so-called Damascus blades was learned by the Saracens from the Persians, who, in their turn, had learnt it from the Hindus. It may have been so, but absolute proof is wanting.

[4] Elliot. I. 37.

Vaṅga are characterised both by keenness and their power of standing blows."[1]

Swords appears to have varied greatly in form and size. Arrian says that in the fourth century B.C. short and broad swords were generally in use. The swords represented at Sanchi generally correspond with this description.[2] On the other hand, Kauṭilya (Bk. II, ch. 18) mentions swords of three distinct varieties, viz., *nistriṁśa* (provided with a crooked end), *asi-yaṣṭi* (shaped like a staff), and *maṇḍalāgra* (provided with a circular head.) It is probable that the first of these resembled the modern *kukri*, incurved with the cutting edge on the inner side; while the second was certainly the typical Indian long sword, with straight and pointed blade (modern *kirich*). The exact shape of the *maṇḍalāgra* is more difficult to determine, but it might have been the same as the modern leaf-shaped '*paṭṭiśa*.'[3] It is note-worthy that all these three types of sword are represented in the frescoes and sculptures at Ajantā, "while *kirich* and *paṭṭiśa* blades have been found in the Tinnevelly urn-burials."[4]

Ancient treatises on sword contain detailed rules regarding the construction and measurements of the weapon. Thus both the Bṛhat Saṁhitā (ch. IV) and the Agni Purāṇa (245, 23) maintain that a good sword must not be longer than fifty finger-breadths nor shorter than twenty-five. In the Yukti-kalpataru (p. 174, vv. 59-60) the characteristics of a good and bad sword are thus described: "A good sword is one which is long, light, sharp, tough and flexible. The chief characteristics of a bad sword are shortness, heaviness, sluggishness, thinness, penetrability and inflexibility."[5]

The component parts of the sword were, of course, the blade and the hilt. In the Arthaśāstra (Bk. II, ch. 18) the materials for the construction of the hilt are specified as the horn of rhinoceros

[1] Cf. also Śār. No. 4672 ff., where in addition to the above, the author mentions the following places as famous for sword manufacture: Videha, Madhyama-grāma, Cedī, Saha-grāma, Cīna and Kālañjara. In No. 4672 and 4675, the author mentions Vaṁśa instead of Vaṅga.

[2] See Maisey, *Sanchi and its Remains*, Pl. XXV, fig. 25-28.

[3] The term *paṭṭiśa* is used in a different sense today.

[4] Ind. Ant. 1930, p. 171. A number of primitive swords have also been discovered at Ādittanallūr. All of them have either a spike at the hilt or a curved pick-shaped piece of iron, on to which a wooden handle was attached. See A. S. R., 1902-3, pp. 131 ff.

[5] Cf. also Auśanasa Dhanurveda (pp. 6-24) for more detailed rules regarding the construction, size and measurements of the sword.

and baffalo, the tusk of elephants, wood and the root of bamboo. The epics refer to hilts made of gold or ivory, and set with jewels.[1] Bāṇa describes Harṣa's sword-hilt as "rough with the pearls which thickly studded it."[2] The Rājataraṅgiṇī (VII, 1517) mentions "heaps of gold and silver sword-hilts." It is probable that swords and sword-hilts made for the rank and file were all plain and coarse; while those meant to be used by leaders and higher classes were embellished with gold and silver. The usual type of hilt represented at Ajantā is provided with an angular V-shaped guard and disc-like pommel, the blade usually being strengthened by long processes running up it either in the middle or along the reverse.[3]

Sword sheaths (*kośa*) were usually made of leather. One passage in the Virāṭa-parva (42, 12 ff.) shows that the leather used was that of the cow (*gavya-kośe*), tiger (*vaiyāghra-kośe*) and goat (*pāñcanakha-kośe*). Another passage in the Śāntiparva (98, 26) describes this leather as dark (*nīlacarma*). But besides leather, sheaths were also occasionally made of wood.[4]

The sword was usually worn on the left side. At Bhārhut and Sānchi it is shown as suspended from the left shoulder by means of a belt.[5] But this was not the only mode of carrying a sword. On some of the Gupta coins, the king's sword is shown as hanging from a waist belt.[6] We find a reference to the same practice in the Agni Purāṇa (251, 7-8), where the author says that "the sword is to be attached to the waist and slung on the left side."

The sword was used both for cutting and thrusting purposes. Occasionally it was also used as a missile in the heat of battle.[7] Swordsmanship was raised to the level of a fine art and proficiency in the art involved an acquaintance with certain special manœuvres. The term for these manœuvres in the Mahābhārata is *maṇḍalāni*, and their number is given as twenty-one.[8] The Agni Purāṇa (251, 4) and the Nīti-prakāśika (ch. III) swell them to thirty-two.

[1] Sabhāparva, 51, 16 mentions *hematsaru and śuddha-dantatsaru.* Droṇaparva, 47, 36 has *maṇimayatsarum.*

[2] Harṣacarita, tr. by Cowell and Thomas, p. 50.

[3] Ind. Ant., 1930, p. 171.

[4] A. S. R., 1902-3, p. 131.

[5] Maisey, *Sanchi and its Remains*, Pl. XXXV, fig. 26-28; Cunningham, op. cit. There is a poetic rqference to this mode of carrying the sword in the Śiśupālavadha XVII, 25.

[6] Allan, *Gupta Coins*, Pl. IX, fig. 15-17; Pl. XII, fig. 15-18. For the Kushan mode of wearing the sword, see A. S. R., 1911-12, Pl. LIII and LV, pp. 122 ff.

[7] Vanaparva, 204, 24; Mat. P. 136, 36.

[8] Cf. Droṇaparva, 13, 31 ff., where we have *maṇḍalāni tatastau tu vicarantau mahāraṇe.* Ib. 190, 37 has *mārgān ekaviṁśatiṁ*, and then follows (37-40) a complete list of these manœuvres.

4. Spears and Javelins

Developed from a sharp-headed stake, the spear may be reckoned, with the club, as among the most ancient of weapons. Spear-heads have been discovered at Mohenjo-Dāro and Harappā, but these are "unaccountably primitive in form, thin and broad in the blade without any strengthening mid-rib, and with a tang instead of a socket."[1] Spears were also known to the Vedic Aryans.[2]

The usual term for the spear in the epic and post-epic literature is *śakti*. In the Mahābhārata, it is said to be of different kinds, but all sharp (*śaktīśca vividhāstīkṣṇāḥ*).[3] It is described as a terrible weapon, made of iron (*āyasī*), sometimes adorned with gold and beryl, sometimes with bells.[4] In the Arthaśāstra (Bk. II, ch. 18), it is defined as a weapon provided with edges like a plough share. The commentator to Kauṭilya says that it was a metallic weapon, four cubits long, shaped like the leaf of a *karavīra*, and provided with a handle like the cow's teat. Māgha (XIX, 59) describes it as made of iron (*lohajā*) and provided with a sharp blade at the end (*abhyagra-phala-śālinī*).[5]

There were some other weapons which seem to have belonged to the generic class of spears and javelins. One such was the *kunta*. Kauṭilya defines it, like the *śakti*, as a weapon with edges like a ploughshare. The commentator says that the best *kunta* measured seven cubits in length, the medium six, and the shortest five. In the Nīti-prakāśikā (V, 22 ff.) it is defined as a lance, six cubits long, provided with an iron body and six edges.[6]

The *tomara* was, in all probability, a javelin. In the Ādiparva (19, 12) it is described as possessed of a very sharp point

[1] Sir John Marshall, *Mohenjo-Dāro and the Indus Civilisation*, I, 35.

[2] Vedic Index, I, 118; A. C. Das, *Ṛgvedic Culture*, pp. 334-5.

[3] Ādiparva, 30, 49; Vanaparva, 289, 23 has *śaktīśca vividhākārāḥ*.

[4] Cf. Bhīṣmaparva, 104, 30; 111, 11 where the *śakti* is *kanaka-vaidurya-bhūṣitā*, *āyasī* and *dṛḍhā*; 116, 52 where it is *sarva-pārasavī*. Cf. also Droṇaparva, 185, 40 ff.; Bhīṣmaparva, 53, 14 ff. In Droṇaparva, 90, 64 it is provided with bells (*saghaṇṭā*); in ibid. 104, 29 the number of bells is said to be eight (*aṣṭa-ghaṇṭā*); in Vanaparva, 285, 3, hundred (*śataghaṇṭāṁ . . . mahāśaktiṁ*).

[5] It is also described in later Nīti-p. (IV, 32 ff.), but the description is extremely vague.

[6] It is also described in Śukra, ch. IV, sec. vii. 1. 382. The Auśanasa Dhanurveda, pp. 41 ff. says that the best *kunta*-head should measure sixteen *aṅgulas* in length, the medium fourteen and the worst twelve. The breadth of the *kunta*-head should measure two to three *aṅgulas*.

(*sutīkṣṇāgra*). In the Karṇaparva (27, 14) it is referred to as iron-mouthed (*ayasmaya*) and gilded (*hema-daṇḍa*), piercing straight through the arms of a combatant. In the Arthaśāstra (Bk. II, ch. 18) it is defined, like the *śakti* and the *kunta*, as a weapon with edges like a ploughshare. According to the commentator, it was a rod with an arrow-like edge, the best measuring five cubits in length, the medium four and a half, and the shortest four. Nīlakaṇṭha (Udyogaparva 154, 3 ff.) says that *tomaras* were darts to be thrown by the hand. The Nīti-prakāśikā (IV, 38 ff.) describes it as a weapon with a wooden body and a metal head.[1]

The *prāsa* (or *prāśa*) appears to have been another weapon belonging to this class. The Mahābhārata contains frequent references to this weapon, but nowhere is its exact nature made sufficiently clear.[2] The only information which we can gather from epic evidence is that it was sharp and broad.[3] The Arthaśāstra (Bk. II, ch. 18), however, leaves no doubt in one's mind that it was a kind of spear or javelin.[4] The later Nīti-prakāśikā (V, 25) also defines it as a spear, seven cubits long, its handle made of bamboo.[5]

The *bhindipāla* (*bhiṇḍipāla* or *bhiṇḍivāla*) may also have belonged to the generic class of spears. Though it is often mentioned in the Mahābhārata (e.g. Udyogaparva, 19, 3; 154, 6; Bhīṣmaparva, 96, 58; 106, 23; Droṇaparva, 24, 59, etc.), its nature is left undefined.[6] In most passages, however, it is described as 'flung,' and in one (Bhīṣmaparva, 106, 23) as 'sharp and frog-mouthed' (*niśitaiśca śilīmukhaiḥ*). In the Arthasastra (Bk. II,

1 Ag. P. (152, 10) says that its functions were four-fold. For a late but detailed description of the *tomara*, see Auśanasa Dhanurveda, pp. 30-31. According to this description, three regions were famous for the manufacture of *tomaras*. These were Avantī, Magadha and the South (Dakṣinātya).

2 Cf. Udyogaparva, 19, 3; 154, 9, 13; Vanaparva, 20, 33; Virāṭaparva, 32, 10; Droṇaparva, 24, 58, etc.

3 Ādiparva, 19, 12 has *prāsāśca vipulāstīkṣṇāḥ*. Karṇaparva, 19, 32 has *suvarṇa-vikṛtān prāsān*, but this gold decoration or gilding is so frequently mentioned (and in connection with all varieties of weapons) that one feels inclined to take it as merely poetic, not real.

4 It is defined, like the *śakti* and the *kunta*, as a weapon with edges like a ploughshare.

5 The Vaijayantī has the following: *prāsaḥ kunto hāṭakastu sa trikaṇṭaka-saṁsthitaḥ* (p. 117, l. 330). On the other hand, a commentator to Amara describes it as a sort of quoit or discus (Wilson, *Works*, IV, 300), while Śukra (ch. IV, sec. vii, l. 428) defines it as a broad sword.

6 Hopkins says that it was a "missile, flung by the hand, and is usually associated with darts, hammers, clubs, etc." J. A. O. S. XIII, 290.

ch. 18), Kauṭilya mentions it along with *śakti, prāsa, tomara,* etc. and defines it, like the latter, as a weapon with edges like a ploughshare. There is no doubt but that Kauṭilya regarded it as a kind of javelin or lance. This conclusion is also borne out by later evidence. The Matsya Purāṇa (160, 10), for instance, describes it as 'made of iron' (*ayomaya*) and 'flung' (*cikṣepa*). The Vaijayantī (p. 117, 1. 331) defines it as a long dart with a large head.

We may also include in the same class such weapons as the *kaṇaya* and *karpaṇa*. The commentator on the Arthaśāstra defines the *karpaṇa* as a dart, thrown by the hand like the *tomara*. Its edges weighed 7, 8 or 9 *karṣas*. "It can go," he adds, "as far as a hundred bows' length when thrown by a skilful person." The same authority describes a *kaṇaya* as a "metallic rod both ends of which are triangular. This is held in the middle and is 20, 22 or 24 inches long."

There are numerous illustrations of spears and javelins in ancient reliefs and coins. One of the earliest specimens may be seen in Cunningham's Coins of Ancient India, Pl. IV, fig. 8. Spears and javelins depicted in Sānchi reliefs have been admirably illustrated in Maisey's Pl. XXXV, fig. 29-34. Spears, in some instances barbed, are also represented on some Yaudheya coins, ranging from about the second to about the fourth century A.D.[1] and the Bull and Horseman type of coins of the kings of Ohind.[2] The weapon is also illustrated in some of the frescoes at Ajantā, where it is depicted as short, with triangular blades and ferules.[3]

5. The Mace

The club or mace is one of the most primitive weapons of India. It was known to the people of the Indus valley,[4] and has continued in use ever since. The epic description makes it more important than the sword.[5] According to the historians of Alexander, it was the chief weapon of the Sibi tribe in the fourth century B.C.[6] Plutarch says that in the capital of the Malloi

[1] V. A. Smith, *Catalogue of Coins in the Indian Museum*, Vol. I, Pl. XXI, fig. 15-20.

[2] Ibid. Pl. XXVI, fig. 1-3, 5.

[3] Ind. Ant., 1930, p. 170.

[4] Maces of stone and copper have been discovered at Mohenjo-Dāro and Harappā. These are usually of three different shapes, of which the pear-shaped mace was the commonest. Marshall, *Mohenjo-Dāro and the Indus Civilisation* I, 36.

[5] J. A. O. S. XIII, 281.

[6] McCrindle, *India and its Invasion by Alexander*, pp. 234 and 366.

Alexander "received a blow on his neck from a club, which forced him to lean for support against the wall with his face towards the enemy."[1] The weapon is also referred to in numerous later works and inscriptions.[2]

Its construction, however, must have differed from age to age. During our period maces of both wood and iron appear to have been in use. In the Arthaśāstra (Bk. II, ch. 18), Kauṭilya mentions *musala, yaṣṭi* and *gadā* as three varieties of mace. The commentator says that *musala* and *yaṣṭi* were "pointed rods made of *khādira*" (Mimosa Catechu), whereas the *gadā* was "a long and heavy rod." In the Mahābhārata, however, the *gadā* is always described as made of iron—*ayomayī* or *āyasī*.[3] "Its general form," says Hopkins, "seems to have been that of a tapering post, girded with iron spikes, and hence heavy and sharp, sometimes plated with gold, or, according to the extravagance of the poet's fancy, bejewelled."[4] In the Bhīṣmaparva (51, 28), it is referred to as four cubits long and hexagonal; elsewhere it is octagonal (Udyogaparva 51, 8) and bound in hempen strings, mixed with wires of gold (Droṇaparva, 15, 13).

We get similar accounts of the mace in later works. In the Nīti-prakāśikā (V, 29-30), for instance, it is described as made of iron, four cubits long, with a hundred spikes at its broad head, and covered on the side with spikes. Śukra (Ch. IV, sec. vii, 1. 424) refers to it as octagonal (*aṣṭāsrā*) in shape, breast-high (*hṛdaya-sammita*), and provided with a strong handle. The Auśanasa Dhanur-veda (pp. 39-40) says that the best mace should measure fifty *aṅgulas* in length, the next best forty, and the worst thirty. It may be of three shapes, viz., *sthūlāgrā* (pear-shaped), *caturasṛā* (quadrilateral) and *tālamūlākṛti* (shaped like the root of palmyra).

The mace is much less represented in ancient sculptures than the bow or the sword. There is, however, a two-handed club in one of the reliefs at Sānchi (Maisey, Pl. xxxv, fig. 35). There is another representation of the same weapon in the famous Kaniṣka statue, now deposited in the Mathura Museum. It is a tapering post, being broader at the base than towards the hilt, and is

Ibid. p. 312.

Cf. Ag. P. 252, 11-12; Śukranīti ch. IV, sec. vii, 1. 424; C. I. I. III, 184; Ind. Ant. XI, 111, etc.

Cf. Śalyaparva, 57, 63: *gadā ayomayī*; Droṇaparva, 15, 4: *sarvāyasī gadā*; Śalyaparva, 32, 37: *skandhe kṛtvāyasīṁ gadāṁ*, etc. *Parigha*, often mentioned in the Mahābhārata and described as *āyasa*, was probably another weapon of this class. In the later Nīti-p. (V, 45), however, it has been interpreted as a battering-ram.

J. A. O. S. XIII, 282.

strengthened with five bands, probably of metal. "The portion between the first two bands nearest the handle is round, the middle portion between the second and the fourth band is sixteen-sided, only half projecting from the garment. The remaining portion is eight-sided, only three sides being actually shown in front and two partly at the sides. The fifth and lowest band is decorated with a *makara* head, which like the bands themselves was probably also of metal."[1]

Like the bow and the sword, the mace had its peculiar manœuvres or circles (*maṇḍala or mārga*).[2] In the Ādiparva (68, 12), the club-fight is said to consist of four methods as *prakṣepa* (hurling at the foe from a distance), *vikṣepa* (engaging in close fight at the point of the club), *parikṣepa* (revolving it about in the midst of foes) and *abhikṣepa* (smiting the foe in front). But this list does not exhaust the armoury of technical manœuvres. In the Śalyaparva (57, 16 ff.), in the course of a description of a club-duel between two knights, we are told that the manœuvres are in fact multifarious (*mārgān bahu-vidhān*) ; and then we have an enumeration of twenty technical names. These have been repeated almost verbatim in the Nīti-prakāśikā of Vaiśampāyana (V, 31-34). In the Agni Purāṇa (252, 11-12), clubmanship (*gadā-karma*) is said to involve twelve manœuvres, which are partly identical and partly different from the list in the afore-said works.

6. Battle-Axe, Hatchet Etc.

The axe is mentioned in the Ṛgveda, but seldom as an instrument of war.[3] In the Mahābhārata it is mentioned under several names, such as *paraśu, paraśvadha, kuliśa* and *kuṭhāra,* and is wielded as a weapon chiefly by the nobility.[4] Kauṭilya (Bk. II, ch. 18) mentions *paraśu* and *kuṭhāra* as two kinds of axes. The commentator explains the latter as "a kind of axe well-known," and the former as a scimitar, 24 inches long and edged like a crescent. The Nīti-prakāśikā (V, 9-10) defines the *paraśu* as follows: "It is a thin stick with a broad mouth. Its face is in front, curved

[1] A. S. R., 1911-12, p. 123. See also *Indo-Aryans* I, 315 for the description of a large mace taken from the hand of a guard at the entrance to the Bhoga Maṇḍapa at Puri.

[2] Hence one skilled in club-fight is described as *gadā-maṇḍala-tattvajñaḥ* in the Ādiparva, 69, 23; or as *gadā-mārga-viśāradaḥ* in Śalyaparva, 58, 23.

[3] A. C. Das, *Ṛgvedic Culture,* p. 335.

[4] J. A. O. S. XIII, 291.

like a half moon; the body is dirty-coloured, but the face is shining. At the foot end is the handle, and it has a head. Its height is the length of an arm. Its qualities are felling and splitting." The Agni Purāṇa (252, 13) ascribes six functions to the battle-axe, but it is difficult to make out their exact meaning.[1]

The battle-axe is also illustrated in ancient sculptures and coins. One early illustration may be seen in Cunningham's Coins of Ancient India, Pl. IV, fig. 4-5. Another taken from Sānchi is shown in Maisey's Pl. XXXV, fig. 37. One type of Śamudragupta's coins (Allan, Pl. IV, fig. 8-16) contains a clear representation of the axe; but the weapon does not appear to be of the ordinary type, the metallic curvature being in the middle, not at the end of the handle. Sir John Marshall reports that in course of archeological explorations at Bhita, near Allahabad, he discovered two hatchet-heads. The first belongs to the Kushan period, and is 7″ long and 3¾″ broad. The second belongs to the Gupta period, and is 3¼″ long and 1⅞″ broad at the edge.[2]

7. Discus or Quoit

The discus (*cakra*) is mentioned in many ancient works and inscriptions.[3] But it does not appear to have ever become a national favourite. Kauṭilya (Bk. II, ch. 18) defines it as a movable machine (*cala-yantra*). The Mahābhārata (Ādiparva, 33, 2 ff.) describes it as a revolving (*paribhramantaṁ*) weapon, made of iron or steel (*ayasmayaṁ*) and sharp-edged (*tīkṣṇa-dhāram*).[4] Māgha (Śiśupālavadha, XVIII, 45) speaks of it as a weapon which is hurled from a distance, and cuts off some limb of the enemy.[5]

[1] The *paṭṭiśa* or *paṭṭaśa*, mentioned in numerous ancient works, appears to have been a kind of bill or halberd. It is often wrongly interpreted as a spear (See Ind. Hist. Quart. VIII, 270; Ep. Ind. XV, 362, n. 4). Kauṭ. puts it in the same class as *paraśu* and *kuṭhāra*. The commentator says that it is the same as *paraśu*, but shaped like a trident at both ends. Cf. also Nīti-p. V, 39; Śukra. ch. IV, sec. vii. 1. 425.

[2] A. S. R., 1911-12, p. 91. For a few other illustrations of the battle-axe, see *Indo-Aryans* I, 316 ff.

[3] In the Ṛgveda (VIII. 96, 9) it is referred to as one of the weapons of Indra; in the Mahābhārata as the favourite of Kṛṣṇa. Describing the education of a prince, the Kalingattu Paraṇi says that he was trained in the use of "the five kinds of weapons, beginning with the discus." (Ind. Ant. XIX, 332). For a few other epigraphic references to *cakra*, see South Ind. Inscr. I, 153; C. I. I. III, 184, etc.

[4] Cf. Raghuvaṁśa VII, 46, where also it is described as sharp and razor-bladed (*kṣurāgra*).

[5] In this case it cuts off the trunk of an elephant.

In the Matsya Purāṇa (150, 195), again, it is described as a wheel with eight spokes and besmeared with oil.[1] The Nīti-prakāśikā (IV, 47) says that it had the form of a circular disc (*kuṇḍalākāraṁ*), with a triangular hole in its midst.[2]

8. Noose and Lasso

The *pāśa* was a sort of lariat or lasso. It is mentioned in the Ṛgveda (ix. 83, 4; x, 73, 11) as one of the weapons of Varuṇa and Soma. One passage in the Mahābhārata (Śalyaparva, 45, 108) describes it as cast from the raised hand (*pāśodyata-kara*); in another (Karṇaparva, 53, 23) it is employed to tie the foot of the foe (hence called *pāda-vandha*).[3] The Agni Purāṇa (251, 2 ff.) describes it as follows: "A *pāśa* should measure ten cubits in length, its end terminating in a loop, and its face should be retained in the hand. It should be constructed of the strings made of hemp, or of flax, or of *muñja* grass, or of *bhaṅga*, or of sinews of animals, or of leather, or of other things of which a strong thread may be made. It may also be made of thirty pieces of thread twisted together. The learners should make a running knot in the *pāśa*; and having held one end of it with the left hand, and twisted it round on the right, they should turn it over their heads, and afterwards throw it on the throat of a human figure covered with skin. After this they should try to throw the string on the neck of a horse at full gallop, or of animals jumping about, or such as are moving fast." Elsewhere (252, 6-7), the author remarks that there were eleven methods in the employment of this weapon and that its functions were five-fold.[4]

9. Śataghnī

The word literally means a "hundred-killer." Halhed in his Code of Gentoo Laws interpreted it as a cannon,[5] while Wilson

[1] Cf. also Mat. P. 178, 39-42 for a description of Viṣṇu's divine discus.

[2] Cf. also Śukra. ch. IV, sec. vii, l. 430; also Auśanasa Dhanurveda, pp. 25-6, which speaks of three kinds of quoits and their distinguishing characteristics. Ag. P. 252, 8 defines the functions of the discus. *Cakras* are seen flying through the air in the Siṁhala fresco at Ajantā. Ind. Ant., 1930, p. 170.

[3] In the Mat. P. it is employed to tie up the arms of an enemy. Nīlakaṇṭha (Udyogaparva, 154, 4) says that it was cast forward in such a manner that it settled round the neck of the approaching foe.

[4] The Nītip. IV, 45-6, says that the *pāsa* was "composed of very small scales made of metal." According to Śukra (ch. IV, sec. vii), it was shaped like a rod, three cubits long, with three sharp needles, and had an iron string attached to it. It is probable that such was the medieval development of the ancient noose.

[5] Halhed, *Code of Gentoo Laws*, Introd. p. lii.

and Oppert, relying on medieval commentators, construed it as a rocket.[1] After a critical examination of all epic references to the weapon, Hopkins showed that it was neither the one nor the other.[2]

What, then, was the real nature of this weapon? The name itself ought not to mislead us, for a name is not always an unerring index to the nature of a weapon.[3] Ancient writers seem to refer to two varieties of *śataghnīs*—the first forming part of a city's defence, and the second used as a sort of projectile along with spears, javelins, etc. The former is often seen planted on the walls of fortresses or fortified towns. Thus in the Ādiparva (207, 34), it is mentioned as a part of the defensive equipment of Indraprastha; in the Vanaparva (15, 7) as that of Dvārakā; in the Rāmāyaṇa (Ayodhyākāṇḍa, 5 11; Sundarakāṇḍa, 2, 21; Laṅkākāṇḍa, 3, 23) as that of Ayodhyā and Laṅkā. The Śānti-parva (69, 45) enjoins that the king should place destructive engines (*yantras*) in all the gates of the city. "He should plant on the rampart of his forts *śataghanīs* and other weapons." The same injunction is repeated in other texts.[4]

It is clear, therefore, that the *śataghnī*, like the *yantra*, formed an essential element in a city's defence. But what was it like? Mr. G. N. Vaidya says that it "must have been some machine in the nature of a catapult."[5] The catapult, it may be noted, was a warlike instrument of the cross-bow type. It was a propelling machine and was used with arrows "for what is now called direct fire." There is not a scrap of evidence to show that the *śataghnī* was a propelling instrument, or that it was ever used with arrows. On the contrary, one passage in the Rāmāyaṇa (Laṅkākāṇḍa, 3, 13), referring to the *śataghanīs* which were placed to defend the gates of Laṅkā, says that they were steel-made (*kālāyasamayāḥ*), sharp (*śitāḥ*) and formidable-looking (*bhīmāḥ*). This agrees remarkably with what we learn about the weapon from later commentators. For instance the commentator on the Arthaśāstra defines it as a "big pillar provided with an immense number of sharp points on

[1] Wilson, *Works*, IV, 302; Oppert, *On the Weapons, Army Organisation* etc., p. 22.

[2] J. A. O. S. XIII, 299 ff.; also cxiv.

[3] For instance, in the Droṇaparva 28, 17 ff. an *ankuśa* is described as *sarvaghāti* (all-killer), while in ibid. 182, 2 a *śakti* is referred to as *ekaghnī* (one-killer).

[4] Cf. e.g. Mat. P. 217, 8.

[5] J. B. B. R. A. S., Dec., 1928, p. 32.

its surface, and situated on the top of a fort wall." The Vaijayantī (p. 118, ll. 337-8) describes it as a huge block of stone (*mahāśilā*), studded with iron spikes.[1] Presumably these heavy objects were kept on the gates and walls of fortresses in order that they might be thrown on a besieging force attempting an assault. Presumably, too, these gigantic blocks of stone or wood were provided with wheels to facilitate movement. Time and again in the Mahābhārata, the *śataghnīs* are described as wheeled (*sacakrāḥ*) instruments.[2] One verse in the Droṇaparva (198, 19) specifies the number of wheels as two and four.[3]

As stated above, there seems to have been a second variety of *śataghnīs,* which were used as ordinary projectiles along with spears and javelins. These are referred to in the Śalyaparva (45, 109-10) as "held in hand" like clubs, swords and hammers. Elsewhere (Karṇaparva, 11, 8; 16, 17) they are stored in a war-car along with a multitude of other weapons. Moreover, like the swords and spears, they are described as "ornamented with bells" (*sakiṁkiṇīḥ*).[4] In all cases, however, these hand-*śataghnīs* are 'flung,' but they produce no greater effect than that of ordinary projectile weapons. In his Raghuvaṁśa (XII, 95-6), Kālidāsa describes Rāvaṇa hurling a *śataghnī,* but it is soon split to pieces. The *śataghnī* itself is described as studded with iron spikes (*ayaḥ-saṅkucitāṁ*). The later Nīti-prakāśikā (V, 48-9) says that the *śataghnī* was made of iron, was provided with thorns and had the look of a hammer (*mudgara*). It is not improbable, therefore, that the second variety of *śataghnīs* resembled the first in general appearance; only they were shorter, lighter, altogether more handy, and hence used as projectiles.[5]

[1] The Uvāsagadasāo (Vol. II, Appendix, p. 60) says that in the war with Vaiśālī, Kuṇiya Ajātaśatru made use of an instrument called *mahāsilā-kaṇṭaga.*

[2] Cf. Vanaparva, 283, 31; Droṇaparva, 177, 46 has *cakra-yuktāḥ śataghnyaḥ;* Karṇaparva, 27, 27 ff.

[3] It should be noted, however, that these "wheeled" śataghnīs are described in the Mahābhārata as being flung like spears and javelins. I think this is due to some confusion in the poet's mind. If they were wheeled, there was no need to fling them like ordinary projectiles.

[4] Cf. Karṇaparva, 14, 35.

[5] This conclusion is borne out by the following definition of the *śataghnī* in the Vaijayantī:

śataghnī tu catustālā loha-kaṇṭaka-sañcitā
ayaḥ-kaṇṭaka-sañcinnā śataghnyeva mahāśilā

Defensive Arms

Defensive arms may be considered under two main heads, viz., shield and body-armour. The usual terms for the former in Sanskrit are *āvaraṇa, carma, phalaka,* etc.; for the latter *varman,*[1] *kavaca, sannāha, tanu-trāṇa,* etc. In the Arthaśāstra (Bk. II, ch. 18), Kauṭilya uses the term *āvaraṇa* in the generic sense of shields, and *varman* for different kinds of body-armour.

1. Shields

We have recorded elsewhere the evidence of the classical authors that in the fourth century B.C. the Indians used bucklers of undressed ox-hide—the bucklers used by the cavalry being somewhat shorter than those of the infantry. The Arthaśāstra (Bk. II, ch. 18) and the Mahābhārata furnish us with ampler details regarding the construction of early shields. Kauṭilya says *"Peṭī* (basketry),[2] *carma* (leather-shield), *hastikarṇa* (elephant's ear, so-called perhaps because of the shape), *tālamūla, dhamanikā* (bladder), *kavāṭa* (door-wing) *kiṭikā* (light shield), *apratihata* (irresistible) and *valāha-kānta* (cloud-edged) are the instruments used in self-defence (*āvaraṇāni*)." The commentator explains *peṭī* as a kind of mat made of *koṣṭhavallī* (a creeper), *carma* as a kind of cover made of leather, *hastikarṇa* as "a board to form a cover to the body," *tālamūla* as a "wooden shield," *kavāṭa* as "a wooden board," and *kiṭikā* as "a kind of shield of reed and leather." The *apratihata* is left unexplained, but the name indicates that it was particularly strong. The *valāhakānta,* however, is said to be the same as *apratihata,* only with the edges wrapped with strips of iron. It is clear, therefore, that in the age of Kauṭilya shields were constructed of a variety of materials such as creepers, bamboo, wood and leather. The same materials were also used in the fabrication of medieval shields.

The frequent mention in the Mahābhārata of the epithet *carma* for shield probably shows that the knights used hide-shields in preference to others. These shields were sometimes prepared from the skin of tigers, more frequently from that of bulls (*ārṣabha*).[3] They were, moreover, elaborately decorated and damascened with

[1] In the Mānas. p. 80, v. 564, the term *varman* is used in the sense of a shield. This is rather unusual. It may, however, be a mistake for *carma,* owing to the confusion between the letters v and c in Sanskrit.

[2] Shām.'s ed. has vetī instead of peṭī.

[3] For tiger-skin see Bhīṣmaparva, 46, 31; Udyogaparva, 154, 8; for bull's skin Bhīṣmaparva, 54, 26 ff.; 116, 19, etc.

golden stars, crescents and moons.[1] A passage in the Śāntiparva (166, 51) mentions a shield (*carma*) studded with three bosses (*trikūṭam*). But besides the hide-shield, there was another kind called *phalaka* (mentioned, for instance, in Sauptikaparva, 8, 56; Śāntiparva, 100, 9). In one passage it is said to have been held in the left hand (*savye ca phalake bhṛśaṁ*); in another it is differentiated from *carma.*[2] The *śarāvara* or *śarāvaraṇa,* mentioned in the Bhīṣmaparva (60, 17; 90, 40) and the Droṇaparva (13, 72) may have been just another name for a shield. Hopkins says that it "may be anything that protects the body from arrows such as shields, helm, breast-plate, etc."[3] But in the passages, referred to above, the interpretation of shield seems most appropriate. In the Bhīṣmaparva (60, 17) it is, like the *carma,* described as decorated with a cluster of golden stars and sun. Elsewhere a knight is said to have unsheathed his sharp sword and taken hold of a *śarāvara.*[4]

The shield is also described in later works like the Mānasollāsa (p. 80, vv. 564-5) and the Yukti-kalpataru (pp. 174-5, vv. 62-5). Someśvara recommends that shields should be round in shape (*vartulāni*) and made of canes, bamboo, wood and hide—the same materials as mentioned in the Arthaśāstra. In the Yukti-kalpataru, the term *carma* is used in the generic sense of shields. "It is of two kinds, according as it is made of wood or hide. It should protect the body, and be firm, light and tough. That which is insufficient to cover the body or is heavy, soft, easily penetrable or made of offensive material is defective."[5]

Shields are also occasionally found represented in ancient reliefs and frescoes. Those at Sānchi have been illustrated in Maisey's Pl. XX, XXVII and XXXV. They are of varying shapes. Some of them are emblazoned with the "Union Jack" device, some with crescents and circular bosses. In the frescoes at Ajantā, three types of shields are usually represented: (1) parrying type,

[1] Cf. Bhīsmaparva, 54, 26: *carma cāpratimaṁ rājannārṣabhaṁ puruṣarṣabha. Nakṣatrair ardhacandraiśca śātakumbhamayaiścitam.* In ibid. 116, 19 the bull-hide shield is decorated with a hundred moons (*śatacandra-pariṣkṛte*) and hundred stars (*tārakāśata-citre*); ibid. 96, 50 has *carmāṇi . . . rukma-citrāṇi.*

[2] Hopkins prefers to take *phalaka* here and elsewhere as a sword. See J. A. O. S. XIII, 305, f.n. But it seems to me that there is no necessity for such forced interpretation.

[3] J. A. O. S. XIII, 304, f.n.

[4] Bhīsmaparva, 90, 40: *niṣkṛṣya tu śitaṁ khaḍgaṁ gṛhītvā ca śarāvaraṁ.*

[5] In the Śiśupālavadha (XVIII, 21), the shield (*carma*) is described as provided with a handle, which is held fast in grip. (*maṇḍuka-śliṣṭa-muṣṭhe*).

(2) round, and (3) curved oblong. Mrs. Codrington says that the first variety was probably made of metal, the second probably of hide, while the third might have been made of black and white bamboo basket-work. "The patterns of these long shields," she continues, "are most interesting and vary greatly. Round hide shields are common in modern India, elephant and rhinoceros hide being chiefly used. The little parrying shield to be seen at Ajantā is iconographical and appears in many southern Indian sculptures."[1]

Shields of different types are also represented at Bhuvaneśvara, Khaṇḍagiri and Kanarak. These have been ably illustrated and described by Rajendralal Mitra.[2]

2. Body Armour

The mention of such terms as *varman* and *drāpi* in the Ṛgveda shows that some kind of body armour or corselet was known to, and used by, the nobles and chiefs of the early Vedic period.[3] Of what material it was made is not known. There are references, however, to sewing (*syūta*), "which may be reckoned in favour of the use of linen corselets such as those recorded by Herodotus." The Atharva-veda (XI. 10, 22) uses the term *kavaca* in the sense of a corselet or breast-plate. The Jaiminīya Upaniṣad Brāhmaṇa (IV. 1, 3) explicitly mentions metal armour,[4] but it is doubtful whether any importance can be attached to this.

Passing over to the fourth century B.C., we feel ourselves on surer ground. Referring to the armour which Porus wore in the battle of the Hydaspes, Arrian says that it was "shot-proof" and "remarkable for its strength and the closeness with which it fitted his person, as could afterwards be observed by those who saw him." But he was "wounded in the right shoulder, where only he was unprotected by mail."[5] Curtius adds that the armour of Porus was embellished with gold and silver, and that it "set off his supremely majestic person to great advantage."[6] It seems reasonable to believe that it was some metal armour which Porus wore, but whether it was of the cuirass type or of the inter-linked chain-mail variety cannot be determined.

Ind. Ant., 1930, p. 170. Indo-Aryans I, 320 ff.

Vedic Index I, 333; II, 271 ff. Macdonell and Keith say that *drāpī* means a 'mantle' or 'cloak.' Sāyaṇa, however, renders the word by 'coat of mail' (*kavaca*).

The combined testimony of the Mahābhārata and the Arthaśāstra, however, proves that both these types of armour, besides wadded coats of quilted cotton, were known near about the same period. In the former work, the *varman* and the *kavaca* are usually described as made of iron or steel, covered with lacquered ornamentation in gold and colours. The decorations used on them, however, are the same as on shields, such as suns, circular bosses, eyes, etc.[1] In the Arthaśāstra (Bk. II, ch. 18), Kauṭilya describes the materials out of which the different kinds of body armour, as known to his age, were fabricated. The relevant passage may be rendered as follows: "Iron-net (*loha-jāla*), little iron-net, (*loha-jālikā*), iron-plate garment (*loha-paṭṭa*), iron armour (*kavaca*), *sūtraka*, and a contrivance of skin, hoof and horn of Delphinus gangeticus, rhinoceros, *dhenuka* (according to Shām., buffalo; according to Gan., Gayal), elephant and cattle are protective clothing (*varmāṇi*)."[2]

The *loha-jāla* or *loha-jālikā* was undoubtedly a hauberk of interlinked chain-mail. It is mentioned in the Mahābhārata also, but here the poet's fancy makes it of gold.[3] According to Bhaṭṭasvāmin's commentary, the *loha-jāla* covered the whole body, including the head, while the *-jālikā* left the head bare. The same authority explains *loha-paṭṭa* as a coat of iron without cover for the arms. The *kavaca* appears to have been a cuirass, composed of breast and back-plates and perhaps resembling those worn in Europe during the Middle Ages. The *sūtraka* (or *sūtra-kaṅkaṭa*, as Gan. reads it), on the other hand, was assuredly a jacket of quilted cotton.

[1] Cf. the following:
varmāṇi cāpa-viddhāni rukma-pṛṣṭhāni, Karṇaparva, 19, 31.
varma jagrāha kāñcanaṁ, Śalyaparva, 32, 63.
śubha-kāñcana-varmabhṛt, Śalyaparva, 36, 64.
kārṣṇāyasaṁ varma hema-citraṁ, Droṇaparva, 125, 17.
varma-mukhyaṁ tanutrāṇaṁ śātakumbha-pariṣkṛtaṁ, Bhīṣmaparva, 95, 47.
sarva-pāraśavaṁ varma kalyāṇa-paṭalaṁ dṛḍhaṁ, Virāṭaparva, 31, 12.
suvarṇa-dṛṣṭaṁ sūryābhaṁ . . . dṛḍhamāyasa-garbhantu śvetaṁ varma śatākṣimat. Virāṭaparva, 31, 15.
śaikyāyasāni varmāṇi, Droṇaparva, 117, 38.
lauhāni kavacāni, Virāṭaparva, 62, 4.
kavacānāṁ . . . tāmra-rājata-lohānāṁ, Virāṭaparva, 62, 7.
vajrāyasa-garbhaṁ tu kavacaṁ tatra kāñcanaṁ, Virāṭaparva, 31, 11.
Śata-sūryaṁ śatāvartaṁ śata-bindu śatākṣimat
abhedya-kalpaṁ Matsyānāṁ rājā kavacam-āharat. Virāṭaparva, 31, 13-14.
abhedyaṁ kavacaṁ . . . sparśa-rūpavaduttamaṁ, Vanaparva, 168, 75.

[2] Here I have followed Meyer. Shām.'s tr. is slightly different.

[3] Cf. Udyogaparva, 154, 10: *rukma-jāla-praticchannā*; Bhīṣmaparva, 19, 30, where we have *hemamayair jālair dīpyamānā ivācalāḥ.*

Lastly, there was a kind of body armour fabricated from hides, hoofs and horns of certain animals.

It is probable that the different varieties of armour mentioned in the Arthaśāstra remained a permanent feature of Indian armoury throughout our period. The dark or dusky-coloured iron armour is repeatedly referred to in Māgha's Śiśupālavadha (XVIII, 20; XIX, 11, 26, etc.). The Mānasollāsa (p. 80, v. 562) mentions coats of mail (*sannāhāḥ*) made of iron, hide, cotton and bark. The Yukti-kalpataru (p. 140, v. 37), however, seems to imply that metal armour, though well-known, was not in common use. The very cost of metal armour, apart from its intricacies, must have tended to make it a monopoly of the higher classes. The rank and file had probably to satisfy themselves either with simple shields or with wadded coats of quilted cotton or with both.[1]

3. Helmet, Neck-protector, Bracer, etc.

Besides shields and body-armour, there were in use other kinds of protective devices. These are summed up by Kauṭilya as follows: "*Śirastrāṇa* (cover for the head), *kaṇṭha-trāṇa* (cover for the neck), *kūrpāsa* (cover for the trunk), *kañcūka* (a coat extending as far as the knuckles), *vārabāṇa* (lit. "arrow-averter"), *paṭṭa* (a coat without cover for the arms) and *nāgodarikā* (finger-gloves.)."

The *śirastrāṇa* (probably the same as *śiprā* of the Ṛv.) is mentioned in a multitude of other works. But it is difficult to make out its exact composition. The Mahābhārata represents it "to be of metal and adorned with gems, chiefly the diamond."[2] It might well have been a steel head-piece, which was worn along with the cuirass or chain-mail; but it might also be mere folds of cloth, adjusted on the head to protect it from a sword-blow. The *kaṇṭha-trāṇa* (neck- protector), too, is mentioned in the Mahābhārata (e.g. Droṇaparva, 125, 18), but here as elsewhere it is a mere name without details. The *nāgodarikā* of the Arthaśāstra is the same as the *aṅgulitra* or *aṅgulitraṇa* of the Mahābhārata.[3] It was a shooting-

[1] On the characteristics of a good and bad armour, the Yukti-kalpataru (p. 140, vv. 34-6) contains the following interesting observation: "Encompassing the body, lightness, toughness and impenetrability—these are the characteristics of a good armour. Possession of holes or fissure, exceptional heaviness, thinness and easy penetrability—these are the characteristics of a bad armour."

[2] J. A. O. S. XIII, 306.

[3] Cf. Bhīṣmaparva, 106, 24; Droṇaparva, 35, 23; 40, 16; 48, 14; Karṇaparva, 19, 40; Vanaparva, 37, 19, etc.

glove used by the bowman for the protection of his fingers, and probably consisted of leathern finger-stalls sewn to corresponding straps.

Besides the shooting glove, the archer used an armguard or bracer to protect his arm from the blow of the string when the arrow was loosed. The term for the bracer in the Ṛgveda is *hastaghna*.[1] Lāṭyāyana has *hastatra*,[2] and the Mahābhārata *hastāvāpa* and *talatra* as its equivalents.[3] The epic evidence proves that it was made of iguana-skin. Rajendralal Mitra asserts, on what authority we do not know, that metal gauntlets were used in later ages.[4]

1 Ṛv. VI. 75, 14; Nirukta. IX, 14 etc.

2 Śrauta Sūtra III, 10, 7.

3 Cf. Vanaparva, 37, 19: *kavacī satalatrāṇo baddha-godhāṅgulitravān*; *talatrāṇa* also mentioned in Droṇaparva, 125, 16; in Bhīṣmaparva, 106, 24, *talatra* and *aṅgulitra* are differentiated from each other. *Hastāvāpa* is mentioned in Virāṭaparva, 55, 54; Droṇaparva, 163, 28, etc. See also J. A. O. S. XIII, 308 f.n.

4 Indo-Aryans, I, 304.

CHAPTER XV

CONCLUDING REMARKS

The history of ancient India is one of almost continuous warfare, broken by occasional periods of short-lived peace. The doctrine of *maṇḍala,* which epitomises the Hindu conception of inter-statal relations, is essentially a doctrine of strife and struggle. And it was no mere abstract theory, but embodied the experience of political leaders through countless generations. The factors which contributed to this frequency of warfare were various. One ancient writer has summarised them as follows. "Usurpation of the kingdom, abduction of women, seizure of provinces and portions of territory, carrying away of vehicles and treasures, arrogance, morbid sense of honour, molestation of dominions, extinction of learning, destruction of property, violation of laws, prostration of the regal powers, influence of evil destiny, necessity of helping friends and allies, disrespectful demeanour, destruction of friends, want of compassion on creatures, disaffection of the *prakṛti-maṇḍala,* and common eagerness for possession of the same object—these and many others have been said to be the sources of war."[1] A more potent factor was the Hindu ideal of *vijigīṣā.* Ancient texts inculcate times without number that fighting constituted the essential function of a king,[2] that pacificism and kingship, so to say, were contradiction in terms. A king's highest duty was not to shun war, but to get ready to smite his foes. "Like a snake swallowing up mice," says Uśanas, a pre-Kauṭilyan author on politics, "the earth swallows the king who refuses to fight and the Brāhman who is unduly attached to wives and children."[3] "Like a fisherman," says Bhāradvāja, "who cannot become prosperous except by catching and killing fish, a king can never attain prosperity without tearing the vitals of his enemy and performing other violent deeds. The armed might of your foe should be completely destroyed by ploughing it up and mowing

[1] Kām. X, 2-5 (tr. by M. N. Dutt, pp. 136-137). The grounds of war as given in the Ag. P. 240, 15-18 are exactly the same.

[2] Manu (VII, 98) says: *yodha-dharma sanātanaḥ* (war is the eternal law of kings).

[3] Śāntiparva, 57, 3.

it down or otherwise afflicting it by famine, starvation and thirst."[1] Elsewhere it is emphasised that "no respect is due to a king that does not somehow or other subdue his enemies. He sinks like a cow in the mud, and is helpless as an ant."[2] "There is," it is said again, "absolutely no rule but conflict for one of the warrior caste."

This incessant harping on war as an instrument of policy was not without purpose. In the congeries of small states into which India was habitually divided, often without natural frontiers marking them off into separate geographical units, military strength was the only guarantee for the continued existence of a kingdom. It was a guarantee not merely against strong rivals in the neighbourhood, but against the subtler forces of internal disintegration. But there was perhaps a deeper reason behind this ceaseless advocacy of war. The Hindus, it is well known, had evolved a synthesis out of the heterogenous mass of customs, traditions, values, tastes and beliefs, held by the various tribes and races inhabiting this vast continent. This synthesis was already a well-established fact before the rise of Maurya empire, and was never seriously disturbed till the advent of Islam. But there was nothing corresponding to this cultural unity in the political sphere. From very early times, therefore, men longed to set up a common political organisation for the whole country. This longing gave birth to the concept of *cakravartin* or *sārvabhauma* (paramount sovereign). "Monarchy at its highest," says the Aitareya Brāhmaṇa (VIII. 4, 1), "should have an empire extending right up to natural boundaries; it should be territorially all-embracing, up to the very ends uninterrupted, and constitute and establish one state and administration in the land up to the seas."[3] Kauṭilya defines a *cakravartin* as one holding sway over the whole land "extending north to south from the Himalayas to the sea and measuring a thousand *yojanas* across."[4] Whether they consciously believed it or not, most of the great war lords of ancient India seem to have acted in pursuance of this ideal. The motive force behind the endless campaigns and expeditions of the Mauryas and the Guptas, of the Gurjara-Pratihāras, the Pālas and the Rāṣṭrakūṭas does not seem to have been mere ambition, a passion for conquering for the sake of

[1] Adiparva, 140, 77-78.

[2] Sabhāparva, 15, 11; Vanaparva, 35, 7.

[3] It should be noted that the Hindus, like the Romans, identified the geographical area with which they happened to be immediately acquainted with the world.

[4] Kauṭ. Bk. IX, ch. 1.

conquering, but a conscious or unconscious urge to bring the whole country under one single hegemony. The success attained was often partial and temporary. It was because the forces of disintegration were too strong to be permanently surmounted. The vastness of the country, the difficulty of intercommunication, the selfish ambition of local chiefs, the lack of general ideas and common interests, the almost total absence, in a word, of all the sources from which every government must draw its life and strength, this general condition rendered all attempts at empire-building infructuous. But nonetheless the ideal was there, consciously held by some, unconsciously by almost all; and its existence accounts for, to some extent at any rate, the frequency of internecine strife in ancient India.

Concurrently with the king's duty to fight, ancient writers have stressed and eulogised the soldier's duties as second to none. The Śāntiparva (63, 24) says: "Among men the highest duties are those performed by the warrior caste. The whole world is subject to the might of their arms. All the duties, principal and subordinate, of the three other orders are dependent for their observance upon the duties of the warrior." And the essence of the warrior's duty, like that of the king, lies in fighting. No matter how challenged, the warrior, who is true to his salt, must respond. He must, moreover, never think of fleeing from the battle-field. "The gods headed by Indra send calamities unto those who forsake their comrades in battle, and come home with unwounded limbs."[1] Not only do they get disrepute in this world, but are condemned to eternal hell after death.[2] Bhīṣma roundly asserts that those who seek to save their own life by deserting their comrades should be slain with staves or clods, or burnt in a fire of dry grass, or slaughtered like a beast.[3]

On the other hand, the man who dies a soldier's death on the battle-field is promised forgiveness of all his sins and the thrilling delights of a sensual paradise. The following passage from the Mahābhārata is illustrative of sentiments shared by all, and expressed almost everywhere:

> "The men their lives who bravely yield
> To death upon the battle-field,
> Their fleeting pangs and sufferings o'er,
> All straight to heavenly mansions soar.

[1] Śāntiparva, 97, 20.

[2] Śukranīti, ch. iv, sec. vii, ll. 656-661.

[3] Śāntiparva, 97, 21-22.

There nymphs divine these heroes meet,
With witching smiles and accents sweet,
Run up and cry in emulous strife,
'Make me,' 'nay, me,' 'nay, me,' 'thy wife'."[1]

Śukra asserts that the great position that is acquired by sages after long and tedious penances is also attained by warriors who meet death in war. "This is at once penance, virtue, and eternal religion. The man, who does not flee from battle, does at once perform the duties of the four *āśramas*." In this world, the author adds, two men go beyond the solar sphere in heaven, viz., the austere ascetic and the soldier who is killed in battle with his face to the foe.[2] Such is the burden of teachings of the ancient authors. The warrior must kill or be killed in the fight; there is to be no third alternative. If he conquers the foe, he attains to fame and glory in earthly life; if he is defeated and killed in the fray, he is transported straightaway to heaven.[3]

There are reasons to think that these maxims, which appealed at once to the basest and the highest in man, left a deep impress on the life of the military communities. They prepared the warriors for suffering and pain, restraint and violence, blood and tears—prepared them to embrace the horrors of destruction and terrors of the tomb cheerfully. Referring to the Mahārāṣṭra country, the Chinese pilgrim, Hiuen Tsiang, says: "Whenever a general is despatched on a military expedition, although he is defeated and his army is destroyed, he is not himself subjected to bodily punishment; only he has to exchange his soldier's dress for that of a woman much to his shame and chagrin. So many times these men put themselves to death to avoid such disgrace." 'Utbi relates how Jayapāla, king of Bhatinda, was on two successive occasions defeated by Subuktagin and his more famous son, Sultan Maḥmūd, and how, smarting under a sense of shame and dishonour, he caused a funeral

[1] Ind. Ant. X, 92.

[2] Śukranīti, ch. iv, sec. vii, ll. 620-21, 624-27, 632-33.

[3] The belief that soldiers dying on the battle-field are transported to heaven is as old as the Ṛgveda (cf. Rv. X, 154, 2-5), and is repeated almost to weariness in the Mahābhārata. For similar sentiments expressed in contemporary and later literature, comp. Kauṭ. Bk. X, ch. 3; Institute of Viṣṇu, III, 44; Parāśara Smṛti, Acārakāṇḍa, III, 37; Raghuvaṁśa, VII, 51, 53; Śiśupālavadha. The same sentiments are also echoed in inscriptions (Ep. Ind. I, 313, vv. 12, 18, 19; ibid III, 101; IV, 49, etc.) and sculptures (e.g. the Begur stone sculpture, Ep. Ind. VI, 46; the virgal or memorial tablet at Sūḍi, a village in the Dharwar district, Bombay, Ep. Ind. XV, 73).

pyre to be erected and perished in its flames.[1] Firishta adds that a custom prevailed among the Hindus that when a Rājā was overpowered twice by strangers, he became disqualified to reign.[2]

The code of military honour included other articles besides victory or death on the battle-field. Wounded and armless opponents, for instance, were to be considered as exempt from slaughter. It was also regarded as a gross offence to refuse quarter to an armed enemy, who had ceased fighting and asked for mercy. Such a person might be imprisoned, but never wounded or slain.[3] Similarly it was forbidden to slay one who was weary or asleep, one who was walking along a road unaware of danger, one who was greatly enfeebled by wounds or stricken with grief, one who lingered trustfully, as well as the insane, the wounded, servants, camp-followers, old men, children and women.[4] Moreover, prisoners of war were to be cared for and treated with humanity. The Śāntiparva (95, 12-14) lays down that captured opponents should either be sent to their homes, or if brought to the victor's quarters, should have their wounds attended to by skilful surgeons, and when cured, set at liberty. Further, weapons which caused unnecessary pain or which inflicted more suffering than was indispensable to overcome the foe were condemned. "When a king fights with his foes," says Manu (VII, 90), "let him not strike with instruments concealed, with barbed or poisoned weapons, the points of which are blazing with fire." The seizure or destruction of enemy's property unless imperatively demanded by the necessities of war was also prohibited. Temples and their property in places under military occupation and the private property of individual citizens were on no account to be seized.[5]

To what extent these conventions of chivalry were observed in actual practice we do not know. It is probable that, like the Hague and Geneva conventions in modern times, these rules were

[1] Elliot, II, 27. The case of Kulchand, the chief Mahawan, was similar. He gallantly fought against Sultan Maḥmūd in 1018 A.D. but was defeated with heavy loss. Considering that life was not worth living after this dishonour, he slew his wife with a dagger and then drove it into his own body (Elliot II, 43). For another example of this nature, see Krishnaswamy Aiyangar, *Ancient India*, p. 93.

[2] Briggs I, 38.

[3] Śāntiparva, 45, 12; 96, 3.

[4] Manu, VII, 90-94; Śāntiparva, 100, 27-29.

[5] Ag. P. 226, 22-25; see also author's article on the "*Philosophy of War among the Ancient Hindus*" in J. I. H. Vol. VII, pp. 157-184. P. N. Banerji, *International Law & Customs in Ancient India*, Chap. VIII.

often forgotten in the bitterness of the conflict. Instances are on record of villages and towns being burnt and destroyed, in which combatants and non-combatants alike suffered,[1] of the desecration of temples and sanctuaries by relentless conquerors,[2] and of the imprisonment of women in violation of the precepts of the Dharmaśāstra.[3] There are instances also of the use of treachery and fraud, of broken pledges, of cruel assassinations in cold blood.[4] War is, and has always been, inherently brutal in its nature. If it "opens up the most fruitful field to all virtues," as Frederick the Great claimed, it also evokes the meanest instincts of human nature.

[1] Thus several southern kings are recorded to have burnt and plundered Citrakūṭa (Ep. Ind. IX, 179; Ind. Ant. XII, 221) The eastern Cālukya prince Guṇaka-Vijayāditya is known to have occupied and burnt the capital city of the Rāṣṭrakuṭas. The Cambay Plates of Govinda IV record the devastation of the city of Mahodaya by Indra III (Ep. Ind. IX, 28). Someśvaradeva of Nāgavaṁśa is stated to have "burnt Veṅgi like the great Arjuna who fired the Khāṇḍava forest" (Ep. Ind. X, 26). Bilhana's Vikramāṅkadevacarita describes a war waged between Vikramāditya VI and his brother Jayasiṁha. In course of this war, it is stated, "villages were plundered and burnt and their inhabitants dragged into captivity" (Ind. Ant. V, 323). For a few other instances, comp. Mysore Inscriptions, p. 331; Ind. Ant. XII, 221; also *vide supra*.

[2] Thus the Hāthi-Gumphā Inscription tells us that when king Nanda conquered Kaliṅga, he carried the throne of Jina belonging to Kaliṅga as the highest trophy. A Gawarwad Inscription (d. saka 993-4) informs us that Rājendra-coḷa, when he invaded Veḷava, burnt down many temples, and defiled and damaged the Jain sanctuaries erected by Permāndi (Ep. Ind. XV, 345). Cf. also Rājat. VIII, 971-1004 for another instance.

[3] Bāṇa tells us that the king of Malwa, after defeating and slaying Grahavarman Maukhari, cruelly misused the latter's queen, Rājyaśrī, "confining her like a brigand's wife, with a pair of iron fetters kissing her feet" (Harṣcarita, tr. by Cowell, p. 153). The Gauḍavaho (p. 191, vv. 695-697) proudly records that Yaśovarman, after having routed and killed the king of Gauḍa, carried the ladies of his harem into slavery and made them ply the *cāmaras* over him in public durbar. The Bilhari Cedi Inscr. refers to the "crowds of captive women of enemies who again and again were made prisoners" (Ep. Ind. II, 265, v. 25). It was sometimes a matter of boast for *praśasti-kāras* that the wives of vanquished princes were lingering in the prisons of their patron kings (Ep. Ind. I, 138). For similar references to women being taken captive, comp. Ep. Ind. III, 91; South Ind. Inscr. Vol. II, pt. v, p. 6; ibid. III, No. 81, 82 and 83.

[4] Kauṭilya and most writers on *nīti* advocate the use of fraud and treachery in warfare. In the Śalyaparva (61, 61-67), Kṛṣṇa appeals to the eternal plea of end justifying the means. "If I had not followed these deceitful ways," he says, "neither victory, not kingdom, nor wealth would have been yours.... The gods themselves, in slaying the Asuras, had followed the same path. That god-trodden path may be followed by all." Historical examples are not lacking. The case of Candragupta (II), who disguised as Dhruvadevī,

On the whole, however, it would seem that wars in ancient India were characterised by less violence and savagery than wars elsewhere. There is no recorded instance of such wanton and cold-blooded atrocity as Athens perpetrated against Melos, Corcyra and Mytilene, or the wearers of the Cross against the defenders of the Crescent in 1099 A.D. Such incidents of war as the indiscriminate slaughter of all men of military age or the enslavement of women and children of the conquered state were hardly known. These wars, moreover, did not usually lead to any great political changes. On the whole, the chiefs were considerate of each other's rights. It was a well-established maxim of statecraft that a victor should acquiesce in the continuance of the laws, beliefs and customs of the vanquished peoples, and that instead of seeking the extermination of the defeated dynasties, he should be content with their submission and tribute.[1] Kālidāsa tersely describes this policy as one of "uprooting and replanting."[2] This was also the Kauṭilyan ideal of *dharmavijaya*,[3] and the typical Hindu method of creating unity out of diversity in the political sphere. The history of India, especially from the Gupta period onwards, offers numerous illustrations of the application of this policy. Samudragupta's Deccan expedition, for instance, was one; the conquest of the Pāṇḍyan kingdom by Parāntaka I was another. Conscious that this was perhaps the best way of harmonising the conflicting interests of imperialism and local independence, later-day empire-builders seem to have transformed this policy into a tradition. "The Indians,"

the queen of his elder brother, Rāmagupta, entered the Śaka camp and killed the Śaka monarch, may be noted (J. B. O. R. S. XV, 134-141). Bāṇa records how Śaśāṅka of Bengal, acting as an ally of the Malwan king, inveigled Rājyavardhana, king of Thaneswar, by fair promises to a conference, and assassinated him when off his guard. In the tenth century A.D. Betuga II of the Western Gaṅga dynasty of Talakāḍ is stated to have resorted to similar methods of treachery to get rid of the Coḷa king, Rājāditya. Pretended overtures of peace were made, and when Rājāditya confidently went to meet his enemy, he was stabbed with a dagger. (Ep. Ind. VI, 57). The Chachnāma relates the story of a war between Rai Chach and Mahrat, the chief of Jaipur. When the two armies met, Mahrat came forward and proposed, as the matter was a purely personal one, to settle the dispute by single combat. "Chach represented that he was a Brāhman, and unaccustomed to fight on horse-back. His magnanimous foe then alighted to meet him on equal terms, when Chach treacherously sprung upon his horse and slew his adversary before he could recover from the surprise." (Elliot. I, 411-12).

[1] Kauṭ. Bk. VII, ch. 16; Bk. XIII, ch. 5; Manu, VII, 201-203; Ag. P. 236, 62-65, etc.

[2] Raghuvaṁśa IV, 37.

[3] Kauṭ. Bk. XII, ch. I.

writes Sulaiman (9th century A.D.) "sometimes go to war for conquest, but the occasions are rare...When a king subdues a neighbouring state, he places over it a man belonging to the family of the fallen prince, who carries on the government in the name of the conqueror. The inhabitants would not suffer it to be otherwise."[1] The pursuit of this policy, however, had two important results. It led to the growth of that class of feudatory chiefs—the *sāmantas, mahā-sāmantas* and *mahārājas*—who figure so prominently and so profusely in the records of Gupta and post-Gupta India. It is also the reason why some of the princely families in India can boast of an ancestry unequalled by any royal house in Europe.

Broadly speaking, moreover, these wars seldom involved any grave disturbance either to the social equilibrium or the economic life of the people. It is a fact of paramount importance to remember that in India the social, economic and religious life of the people pursued their course irrespective of the activities of the state, and, consequently, wars and campaigns were generally regarded as the business of chiefs and kings and the professionals who chose to serve them. The bulk of the people were indifferent to the fortunes of war, and did not believe that they had any great interest whether their king "was called Harold or was called William." This was partly due to the growth of despotism, which became the prevailing form of government, and the consequent dissociation of the people from the activities of the state, and partly to the comparative immunity from violence and molestation which the wealth-producing classes in the country enjoyed. As early as the 4th century B.C. Megasthenes noticed this peculiar trait of Indian warfare. At the very time when a battle was going on, he says, the neighbouring cultivators might be seen quietly pursuing their work,—"perhaps ploughing, gathering in their crops, pruning the trees, or reaping the harvest." We have an Indian corroboration of this assertion in an incidental statement occuring in the Abhidharma-kośavyākhyā. "Philosophers," we are told, "while destroying the opinion of their adversaries must carefully respect the principles of logic, because these principles are useful to them; just as kings, while destroying the soldiers of their enemies, respect the field-labourer who is the common help of both armies."[2] Hiuen Tsiang affirms that although there were enough of rivalries and wars in the 7th century A. D., the country at large was little injured by them.

[1] Elliot. I, 7.

[2] I. H. Q. I, 369.

A question which inevitably faces every student of India's past, especially of her military system, is—what were the causes which led to the fall of the Hindus; why, in other words, did the Indian states fell an easy prey to the Muhammadan Turks in the 11th and 12th century A.D.? It is difficult to answer this question in a few paragraphs. These causes were so numerous and so involved, they were at work through so long a time, the full understanding of their operation requires so extensive a knowledge of the laws which govern the growth and decline of peoples, that a volume may be required for a clear presentation of the subject. A brief account of the matter is made still further difficult from the fact that the fall of the Hindus has been very often made the subject of partial and incomplete treatment in order to prove some particular point, perhaps to make vivid the disabling effects of the doctrines of *ahiṁsā* and *karma;* perhaps to make manifest the malign influence of caste on the life of the people. Undoubtedly, the doctrine of *ahiṁsā* tended to create in certain sections of the people a deep abhorrence to all forms of violence; and the theory of *karma,* as popularly interpreted, produced a fatalistic outlook and disinclination for effort. But it would be as erroneous to attribute the downfall of the Hindus to the effects of these doctrines, as it is to ascribe to Christianity the downfall of the Roman empire. In both cases other and deeper causes were at work, sapping the foundations of vitality and strength; and just as the Roman empire would have fallen, as it did, even if Christianity had not found many adherents within its borders, so would the Hindu states have succumbed to the Muhammadan Turks, even if they had never known the doctrines of *ahiṁsā* and *karma.*

Undoubtedly also, the caste system exercised a pernicious influence on the life of the people. It divided the community into classes separated by intractable barriers, inhibited freedom of choice, promoted rigid sectional attributes and impeded the growth of a common national consciousness. Nevertheless to explain the downfall of the Hindu states by this one premise is to simplify a problem which is inherently complex. It should be borne in mind that in spite of the prevalence of the caste system, Candragupta Maurya drove out the remnants of the Greek hosts left behind by Alexander and beat back Seleucos Nikator, Skandagupta and Yaśodharman repulsed the Huns, the Hindu kingdom of Vijayanagar checked the onrush of the armies of Islam for well over two hundred years (1336 to 1556 A.D.), and the Marathas became a mighty power on the ruins of the Moghul empire. Some writers would have us think that the caste system, by restricting the field of recruitment, diminished the fighting strength of the Hindu states, and thus prevented them from becoming what may be called "nations in arms." It has been already shown that the theory that troops were recruited from the Kṣatriyas alone has no foundation in fact;[1] and a "nation in arms" is an entirely modern concept—a legacy of the French Revolution to the world. Nor is there much truth in the statement that caste prevented the growth of a feeling "that fighting for or defending one's own country was everyone's business and not of a particular class of people;"[2] for such consciousness was equally absent in other medieval countries and communities where hereditary caste system of the Indian type was never known. In medieval Europe, for instance, fighting was almost wholly done by the feudal knights, and at the beginning of the modern age, by professional standing armies maintained by absolute monarchs. As in India, so in Europe down to the eighteenth century, the mass of the people seldom mixed themselves up in wars undertaken by their masters.

The immediate causes of the fall of the Hindu states may be roughly divided into two groups—first, political causes; second, military. Among political causes may be mentioned the fact that the commencing years of the eleventh century, when the Turkish tempest beat upon the western flank of the Hindu world, were an age of decaying dynasties and of kingdoms that were falling to pieces. After the break-up of the Gurjara-Pratihāra empire, northern India split up into many small kingdoms. Some of them were formed by tribal chiefs, some by military adventurers; their boundaries were shifting, and they were continually at feud with one another. This division and disunion did not make it easy for the Hindu princes to unite for a common defence and repulse of the enemy. Mr. McCrindle's remark that "if Alexander had found India united in arms to withstand his aggression, the star of his good fortune would have culminated with the passage of the Indus" is not wholly inapplicable to Muhammad bin Kasim, Sultan Maḥmūd or Muhammad of Ghor. This division and disunion also enabled the crafty invaders from the north to exploit the differences within the country, for the dread of the foreigner was apt to be less than the dread of the strong neighbour.

But the disruptive forces did not merely split up the country into numerous small kingdoms; they worked deeper than that. Ever since the days of the Guptas feudal tendencies had been

[1] *Vide supra*, pp. 78-82. [2] Modern Review, August, 1930, p. 153.

steadily developing in northern India, and there are good reasons to think that with the passing away of the old powerful dynasties, they reached their maturity about the eleventh century A.D. The consequence was that the numerous kingdoms, into which northern India was divided, were themselves subdivided into a multitude of territorial fragments, ruled over by petty chiefs or lords. The exact relationship between the overlord and the feudatory chiefs cannot be determined with any amount of exactitude; but in broad outline it does not seem to have been very different from what obtained between kings and their vassals in feudal Europe. That is to say, while enjoying virtual autonomy in their own domains, the feudatory chiefs were bound by some kind of allegiance to their overlord and were expected to help him in times of war. There is, however, ample testimony that the feudatories were often intensely jealous of one another and did not look upon their subordination with equanimity. Whenever due to external or internal reasons there was a decline in the fortunes of the overlord's family, the more powerful among the feudatory chiefs threw off their dependence and forced the smaller vassals in their neighbourhood to change their allegiance. In fact, most of the Hindu states of this period seem to have been organised on such unstable, semi-feudal basis. Consequently the armies with which they fought, being mostly composed of the retainers of their subordinate chiefs, lacked that uniformity of organisation and unity of control and command which is one of the essential requisites of success in war.

This brings us to a consideration of the military causes. "The Hindu defenders of their country," V. A. Smith rightly remarks, "although fully equal to their assailants in courage and contempt of death, were distinctly inferior in the art of war, and for that reason lost their independence."[1] Success in war, it is well known, depends primarily on three factors, viz., moral qualities, organisation and equipment, and leadership. An exact comparison and assessment of the Hindus and their northern antagonists on these three counts would be a difficult task. The contemporary or semi-contemporary Muhammadan chronicles, from which the story of the military operations of the time is mostly derived, are often one-sided and misleading in their statements. Yet certain facts seem to stand out in glaring light, and certain inferences are possible on the basis of those facts.

By moral qualities are meant virtues like courage, energy and determination. Although the Hindus were not lacking in these

[1] Smith, *Oxford History*, p. 220.

virtues, the Muhammadan Turks seem to have possessed them in a larger measure. It is an amply-proved fact of history that during the simpler and more primitive stages of racial and tribal existence the moral qualities of courage and self-sacrifice, the complete subordination of individual advantage and individual comfort to the good of the community, are most apparent as a natural growth, and seem to need least artificial cultivation. A civilized and prosperous community, on the other hand, is not a congenial soil for the natural development of these virtues; and the Hindus were infinitely more civilised and prosperous than the Turks. Moreover, with this rude vigour of semi-civilised barbarians they combined the fierce religious zeal of neo-converts. "The great missionary creed of Muhammad, which to the Arabs and Persians had become a familiar matter of routine, was a source of fiery inspiration to the fresh untutored men of the steppes. To spread the faith by conquest doubled their natural zest for battle and endowed them with the devoted valour of martyrs."[1] "The best soldier," said Oliver Cromwell, "is the soldier who knows what he is fighting for and loves what he knows." Like Cromwell's Ironsides, the Turks derived strength and fortitude from the belief that they were fighting on behalf of God, and that God's benign protection was always with them. The Hindus, on the other hand, lacked a common ideal for which to fight and die. Nationalism and patriotism as controlling forces of history were not yet born, here or elsewhere; and the very nature of their religion, which was a blend of many different elements—a synthesis of diverse customs, thoughts and beliefs,—made them incapable of being fanatically intolerant. It is true that common antipathy against the foreigners, who plundered and destroyed their temples and sanctuaries, and who trampled under foot all that they had for ages held dear and sacred, united on a few occasions some of the ruling princes in a common endeavour to oust the intruders; but it was not a strong enough cohesive force to survive a disaster or keep in check the disruptive tendencies within the country. In short, the absence of a higher, ennobling ideal rendered the Hindus incapable of combined effort, involving any continuous strain of risk or hardship.

The comparatively inferior morale of Hindu India became evident as the drama unfolded itself. Sultan Maḥmūd met with stubborn resistance in his first encounters with Jayapāla (1001 A.D.) and Ānandapāla (1008 A.D.); but the resounding victories which he won against the kings of Bhatinda (Bathindah) seem to have

[1] Lane-Poole, *Medieval India*, pp. 17-18.

sent a thrill of consternation among the other ruling princes of India. Their demoralisation, indeed, became so complete that sometimes we hear of them fleeing their capitals and hiding themselves in forests and inaccessible hills without striking a single blow.[1] The panic with which they were seized is strikingly illustrated in a letter which Bhimpāl is said to have written to the Cāndella king, Gaṇḍa, "Sultan Mahmud," runs the letter, "is not like the rulers of Hind, and is not the leader of black men. It is obviously advisable to seek safety from such a person, for armies flee away before the very name of him and his father. I regard his bridle as much stronger than yours, for he never contents himself with one blow of the sword, nor does his army content itself with one hill out of a whole range. If therefore you design to contend with him, you will suffer, but do as you like—you know best. If you wish for your own safety, you will remain in concealment."[2] One notices a similar demoralisation overtaking the Hindu princes after the second battle of Tarain (1192 A.D.), where Pṛthvīrāja with his confederate hosts had fought and lost. There was no longer any organised resistance after this great disaster; instead pusillanimity, vacillation and weak surrender.[3] The Dabhoi Inscription (c. 1200 A.D.) remarkably illustrates the dread of the Hindu princes of this period when it says: "So many god-like kings are there on this earth; but they all become uneasy at heart even at the mention of the Turuṣka king."[4]

Nor in battle efficiency were the scales exactly even between the Hindus and the Turks. Although the weapons used by the two adversaries were much the same, they do not seem to have been wholly on a par in the matter of equipment. As it has been pointed out before, whereas the Hindus put excessive reliance on the "illusory strength of elephants,"[5] their enemies depended for their success on the skilful use of a well-trained and well-equipped

[1] Elliot. II, 28, 45, 49, etc.

[2] Elliot. II, 48. Gaṇḍa, however, got ready for battle. Sultan Maḥmūd is said to have trembled when saw the huge army which the Cāndella king put on the field of battle (*vide supra*, p. 13). But to the great surprise and delight of Maḥmūd, Gaṇḍa fled at night, leaving his entire baggage and other materials of war. Iswari Prasad, *History of Medieval India*, p. 81.

[3] The writer is aware that a few Hindu princes (Jayacandra of Kanauj, for instance) fought hard to save their independence. But these were exceptions rather than the rule. The majority seem to have been seized with a dark fear that the Turk was invincible and all resistance fruitless.

[4] Ep. Ind. I, 26.

[5] Cf. Chap. VI.

cavalry. The cavalry gave the Muhammadan forces an overwhelming superiority in mobility, an advantage emphasised by the vastness of the theatre of war and the peculiarities of its terrain. It enabled the Turkish generals to employ what is known as shock tactics, and gave them such elements of tactical advantage as surprise, advantage of ground and simultaneous attack from several quarters. In the matter of organisation, too, the Turks were at an advantage. They fought under one undivided command and obeyed one will. This rendered combination among the subordinate leaders possible, and on this combination their success in no small measure depended. The Hindu armies, on the other hand, as stated above, were often organised on a semi-feudal basis; and feudal contingents are seldom as effective in action as they are impressive in size. It is probable also that the confederacies which were formed by some Hindu kings, as in the time of Jayapāla, Ānandapāla and Pṛthvīrāja, suffered from a similar organisational weakness. We may well believe that the troops of the allied states were not trained and organised on uniform lines and prepared for being moulded into one army.

But nowhere is the contrast between the two adversaries more evident than in higher leadership. Hindu generals like Jayapāla, Ānandapāla and Pṛthvīrāja were endowed with great gallantry and personal courage. But they were surprisingly lacking in strategical enterprise and tactical initiative. It is curious that throughout this long-drawn struggle they never posted frontier guards along the narrow passes of the North-western Frontier and never sought to cut off the enemy by an ambuscade while passing through the hills. Pṛthvīrāja, the last of the stalwarts, who has become a hero of poetry and romance, had won military laurels for himself before his engagement with Muhammad of Ghor, and he seems to have based on this limited experience an exaggerated belief in his own military abilities. It is sad to reflect that after the first battle of Tarain (1191 A.D.), in which he won a signal victory over his Muhammadan adversary, he did not press his advantage to the farthest limit. Instead he halted his troops, leisurely besieged the fortress of Sarhind, and neglected to take adequate precautions against the return of the Ghorian chief. It is true that when next year Muhammad came back with a yet larger force, Pṛthvīrāja fought out the issue with courage and determination; but no gallantry and no heroism can save a people from the results of neglecting war preparation. Moreover, a common mistake which most Hindu chiefs of this period seem to have committed was their persistent adoption of defensive tactics. It was a mistake which robbed them of the chief elements of tactical advantage and surrendered them to the enemy. The Hindu chiefs forgot that an army condemned to eternal defensive can never deal a decisive blow. They forgot that the moral force of a confident anticipation of victory lies ever with the attack.

The Turks, on the other hand, were more fortunate in their generals. Both Sultan Maḥmūd and Muhammad of Ghor were men capable of animating their troops with a spirit of deep devotion. They appealed not merely to their greed and lust, but awakened in them an indomitable sense of duty towards religion. Moreover, not only did they possess the traditions of Parthian strategy, but also a complete system of tactics carefully elaborated to suit the requirements of the age. In craft and resourcefulness, too, they far surpassed their Indian antagonists. Above all, whereas the Hindu love of *vyūhas* committed the armies of India to a cult of positions and defensive tactics, they regarded it as a fundamental proposition of warfare that offence was better than defence, that the sword was better than the shield. It will be too much to believe that the Muhammadan generals did not commit mistakes; yet a ruthless offensive spirit seems to have so saturated the minds of the Ghaznavite and Ghorian officers and men that it sufficed, notwithstanding errors in detail, to guide them in the right path of victory.

Of the Muhammadan generals, who figure prominently in the annals of the time, Sultan Maḥmūd in particular deserves to rank as one of the great commanders in history. A man of infinite courage and of indefatigable energy of body and mind, he never owned a defeat during more than thirty years of almost incessant warfare. He was not merely a great planner of campaigns and a shrewd marshaller of hosts, but the stoutest lance in his own army.[1] It is amazing how with comparatively small armies he achieved conquests which added vast tracts of territory to the inheritance left by his father. He trusted to skilful tactics, to the mobility of his troops and to the rapidity of his marches to overcome the larger and more clumsy masses of his opponents.[2]

[1] He usually plunged into the thickest part of the battle and is said to have received seventy-two cuts and wounds during his numerous wars. Muhammad Nazim, *The Life and Times of Sultan Mahmud of Ghazna*, p. 154.

[2] His rapid marches often baffled the calculations and belied the anticipations of his enemies. "He thundered at the gates of Multan while the rebel Sukhpāl was slumbering in security, and he surrounded the town of Quṣdār before its ruler was well aware of his approach. Even when he was in the

Muhammad of Ghor, though not as great a captain as Sultan Maḥmūd, was certainly superior to his Indian antagonists. He seems to have known the great precept which modern military science has claimed as its own that "in a cavalry combat the side which holds back the last reserve must win." In the second battle of Tarain, which was his crowning achievement, he demonstrated the truth of this dictum and also the tremendous efficacy of shock tactics. Minhāju-s Sirāj writes that "The Sultan drew up his battle array, leaving the main body in the rear, with the banners, canopies and elephants, to the number of several divisions. His plan of attack being formed, he advanced quietly. The light unarmoured horsemen were made into four divisions of 10,000, and were directed to advance and harass the enemy on all sides, on the right and on the left, in the front and in the rear, with their arrows. When the enemy collected his forces to attack, they were to support each other, and to charge at full speed. By these tactics the infidels were worsted, the Almighty gave us the victory over them, and they fled."[1] Firishta adds that the battle raged back and forth from sun-rise to sun-set, and when the Hindu army was well-nigh exhausted by a continuous succession of shocks, Muhammad "put himself at the head of 12,000 of his best horses, whose riders were covered with steel armour, and making one desperate charge, carried death and destruction throughout the Hindoo ranks."[2] It is thus clear that the second battle of Tarain, like the battle of the Hydaspes fought many centuries earlier between Porus and Alexander, was essentially a general's battle—the triumph of genius in command, not of mere valour.

At the commencement of this work we stated that throughout more than a millennium the art of war in India followed a stereotyped course, marked by no remarkable improvements in any of its branches. Strabo, borrowing from Megasthenes, says that the Indians did not pursue accurate knowledge of any kind, except that of medicine; and "in the case of some arts, it is even accounted vicious to carry their study far, the art of war, for instance."[3] But the causes of this static character of Hindu military system seem to have been deeper than a mere sense of its inherent viciousness. A similar lack of progress is noticeable in the political thought of India after Kauṭilya. These seem to point to the fact that the creative power of antiquity in certain spheres of speculation and

grip of his fatal malady, the swiftness of his movements surprised Mīnūchihr and forced the Seljuks to clear out of Khurasan." Ibid. pp. 155-156.

[1] Elliot. II, 296-297. [2] Briggs. I, 177. [3] Strabo XV, c. 701.

achievement was exhausted. This exhaustion became manifest in other spheres as centuries rolled on. Having brought civilisation up to a certain point, the Hindus seem to have been able to carry it no further. Even in those fields where the most remarkable results had been attained, as, for example, in that of philosophy and metaphysics, nothing further seemed to be possible, except to work over the old results into new forms. Berūnī bears testimony to the fact that by the 11th century the Hindus had completely lost their old genius for assimilation and absorption, and had become a grossly superstitious and vegetating people. "According to their view," says the Muhammadan savant, "there is no other country on earth but theirs, no other race of men but theirs, and no created beings have any knowledge or science whatsoever. Their haughtiness is such that, if you tell them of any science or scholar in Khurasan and Persia, they will think you to be both an ignoramus and a liar." This dismal attitude of mind, which refused either to learn or unlearn anything—a characteristic of the Bourbons— this pathetic state of intellectual stolidity was at once a cause and symptom of decay. In the first century A.D. the Roman Tacitus wrote his Germania, telling his countrymen that the barbarians living beyond the Rhine and the Danube should not be despised, and that they possessed certain intrinsic virtues which the more civilised Romans might cultivate with profit. The Romans paid no heed to that warning, with the result that their great empire was overwhelmed by the inflowing tide of vigorous fighting barbarism. The Hindus committed a similar blunder. They shut themselves up in a world of isolation, narrow, cramped, torpid. They set up insurmountable barriers which no gust of wind and no ray of light could penetrate. The result was stagnation; stagnation brought decay, and decay disaster. The saying of Emerson is ever true that a thing cannot be crushed by a blow from without until ready to perish from decay within.

INDEX

BIBLIOGRAPHY

I. VEDIC

Ṛgveda Saṁhitā. With Sāyaṇa's commentary, *pāda*-text, grammatical analysis, and Marathi translation of the text and commentary. Edited by Kasinath Vamana Lele. Wai, 1909-11.

The Hymns of the Ṛgveda. Translated by Ralph T. H. Griffith, 2 vols. 2nd edition, Benares, 1896-7.

The Veda of the Black Yajus School entitled Taittirīya Saṁhitā. Translated by A. B. Keith. 2 vols. Cambridge, Mass., 1914. (Harvard Oriental Series. Vols. 18 and 19).

Yajur-veda Saṁhitā (Vājasaneyi-Saṁhitā). With Mahīdhara's commentary. Edited with Bengali translation and notes by Durgadas Lahiri, Howrah (1909-).

Atharva-veda Saṁhitā. Translated by W. D. Whitney. Revised and edited by C. R. Lanman. Cambridge, Mass., 1905.

Śatapatha Brāhmaṇa. Translated by Julius Eggeling. Sacred Books of the East Series, Vol. XII, XXVI, XLI, XLIII and XLIV.

Jaiminīya Upaniṣad Brāhmaṇa. Edited by Pandit Rama Deva, 1921.

Original Sanskrit Texts by John Muir. 5 vols. 1868-1884.

II. EPIC

Mahābhārata. Edited by Pañcānana Tarkaratna. 2 vols. Calcutta, 1904.

Mahābhārata. Translated into English from original Sanskrit text by P. C. Roy. New edition (revised by S. L. Bhaduri), Calcutta, 1919.

Rāmāyaṇa. With Bengali translation. Edited by Pañcānana Tarkaratna. Third edition. Calcutta, 1904.

Rāmāyaṇa. Translated into English prose by M. N. Dutt. 7 vols. Calcutta, 1892-94.

N.B.—References and quotations from the Mahābhārata and the Rāmāyaṇa are taken from the above editions. In the Bombay edition they are slightly different.

III. DHARMASŪTRA AND DHARMAŚĀSTRA

Āpastamba, Dharmasūtras. Translated by G. Bühler. Sacred Books of the East Series, Vol. II, Pt. I.

Baudhāyana, Dharmasūtras. Translated by G. Bühler. S. B. E. Vol. XIV.

Bṛhaspati, The Minor Law Books. Translated by Julius Jolly. S. B. E. Vol. XXII.

Gautama, Dharma-sūtra. Translated by G. Bühler. S. B. E. Vol. II.

Gṛhya Sūtras (Rules of Domestic Ceremonies). Pt. I. Translated by Hermann Oldenburg. S. B. E. Vol. XXIX. Pt. II. Translated by Hermann Oldenburg and Max Muller. S. B. E. Vol. XXX.

Āśvalāyana Gṛhya Sūtra. Edited by T. Gaṇapati Śāstrī. Trivandrum Sanskrit Series, No. 78.

Manu-saṁhitā. Translated by G. Bühler. S. B. E. Vol. XXV.

Manu-saṁhitā (Manu-smṛti). Translated by M. M. Ganganath Jha. Published by the Calcutta University, 1920-

Nārada, Dharmaśāstra. The Minor Law Books. Translated by Julius Jolly. S. B. E. Vol. XXXIII.

Vaśiṣṭha, Dharmaśāstra. Translated by G. Bühler. S. B. E. Vol. XIV.

Yājñavalkya, Dharmaśāstra. Translated into English by V. N. Mandalik. Bombay, 1880.

Ūnaviṁśati Saṁhitā. Edited by Pañcānana Tarkaratna. Calcutta, 1903.

IV. ARTHAŚĀSTRA AND NĪTI-ŚĀSTRA

Kauṭilya, Arthaśāstra. Revised and edited by R. Shamasastry. Mysore, 1919.

Kauṭilya, Arthaśāstra. Translated by R. Shamasastry. Second edition. Mysore, 1923.

Kauṭilya, Arthaśāstra. With the commentary Śrīmūla by T. Gaṇapati Śāstrī. Trivandrum Sanskrit Series. 3 vols. Trivandrum, 1924.

Meyer, J. J., Das Altindische Buch vom Welt—Und Staatsleben. Leipzig, 1926.

Kāmandaka, Nītisāra. Edited by T. Gaṇapati Śāstrī. Trivandrum Sanskrit Series. No. 14. Trivandrum, 1912.

Somadeva Sūri, Nītivākyāmṛta. Published in the Grantharatna-mālā. Bombay, 1890.

Someśvara, Mānasollāsa (or Abhilaṣitārtha-cintāmaṇi). Edited by Gajanan K. Shringodekar. Gackwad's Oriental Series. No. 28.

Someśvara, Abhilaṣitārtha-cintāmaṇi. Edited by R. Shamasastry. Mysore, 1926.

Bhojarāja, Yukti-kalpataru. Edited by Iswar Chandra Śāstrī. With a foreword by Narendra Nath Law. Calcutta, 1917.

Vaiśampāyana, Nīti-prakāśikā. Edited by Gustav Oppert. Madras, 1882.

Śukrācārya, Nītisāra. Translated into English by B. K. Sarkar. Sacred Books of the Hindus. Allahabad, 1914.

V. THE PURĀṆAS

Agni Purāṇa. With Bengali translation by Tārākānta Kāvyatīrtha. Edited by Pañcānana Tarkaratna. Calcutta, 1907.

Garuḍa Purāṇa. Edited by Pañcānana Tarkaratna. Calcutta, 1907.

Garuḍa Purāṇa. Translated into English by Ernest Wood and S. V. Subramanyam. Sacred Books of the Hindus, Vol. IX, Allahabad, 1911.

Matsya Purāṇa. Edited by Pañcānana Tarkaratna. Calcutta, 1909.

Matsya Purāṇa. Translated by a Taluqdar of Oudh. Sacred Books of the Hindus. Vol. XVII. Allahabad, 1916-1917.

Viṣṇu Purāṇa. Edited by Pañcānana Tarkaratna. Calcutta, 1907.

Viṣṇu Purāṇa. Translated into English by H. H. Wilson. Works of H. H. Wilson. Vol. VI-X.

VI. DHANUR-VEDA

Auśanasa Dhanur-veda Saṅkalanam. Edited by Pandit Rajaram. Lahore, 1923.

Kodaṇḍa-maṇḍana or Bāṇa-vidyā. Moradabad, 1901.

Dhanur-veda Saṁhitā of Vaśiṣṭha. With a Hindi translation attributed on the title page to Haradayālu Svāmī, and in the colophon to Rāmarakṣapāla. Bombay, 1902.

Dhanur-veda Saṁhitā of Vaśiṣṭha. With a Bengali translation by Pandit Iswar Chandra Śāstrī and Arun Chandra Sinha, M.A. Mymensingh (Bengal), 1922.

VII. MISCELLANEOUS WORKS IN SANSKRIT, PALI AND PRĀKṚT

The Jātaka. Translated under the editorship of E. B. Cowell. Cambridge, 1895. 6 vols.

The Jātaka. Edited by V. Fausboll. 7 vols. London, 1877-97.

Aśvaghoṣa, Sūtrālaṅkāra.

Mahāvaṁśa, or the Great Chronicle of Ceylon. Translated into English by W. Geiger and M. H. Bode. Pali Text Society. Oxford-London, 1912.

Saṁyutta-Nikāya of the Sutta-Piṭaka. Edited by Léon Féer. Pali Text Society. 6 vols. London, 1884.

Vākpati, Gauḍavaho. Edited by Shankar Pāṇḍu-rang Paṇḍit. Bombay Sanskrit Series, No. XXXIV, Bombay, 1887.

Bāṇa, Harṣacarita. Translated into English by E. B. Cowell and F. W. Thomas. (Oriental Translation Fund), 1897.

Kalhaṇa, Rājataraṅgiṇī. Translated with an introduction, commentary and appendices by Sir Aurel Stein. 2 vols. 1900.

Kālidāsa, Raghuvaṁśa. Edited by Gajānana Mahādeva Gurjara. Bombay, 1905.

Māgha, Śiśupālavadha. Edited by Pandit Durgaprasad and Pandit Sivadatta. Revised by T. Srinivasā Venkatarama Sarma. Bombay, 1923.

Daṇḍī, Daśakumāra-carita. Edited by P. V. Kulkarni. Bombay, 1919-

Somadeva, Kathā-sarit-sāgara. (The Ocean of Story). Translated by C. H. Tawney. Edited with introduction, notes and terminal essay by N. M. Penzer. 10 vols.

Pālakāpya, Hastyāyur-veda. Ānandāśram Sanskrit Series, 1894.

Hemasūri, Aśva-śāstra (Science of Horses). Translated into English by Pandit Vijayaraghavacharya, 1928.

Śārṅgadhara Paddhati. Edited by Peter Peterson, Kāvyamālā Series.

Varāha Mihira, Bṛhat Saṁhitā. With Bengali translation by Dhīrānanda Kāvyanidhi. Edited by Pañcānana Tarkaratna. Calcutta, 1910.

Viśākhadatta, Mudrārākṣasa. Edited with English translation by M. R. Kale. Bombay, 1911.

Vaijayantī. Edited with a Sanskrit-English vocabulary by Gustav Oppert. Madras, 1893.

Uvāsagadasāo, being the seventh Aṅga of the Jainas. Edited with the Sanskrit commentary by Abhaya Deva, and an English translation and notes by A. F. R. Hoernle. Calcutta, 1885.

VIII. FOREIGN ACCOUNTS

(a) *Classical*

Herodotus, History. Translated by G. Rawlinson. London, 1858-60.

McCrindle, J. W. Ancient India as described by Ktesias the Knidian, 1882.

„ „ Ancient India as described by Megasthenes and Arrian, 1926.

„ „ Ancient India as described by Ptolemy, 1885.

„ „ Ancient India as described in classical literature, 1901.

„ „ The Invasion of India by Alexander the Great, 1896.

(b) *Chinese*

Beal, Samuel, Buddhist Records of the Western World, 2 vols., 1906.

Beal, Samuel, The Life of Hiuen Tsiang, London, 1911.

Watters, Thomas, On Yuan Chwang's Travels in India. Edited by T. W. Rhys Davids and S. W. Bushell. 2 vols. Oriental Translation Fund, new series, Vol. XIV. London, 1904-5.

(c) *Muhammadan*

Sachau, E. C., Alberuni's India. 2 vols. London, 1901.

Elliot and Dowson, History of India as told by her own Historians. Vols. I and II.

Briggs (John), Firishtah. 3 vols. London, 1770-72.

Aḥmad b. Yaḥya, al-Balādūrī, Futūḥ al-Buldān. Translated into English by Clark Margotten.

IX. ARCHEOLOGICAL

(a) *Monumental (including sculptures and frescoes)*

Annual Reports of the Archeological Survey of India

Catalogue of the Museum of Archeology at Sānchi, Bhopal State, 1922.

Cunningham, Sir Alexander, The Bhilsa Topes, 1854.

" " Tree and Serpent Worship, 1873.

" " The Stupa of Bhārhut, 1879.

Egerton, Hon. Wilbraham, An Illustrated Handbook of Indian Arms. London, 1880.

Herringham (Christiana Jane), Lady, Ajantā Frescoes: being reproductions . . . after copies taken, 1915.

Marshall, Sir John, A Guide to Sānchi. Calcutta, 1918.

Marshall, Sir John, Mohenjo-Dāro and the Indus Civilisation. 3 vols. London, 1931.

Maisey, F. C., Sānchi and its Remains, 1892.

Memoirs of the Archeological Survey of India.

Mitra, Rajendralal, The Antiquities of Orissa. Calcutta, 1875.

Smith, V. A., A History of Fine Art in India and Ceylon. Oxford, 1911.

Yazdani, G., Ajantā. The colour and monochrome reproduction of the Ajantā frescoes based on photography. London, 1930.

(b) *Epigraphic*

Corpus Inscriptionum Indicarum. Vol. I. (Revised edition by F. Hultzsch) Vol. III. by J. F. Fleet.

Epigraphia Carnatica by Lewis Rice. Vols. I to IV. Bangalore, 1886-98. Vol. V. Mangalore, 1902. Further volumes, Bangalore, 1902-5.

Epigraphia Indica.

Epigraphia Zeylonica.

Indian Antiquary.

Madras Government Epigraphist's Reports.

Maitreya A. K. Gauḍalekha-mālā, 1912.

Majumdar, N. G. Inscriptions of Bengal, Vol. III.

(c) *Numismatic*

Allan, John. Catalogue of the coins of the Gupta Dynasties and of Saśāṅka, king of Gauḍa. London, 1914.

Cunningham, Sir Alexander. Coins of Ancient India from the earliest times down to the seventeenth century A.D. London, 1891.

Gardiner, P. Coins of the Greek and Scythic kings of Bactria and India. B. M. Cat., 1886.

Lane-Poole, S. Coins of the Sultans of Delhi in the British Museum. Vol. I. London, 1884.

Rapson, E. J. Catalogue of the Coins of the Āndhra Dynasty, the Western Kṣatrapas, Traikūṭaka Dynasty, and the "Bodhi" Dynasty. London, 1908.

Smith, V. A. Catalogue of Coins in the Indian Museum, Calcutta. Vol. I. Oxford, 1906.

Whitehead, R. B. Catalogue of Coins in the Punjab Museum. Lahore, 1914.

X. MODERN WORKS

Aiyangar, S. K. The Beginnings of South Indian History, 1918.

Aiyangar, S. K. Some Contributions of South India to Indian Culture (Calcutta University Readership Lectures, 1923).

Aiyangar, S. K. Evolution of Hindu Administrative Institutions in South India. (Sir William Meyer Lectures, 1929-30, Madras University).

Aiyangar, S. K. Maṇimekhalai in its Historical Setting. (Madras University Special Lectures). London, 1928.

Altekar, A. S. A History of Village Communities in Western India. (University of Bombay Economic Series. No. 5). Bombay, 1927.

Appadorai, A. Economic Conditions in Southern India. Madras University Historical Series, No. 12, 1936.

Banerji, R. D. Vāṅglār Itihāsa.

Banerji, R. D. The Pālas of Bengal. Memoirs of the Asiatic Society of Bengal, Vol. V.

Bernier, F. Travels in the Moghul Empire, 1656-1668 A.D. A revised and improved edition, based upon Irving Brock's translation, by A. Constable. 1891

Bhandarkar, D. R. The Carmichael Lectures. Calcutta University, 1919.

Bhandarkar, R. G. Early History of the Deccan. 3rd edition.

Cambridge History of India. Vol. I. Cambridge, 1922.

Chanda, R. P. Gauḍa-rājamālā, 1912.

Cunningham, Sir Alexander. Ancient Geography of India. London, 1871. New edition entitled Cunningham's Ancient Geography of India, edited with introduction and notes by S. N. Majumdar Sastri. Calcutta, 1929.

Das, A. C. Ṛgvedic Culture. Calcutta, 1925.

Date, G. T. The Art of War in Ancient India, 1929.

Davids, T W. Rhys. Buddhist India (Story of the Nations Series). London, 1903.

Dikshitar, V. R. Ramachandra. The Art of War as practised in South India (Reprinted from the Annals of the Bhandarkar Institute, Vol. VIII, 1927).

District Gazetteers of the United Provinces. Vol. XXI.

Eastern States (Bundelkhand) Gazetteer. Vol. VI-A.

Ghoshal, U. N. Contributions to the History of the Hindu Revenue System, 1930.

Hopkins, E. W. Epic Mythology, 1915.

Hopkins, E. W. The Great Epic of India, 1920.

Hopkins, E. W. The Social and Military Position of the Ruling Caste in Ancient India, as represented by the Sanskrit Epic. Journal of the American Oriental Society, Vol. XIII.

Irvine, W. The Army of the Indian Moghuls, 1903.

Irvine, W. Storia do Mogor of Niccolao Manucci. Translated into English (Indian Texts Series), 1906-8.

Iswari Prashad, History of Medieval India. Allahabad, 1928.

Jayaswal, K. P. Hindu Polity, 2 vols. 1924.

Kanakasabhai Pillai, V. The Tamils Eighteen Hundred Years Ago. Madras, 1904.

Keith, A. B. History of Sanskrit Literature. Oxford, 1928.

Law, N. N. Studies in Ancient Hindu Polity, 1914.

Macdonell, A. F. Vedic Mythology, 1897.

Macdonell, A. F. History of Sanskrit Literature, 1928.

Macdonell and Keith, Vedic Index. 2 vols.

Monahan, F. J. The Early History of Bengal. Oxford, 1925.

Majumdar, R. C. Corporate Life in Ancient India. Second edition, 1922.

Majumdar, R. C. Ancient Indian Colonies in the Far East. Vol. I, Champā.

Majumdar, R. C. The Gurjara-Pratīhāras. Reprinted from the Journal of the Department of Letters, Calcutta University, Vol. X.

Mukherji, R. K. Local Government in Ancient India, 1920.

Natha, Prana. A Study in the Economic Condition of Ancient India. Royal Asiatic Society's Monograph. London, 1929.

Nazim, Muhammad. The Life and Times of Sultan Mahmud of Ghazna. Cambridge, 1931.

Oppert, Gustav. On the Weapons, Army Organisation and Political Maxims of the Ancient Hindus, 1880.

Rawlinson, George. The Seventh Great Oriental Monarchy. New York (1876?). 2 vols.

Ray, H. C. The Dynastic History of Northern India. 2 vols. Calcutta, 1931 and 1936.

Ray, H. C. Notes on War (Journal of the Department of Letters. Vol. XIV, 1927).

Raychaudhuri, H. C. Political History of Ancient India. 3rd edition. Calcutta, 1932.

Rice, Lewis. Mysore and Coorg from the Inscriptions. London, 1909.

Rajputana Gazetteer. Vol. II-A.

Saletore, B. A. Social and Political Life in the Vijayanagara Empire. 2 vols. 1934.

" " The Wild Tribes in Indian History. Lahore, 1935.

Sarkar, B. K. Positive Background of Hindu Sociology, 1914.

" " Hindu Achievements in Exact Science. 1918.

Sewell, Robert. A Forgotten Empire. London, 1900.

Smith, V. A. The Early History of India. Revised by S. M. Edwardes. Oxford, 1924.

Smith, V. A. Oxford History of India. Revised and continued to 1921 by S. M. Edwardes. Oxford, 1923.

Stein, Sir Aurel. On Alexander's Track to the Indus. London, 1929.

Thomas, Edward. Chronicles of the Pathan Kings of Delhi. London, 1871.

Vaidya, C. V. Epic India. Bombay, 1907.

" " History of Medieval Hindu India. Vol. I. circa 600 to 800 A.D., Poona, 1921; Vol. II. 750 to 1,000 A.D., Poona, 1924; Vol. III Downfall of Hindu India, 1926.

Weber, Albrecht. The History of Indian Literature. Translated from the second German edition by J. Mann and T. Zachariae. London, 1878.

Winternitz, M. A History of Indian Literature. Vol. I. Translated from the original German by Mrs. S. Ketkar. Published by the University of Calcutta, 1927; Vol. II, translated by Mrs. S. Ketkar and Miss H. Kohn. Published by the University of Calcutta, 1933.

Works of H. H. Wilson. Vol. IV. London, 1864.

Yule (Sir Henry). The Book of Ser Marco Polo. Translated and edited with notes. 2 vols. London, 1903.

Zimmer (Heinrich), Altindisches Leben. Berlin, 1879.

CORRIGENDA

p. 2 l. 15 *for* Ep. Ind. 11, 3 *read* Ep. Ind. II, 3

p. 20, l. 2 *for* but was *read* but is

p. 27, n. 1 *for* Yukti. Kalpataru *read* Yukti-kalpataru

p. 38, l. 10 from foot *for* Sanchi *read* Sānchi

p. 38, l. 7 from foot *for* Sanchi *read* Sānchi

p. 66, n. 1, l. 5 from foot *for* Mc.Crindle *read* McCrindle

p. 77, l. 8 *omit* , *after* (Saindhava)

p. 78 l. 21 *for* Brahman *read* Brāhman

p. 78, l. 23 *for* Prthvīsena *read* Pṛthvīsena

p. 83, l. 18 *for* Vāhini read Vāhinī

p. 87, l. 12 *for* (58-9) *read* (58, 9)

p. 95, l. 4 from foot *omit* , *after* Kauṭilya

p. 97, n., l. 5 from foot *for* Āśvin *read* Āśvina

p. 102, l. 17 from foot *insert* the *after* keep

p. 108, l. 1 *for* āṭṭālaka *read* *aṭṭālaka*

p. 114, l. 17 *for* movemnt *read* movement

p. 124, n., l. 11 from foot for *Paṇvānaka* read *paṇavānaka*

p. 139, l. 9 from foot *for* Loharokoṭṭa *read* Loharakoṭṭa

p. 143, n., l. 12 from foot *for* fort Āsī *read* fort of Āsī

p. 154, l. 14 *for* king *read* kind

p. 164, l. 5 *for* Sanchi *read* Sānchi

p. 165, n. 1 for *hematsaru and śuddha-dantatsaru* read *hematsaru* and *śuddha-dantatsaru*

CORRIGENDA

[illegible]